Beneath the Mountains

Beneath the Mountains

Exploring the deep caves of Asturias

David Rose and Richard Gregson

Hodder & Stoughton

LONDON SYDNEY AUCKLAND TORONTO

British Library Cataloguing in Publication Data

Rose, David
  Beneath the mountains: exploring the
  deep caves of the Asturias.
  1. Speleology   2. Caves—Spain—
  Asturias
  I. Title   II. Gregson, Richard
  796.5'25'094619   GB608.61

  ISBN 0-340-38791-2

For Keith
hombre

Illustrations

between pages 112–13

The Xitu streamway near the Samaritan pitches[1]
Helectite formations in the Snowcastle series[1]
The first Samaritan pitch[2]
Flat Iron pitch[2]
A soaking on Pafs Pot[1]
The Xitu camp[1]
Flat Iron shaft[2]
David Rose before the Marble Steps[3]
Phil Rose attempts to emerge in 3/5[4]
The Culiembro streamway[5]
The Classic Numbers[1]
Fred Wickham enjoys the Perdices entrance series[5]
The Corkscrew, Pozu Optimistu[1]
The Oubliette, Optimistu[1]
Camshaft, Pozu la Cistra[5]
Richard Gregson in the Meander of the Argonauts[1]
Near Obelix pitch in Perdices[5]
The lower reaches of Pozu la Cistra[5]
Looking out to daylight from Ridge Cave[5]
Dinosaur Beach, Ridge Cave[5]
Cueva Culiembro[5]
The Snowcastle[1]

CREDITS
1 George Hostford 2 Clive Westlake 3 Mick Clarke 4 Geoff
Hogan 5 Martin Hicks

PLANS

Contents

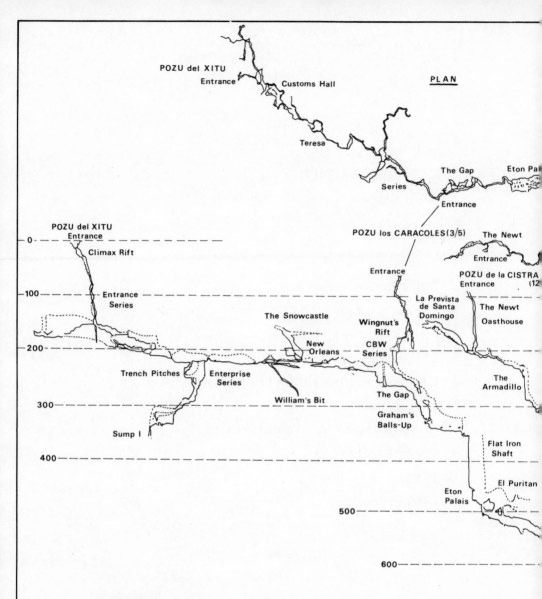

PLAN

POZU del XITU
Entrance   Customs Hall

Teresa

Series   The Gap   Eton Pa

Entrance

POZU los CARACOLES(3/5)   The Newt

POZU del XITU
Entrance   Entrance

0 — Climax Rift   POZU de la CISTRA
                                             Entrance   (12

100 — Entrance   La Prevista   The Newt
       Series   de Santa
                              Domingo   Oasthouse

                  The Snowcastle   Wingnut's
                                    Rift
200 —   New   CBW
                  Orleans   Series

      Trench Pitches   Enterprise   The
                       Series   Armadillo
                              William's Bit   The Gap

300 —   Graham's
                                              Balls-Up
                                                         Flat Iron
      Sump I   Shaft

400 —   El Puritan
                                              Eton
                                              Palais
500 —

600 —

SISTEMA XITU

Depths in metres

Conjectured roof lines   -----------

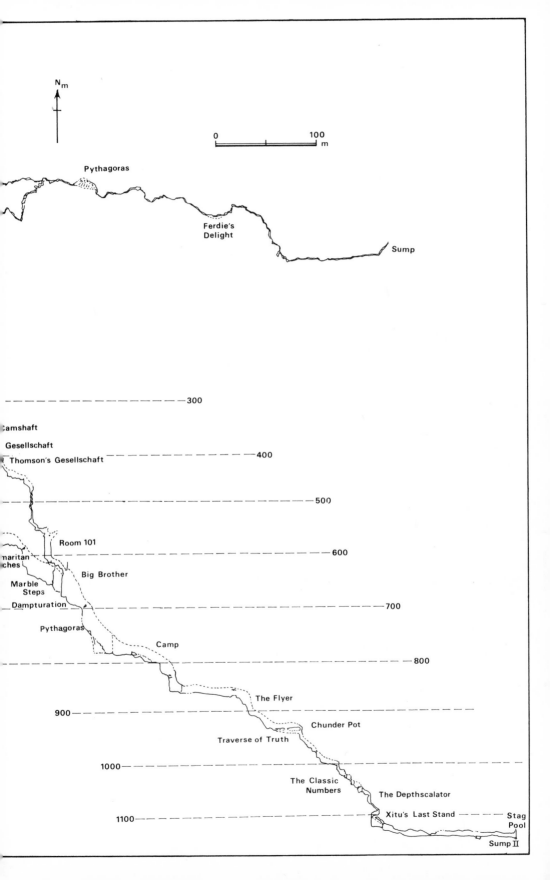

N_m

0   100
m

Pythagoras

Ferdie's
Delight

Sump

300

Camshaft

Gesellschaft

Thomson's Gesellschaft   400

500

Room 101   600

maritan
ches

Big Brother

Marble
Steps

Dampturation   700

Pythagoras

Camp

800

The Flyer

900

Chunder Pot

Traverse of Truth

1000

The Classic
Numbers   The Depthscalator

Xitu's Last Stand   Stag
Pool

1100

Sump II

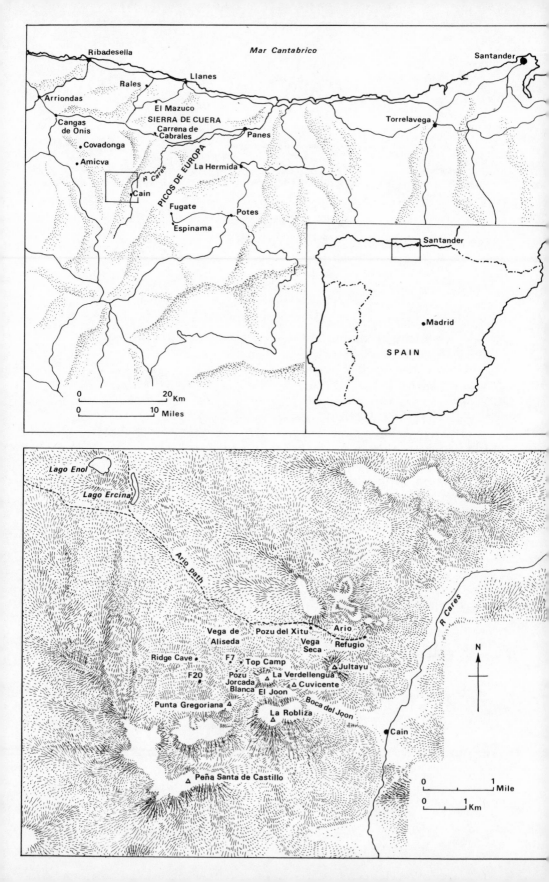

Preface

This is the record of several years' work by a large number of people. If it appears from these pages that the two of us have played a disproportionately important part in the expeditions, then we must apologise. It is neither true nor the impression we wished to give.

Like the trips themselves, writing the book has been team-work. The name in capitals at the start of each section indicates who is to blame for what follows. We must thank: the photographers whose work is represented here, Mick Clarke, Simon Fowler, Martin Hicks, Geoff Hogan, George Hostford and Clive Westlake; the Spanish caving authorities, the FNE and CRNE, for allowing us to work unhampered in the Picos de Cornion, the Grupo SIE of Barcelona for many years' cooperation and friendship; and the successive wardens of the Refugio MVA de Ario, Manolo, Eduardo, Alvaro, Vlas and Julia. Amador Gonzalez Ramon, who allowed his restaurant to be taken over by speleologists and gave them free showers, deserves special thanks, and he also has a part of Xitu named after him.

We don't really need to thank all those who took part in the expeditions, who shivered in cold dark tunnels and sweltered up the mountains with huge packs. They, like us, are obsessed by the caves in an obscure range of mountains of which most of their friends have never heard; and in many cases their obsession has continued long after they stopped being students and took up more suitable employment. Why this is so may seem a mystery, to which no amount of words or descriptions can give an explanation. But we have tried.

David Rose and Richard Gregson
Bradwell, May 1986

11

1

Learning to Crawl

DAVID It was the afternoon of my twenty-first birthday. I was dangling on a rope above a pit of unknown depth, and I was scared.

From below came the sound of falling water. Above, the roof was invisible, but I knew that beyond it was rather more than 300 metres of solid rock. As I worried and fretted about how to get down this hole, my friend Kevin offered encouragement. "Can't you get a move on? I'm freezing." It was all right for him, he was on a comfy ledge. I mumbled an apology and carried on with my work, the driving of a steel expansion bolt into the rock to provide an anchor for a safe descent. The principle was similar to putting a rawl plug into plaster. The execution was more difficult.

At last I tapped the bolt home and clipped in the rope. "OK, Kev, I'm off." Weak cheers. I wound the line through my descender and set off. I didn't know what was at the bottom of this shaft. This had been my first bolt, and as the blackness unfolded between my feet I felt the intoxicating lurch of high-grade adrenalin.

There were boulders, big ones, coming into view. Twenty-five metres down I touched bottom. Reassuringly confined at the top, the shaft had belled out: I was standing in a large cavern, curved strata stretching beyond vision in stacks against the walls. A little waterfall flowed into a pool and began a streamlet, flowing away into the high corridor beyond. I filled my lungs and shouted, testing the echo: "Kev! Rope free! It's enormous . . ."

Kev joined me, warm again with his own excitement. Together we rushed into the tunnel carrying the stream, clambering over boulders, down a small cascade, turning sideways to edge past places where the passage narrowed. We came to a longer drop which looked too hard to free climb: hastily we knocked up a rig made of knotted lengths of nylon tape and shinned down. Kev was first. He disappeared round the corner.

A few yards further I caught up with him on the edge of a further fall of 4 metres. He looked mesmerised. We leaned over the edge, looking into a small chamber with a slot at the far end. Kev picked up a rock. "Just listen to this," he said. He tossed the rock through the slot. I expected to hear it land, but there was silence. After a long age of seconds a stupefying, far-off boom rumbled from below. We climbed down into the chamber and threw more rocks, hiding our terror with hysterical laughter.

"Six seconds before they hit the bottom, Kev. That makes it 180 metres deep. The height of the Post Office Tower. God's Holy Trousers!"

RICHARD The idea of a caving expedition to Spain began in 1960 with some Oxford archaeologists, and their hopes of finding cave paintings like those in the famous cave of Altamira. The archaeologists soon dropped out, but their idea had taken root among the members of the university caving club. They scoured the geographical and topographical map collections in the Bodleian Library for promising country. The place they eventually found was on a map made by the Nazis during the Spanish Civil War. About halfway along Spain's north coast were the limestone mountains of the Picos de Europa. In the western massif of the Picos, the Macizo de Cornion, there was a track leading up into the mountains from a village called Covadonga to a couple of lakes. This place, Los Lagos, was to be a base camp used from the 'sixties onwards.

Covadonga was not quite unknown to the world. Although it is now a tiny village, it was the site of a crucial battle in the eighth century, when the local Visigothic tribe, led by their chief, Pelayo, defeated the army of the Moors. Covadonga and all of the remote mountains around it were never conquered by Islam, and it was from this village that the 'reconquista' is said to have begun. Today there is a large basilica and a shrine on this spot, and people drive out to pray there from Cangas de Onis, the nearest town. Poor Cangas was once the capital of all Christian Spain, but now is a provincial market town where the peasant farmers who make a tough living on the limestone mountains come to buy what they need.

The track that was marked on the map snaked upwards from Covadonga into the mountains proper, to an altitude of 1,000 metres. It was built, in fact, by an Englishman. Earlier in the century there had been an iron mine at Los Lagos, and the British mining engineer constructed the track to supply it. He had also constructed the mine, and when it collapsed, killing some local miners, the survivors of the accident lynched him. There is nothing at Los Lagos today. Nothing, that is, save for a couple of bars, an ice-cream seller and a campsite for tourists. In 1961, when the Oxford undergraduates left for Spain, there was not even that.

There were many Oxford expeditions to Spain after 1961. They explored caves very much like those in Britain, in low-lying hills around Los Lagos and other areas along the northern coast, where subterranean streams had cut out mainly horizontal cave systems. The early expeditions didn't have the technical capability to cope with caves of a more vertical nature, with many large underground drops; overhanging, smooth and wet. The largest drop they could manage was about 120 metres, roughly the size of Gaping Gill Main Shaft in Yorkshire.

The second method of descending these large underground drops was by lowering the explorer on a rope and hauling him out whilst he steadied himself on a rope ladder. This was the way Edouard Martel had first descended Gaping Gill, the largest shaft in Britain, in 1895. The earlier method was simply to hurl the poor chap down and forget about him, this being the way that Dominic Noon first explored the cave in Ireland which now bears his name.

The first expedition to crack the magic 1,000 metres and explore a cave over a kilometre deep was led by Jean Cadoux in the Alps in 1956. The stream they followed underground at the Gouffre Berger finally slid into a pool, 1,148 metres below the entrance. To get to that spot Cadoux had left one or sometimes several men at the head of every underground drop to help haul up cavers on the return. It was a siege approach that required huge resources. Little wonder that by 1970 only two caves had been discovered over 1,000 metres deep, the Gouffre Berger and Pierre St Martin in the Pyrenees. In 1970, however, the caving world was on the brink of a technological revolution.

Climbers who intend to fall into crevasses have long since used a method of climbing up the rope which has, we hope, broken their fall, by means of knots which will slide up the rope but not down. The knots, called prusik knots after their American inventor, are attached to the climber's feet, and to his body harness. Standing up and sitting down alternately while moving each knot up in turn enables the climber to ascend. The process is quicker with metal camming devices; these will similarly slide up if no weight is on them but jam when loaded from below, like ratchets. It is quicker still if both feet are used instead of the traditional one. Climbers seem to think the use of both feet together is unethical, preferring instead to hang horizontally, so that an enormous amount of strength is required to make each step. Cavers, as ever more practical, keep themselves held vertically into the rope by means of a chest harness, so that all their stepping is converted into upward motion. Suffice it to say that the record for climbing 100 feet at the annual British Cave Research Association conference stands at 32.1 seconds. The caver is at the top while our crevassed climber is still undoing his shoelaces.

Gone was the idea of climbing up and down ladders. Instead you simply hung a single nylon rope down the underground drop, abseiled down it and prusiked up. This 'Single Rope Technique', or SRT, allowed light-weight expeditions to explore many huge new systems in the Alps, and a contest developed to discover the deepest cave yet explored.

In Britain, where the caves are never so deep, and the cavers never so imaginative, SRT caught on very slowly. One group planned to put Britain back into the deep caving spotlight: Dave Judson and his friends decided to find a completely new cave, in a completely new caving area, which would, they hoped, be the world's deepest. They decided to look away from the Alps and the Pyrenees, and Dave Judson himself came to eye up the Picos de Europa where Oxford had been enjoying themselves year after year.

He came to Los Lagos, but instead of staying there he walked up the mountain behind to look at the higher country, before dismissing the mountains as being too shattered to be of much promise and turning instead to Iran. There the British team explored a cave called Ghar Parau, in 1972, returning the following year to finish the promising cave off, only to find that it ended one pitch further in an impassable sump. At 720 metres deep it was the deepest cave explored by British cavers up to that time, yet still failed to make it into the big league.

Oxford, too, were 'Ghar Parau-ed'. Their expedition in 1976 was supposed to explore a cave that lay just above Lago Enol. It had been found and partly explored by a Barcelona caving group to 360 metres deep; they had given up there and now gave the Oxford team a free hand to finish the cave. This should have been the start of a new era for Oxford – for the first time a sustained effort was being planned on a cave high in the mountains, and using SRT. By July 6 all the tackle arrived at Los Lagos; by July 8 the end of the cave had been discovered, only a few metres further on from the limit of exploration. The British cavers re-surveyed the cave and found that the Barcelona team had found another way to get into the big league. The Oxford journal recorded: "below the sixth pitch the depth of the system is consistently and greatly exaggerated" – the cave was only 258 metres deep in all.

Dave Judson had written the Picos off, but one of the 1976 Oxford Expedition members refused to do so. He was Martin Laverty, a man of great vision and massive beard. Late in the summer of 1976 he walked up a path that led from Lago Ercina, the higher of the twin lakes. Some 7 kilometres away it led to a high alp called Ario. As Dave Judson had said, much of the landscape at this higher altitude *was* frost-shattered, but Martin persuaded himself that this was the place deep caves might exist. Ario was a purer, more rugged landscape than Los Lagos. It was above the cloud for much of the time, with soaring limestone edges and staggering views across the Cares Gorge – a 1,800-metre deep gash cut right through the whole of the Picos massif. From the top of Jultayu, a peak quite close to Ario, one could look almost vertically down on the village of Cain, a hamlet nestling in a crook of the gorge, as if from an aeroplane. At Ario itself there were few people; a small colony of shepherds and the guardian of a mountain refuge hut built for passing walkers. Gazing at this beautiful spot, Martin planned another expedition.

The winter of 1978–9 was one of the coldest in living memory. Martin had arranged for the cave club to stay in a ramshackle farmhouse in the Yorkshire Dales over the New Year, and as I arrived at the foot of the steep hill that led up to the ruin there was a lonely figure hitch-hiking in the blizzard. I stopped, and wound down the window of my ancient Triumph Herald to be greeted with, "I say, aren't you OUCC?"

I knew who it was – William Stead, a figure you could never forget. Like me he had joined the Oxford University Cave Club a few months earlier, and had been pleased to find, probably for the first time in his life, a group of people who were as odd as himself. He had left Eton a year earlier. I told him to get in, and together we drove up the hill towards the ancient ruin Martin had selected for our new year meet.

Next morning after a greasy breakfast we marched down from the farm across a field on a compass bearing which led us to the spot where the minibus was parked in the valley below. The minibus conveyed us to a car park where, in the icy grip of winter, we stripped off naked and put on our wetsuits, which were stiff with the cold. Halfway through this torment, I noticed that William and I were standing alone on the frozen gravel. Where were the experienced men? Where was Martin, our 'leader'? The question was soon answered. They had changed inside the public toilets and had been taking turns directing the hot-air hand-drier down their trousers. It was obvious that we had a lot to learn.

Later, as we trudged up to the caves we passed a sign on the edge of the open moor: 'What the Well-Dressed Walker Should Wear'. There was a picture of a merry chap striding along in his big boots, with an anorak, a rucksack, a map and a compass. Inside his rucksack were extra clothes and some food. I looked at this picture. Why, I asked myself, was I wearing a neoprene wetsuit and wellingtons?

In fact, I was one of the best-dressed in the party. Quite unlike climbing, where the better you are the more flash and poncy your gear is, caving kudos can only be gained by putting up with gear that is constantly about to fail. The more holes in your wetsuit the tougher you are, the dimmer your light the obvious-ly more vast your experience. Sometimes in a popular cave you come across a party of potholers who are blundering along dressed in rags and with only one yellow glow from their leader's lamp for them all to see by. In your bright new wetsuit and with your bright new light shining down the passage you press yourself against the rock and let them pass, in awe.

Martin was admired by everyone in the cave club because his gear was so absolutely dreadful. When term began again he was there on the Wednesday night meetings in Brasenose College bar, sitting in the corner stroking his beard, and watching the new recruits to the cave club. Of the dozens who had signed up the term before, only four of us had returned after the ordeal in Yorkshire; myself and William, and two physicists, John Singleton and Graham Naylor.

These two were as unlike each other as it is possible to be. John was large and square, and seemingly impervious to pain or discomfort. He looked rather like the product of spare part surgery, and perhaps what had happened was that they had left out the pain centre. Graham, by contrast, was small, shy and exceptionally strong. He was very good at getting through the tighter sections in caves, and he did this by intelligent wrig-glings, whereas John made his way by battering his body against the rock until it gave way. In the contest between John's flesh and the age-old hardened limestone, John invariable won.

As we talked, Martin eyed us up. If these four could come back for more after the ordeal by snow in Yorkshire, they could take anything. He bided his time, as ever saying little, waiting for the moment when our heads were dulled with beer.

"How do you feel about a caving expedition to Spain?"

Our minds filled with images of wine, flamencos, cheap restaurants and no snow. It seemed a wonderful idea. Martin also said that there would be the chance of discovering a cave system that would be amongst the world's deepest. We pressed him – would our bums be frozen off again? There was a long pause. Probably not, he answered slowly. We didn't know then that it would be the sort of trip where you could have margarine on your bread, or jam, but not both.

Martin's SRT gear was as old as his wetsuit; nevertheless he organised a series of sessions in an Oxford gymnasium to show us how it was done. We dangled ropes down from a girder in the roof, and Martin climbed up, using his 'ropewalking' system. Unlike the 'frog' or sit-stand system, which is roughly what the crevassed climber uses, the ropewalking system used three jammers – one for each foot and another attached to the chest – and it was much more difficult to use. There was no one else in the club, however, who had had any experience of SRT at all, and we had followed our leader in purchasing the gear he recommended.

Working each foot independently, Martin climbed the rope in a series of ungainly spasms until his head hit the roof. As he lay there panting, he explained that SRT was an exceptionally safe technique, because it was almost impossible to detach oneself from the rope. He proved his point by having considerable difficulty in getting down again. What he was trying to do was a 'changeover', an essential manoeuvre in SRT. He had to get his weight off each jammer in turn, and then finally transfer it onto his abseiling device. At the critical moment the descender kept slipping before he could unclip the last jammer, and again and again he ended up hanging from the descender with one foot high above his head still fixed to the rope, well beyond his reach. We got out the vaulting horse and he climbed down onto Simon's shoulders.

"Normally you don't have to do this underground," he said, "you can just step off the rope at the top of the pitch."

Just as well, I thought. There are no vaulting horses underground.

The other change we would have to make for our equipment in Spain was our lamps. In England we used the traditional helmet-mounted electric miners' light, powered by batteries carried on a belt. Without mains electricity at our campsite, we shouldn't be able to re-charge them in Spain, and instead we had to use carbide lamps, or 'stinkies'. These produce acetylene gas from water dripping onto calcium carbide, and the gas burns to give a sooty bunsen burner issuing from our foreheads. They tend to break down a great deal, but can be mended underground, and the length of time they provide light is limited only by how much carbide you carry with you.

On July 8, 1979, the team left for Spain, seventeen strong. After all my preparation, I could not get the time to go, nor could some other members of the club. So Martin invited two cavers from Birmingham, chiefly because they could provide a Land-Rover. 'Skunk' and 'Skippy' had also done a lot more caving than any of the students from Oxford, and they lived in the *real* world: Skunk was a tester at British Steel, and Skippy was a radiographer.

"Only a few miles from the Picos we stopped at a town called San Vincente," the expedition log-book recalls, "to have a last lunch. There are to be no lunches on this caving expedition."

Not only was there to be no lunch, there was to be nowhere to wash. It rained for three days continuously after their arrival at Los Lagos, and the campsite became a quagmire, with mud creeping into everything. It was possible to wash in Lago Ercina, except that the Spanish tourists tended to use it as a latrine. The other lake, Lago Enol, was about half an hour's stiff walk away and ice-cold. Some of the cavers washed in Lago Enol and some washed in the ice-cold spring. Martin decided not to wash at all for the duration of the expedition, earning himself the nickname 'the thing in Martin's tent'. This abstinence meant that it was easy to get to the counter at one of the two bars. The nearest bar is nothing more than a hole in a wall and some tarpaulins, but at the top of a steep and muddy hill is the Refugio Entelagos, a much more substantial building, whose owner, Amador, soon became great friends with the English cavers. Whenever it was misty, and the camp by the lakeside became a misery, the cavers would retire to his bar. It is almost always misty at Los Lagos, and the expedition might have floundered were it not for the fact that there was another bar, or rather a mountain refuge which occasionally sold alcohol, 600 metres higher, at Ario. The extra height meant better weather.

Three of the team went up to Ario. For once the ascent did not bring them out of the mist, and without the yellow paint blobs on the path they would have become lost. Simon Fowler recorded the trip in the log-book:

A hole at the edge of the mist looked interesting – we tossed a stone down to judge its depth: it obviously wasn't deep.

Continuing along the path, we soon reached the solid comforts of the Ario refugio. With the thick mist we could do little else that evening, so we took our single caving ladder and returned to the small shaft we had found. We had decided to call Ario 'Area 5', so this cave would be 1/5.

The shaft was an easy free-climb, but a narrow rift which led off needed our ladder; at the bottom there was a small chamber with a smelly Alpine choughs' nest, and no exit except a narrow and unpromising slot that continued the trend of our entrance. It looked uninviting, but what the hell.

Simon went into the rift, and found that a few feet in, the floor dropped away. To stop himself falling down and becoming stuck in the narrow part below he had to wedge himself high up in the roof.

The clean white walls reminded me that I was the first person to disturb the peace of this cave. I lost contact with the others as the rift got more serious. Reversing out would have been very hard, but I could see that the passage ended at a small alcove just ahead. It would be possible to turn around there.

With a feeling of relief I squeezed through the last, tightest section, letting gravity pull me into the cleft below.

As my head popped out into the alcove I got an unexpected shock. Instead of standing in a convenient turning place, I was perched above an impressive shaft. Roof and floor were out of sight. There was a fortuitously positioned but tiny ledge, which provided a vital foothold, and I could see by the dim light of my carbide flame that there was a large ledge perhaps 15 feet further down. Without much thought for the return journey, I climbed down a difficult flake to the standing room of the ledge. The 30-foot drop that followed looked too wide for me to attempt, but by throwing stones, I estimated that there was another drop beyond of 60 feet or more.

Getting back up and into the rift severely taxed Simon's climbing ability, and getting back along the rift itself was extremely tricky. When he got back to the others though, he had only one comment to make: "Yes, this is the deepest cave in the world."

Jim Shepherd, a veteran of several expeditions of the early 'seventies, was the only one with much experience at rigging a shaft system for SRT, so he went up to Ario to do this with Skunk. They rigged shaft after shaft in Simon's new cave, until the last and biggest drop ended down a miserable slit too small even for Skunk. Halfway down the 40-metre drop Skunk had noticed a horizontal tunnel leading off, and he managed to gain this by swinging across on the rope. From a shingly ledge an old, dry passage led into the mountain and down to a roomy chamber which the pair christened 'Customs Hall'.

Now it was possible to make downward progress without having to rig more pitches – real caving. There were climbs in a dry passage, and at last Jim and Skunk made a real breakthrough: a winding, lofty stream passage. Skunk wrote: "Looking like Oxo. Black limestone with calcite bands. Very impressive. A short cascade was freeclimbed. Were finally halted by a short, annoying pitch. A memorable trip, the epitome of cave exploration."

Skunk's economical style conveys nothing of the excitement with which this news was greeted by the rest of the expedition. Rather than a mere number, the cave was given a name now. As it was right next to the viewpoint, one suggestion was 'Viewpoint Cave'. A Spanish caving group was also at the refugio, and they insisted on this name being translated; the cave that Simon had found in the mist thus became 'Pozu del Xitu'.

These Spanish cavers, the Barcelona SIE, were sceptical about the prospects for the Oxford cave. The cave they had come to explore was called Cabeza Muxa, a gigantic shaft. It was already 500 metres deep, with vast pitches that made Xitu look Lilliputian. Whilst Jim and Skunk were 'crabwalking' sideways along the narrow Xitu streamway, the SIE cavers were bolting their way down the walls of a shaft they called 'El Gran Abisu'; a shaft 247 metres deep. They believed that these big shafts were essential for big caves, but on the day after finding the streamway Skunk was joined on his second push by Francisco, a member of the SIE.

Francisco was dead keen, but fat. The rift gave him a lot of trouble. In a series of attempts to get through he removed his harness, his SRT gear, his oversuit and finally everything before he could manage the squeeze into the alcove. Further down, Xitu carried on like a Yorkshire pothole, writ large; Francisco, though, was dismissive.

"It will never go," he said, "as it's much too small. Quite an interesting cave, but you can be sure that it will be no deeper than 250 metres."

Five days later, when the Oxford expedition left to return to Britain, Xitu was 354 metres deep, nearly a kilometre in length, and it hadn't ended.

2

Depth in the Afternoon

DAVID Between Chesterfield and the M1 there is a fine dual carriageway 6 miles long, which takes no more than a few minutes by car. I was walking up it on the evening of December 27, 1979 and my hands were very cold.

A thin winter fog muffled the distant lamps of the town. Jim Shepherd was swearing: "Bloody geology department. Grr, God, bloody geology department, grr disgraceful, geology department pederasts." Said department had hired us its van and the alternator had fallen out. The AA had towed it to a garage which might have a spare next day but we had to walk. Graham lived in Chesterfield and we could spend the night on his mother's floor. This was my third trip with OUCC, and I was beginning to be underwhelmed: on the second, a beginner's visit to the Mendips, we had had to call the rescue when a chilled medic refused to climb a waterfall.

Simon Fowler was trudging up the road next to me and seemed to feel a vague responsibility for the setback. Like me, he was a member of Magdalen College; as an historian I was apparently the first arts student potholer for many years and he seemed anxious that I shouldn't be put off. He kept on and on about a cave called Xitu in Spain and seemed to be urging me to sign away six weeks of my summer vacation there and then. Surely he must be joking? Could this lot be seriously planning to explore deep holes in Spain when they couldn't even get to Yorkshire?

Simon was irrepressible. "Virgin passage. It's incredible. It could easily be up to 500 metres deep and there are already two ways on." Simon, I soon gathered, was leading this jaunt. I had learnt to be wary of students trying to persuade other students to join things. Now, I was in my second year: but I had been lucky not to have been bludgeoned into joining several choirs, the darts circle and the Monday Club before the end of my first week at Oxford.

At last we made it to Yorkshire and took up residence at Bull

Pot Farm, high on the slopes of Casterton Fell, surrounded by the many entrances of Britain's longest cave, the Easegill Caverns–Pippikin Pot system. The single track lane leading to the cottage was covered in ice, making driving impossible: each day we visited parts of the underground network to emerge after dark, jogging four miles down the hill to the pub and slogging tipsy back to bed through snow that sparkled with starlight. One day I tried my first abseil, into the 35-metre entrance shaft of Lancaster Hole. I had a makeshift harness made of nylon tape that squeezed my groin. But 6 metres down the pitch belled out into a beautiful cavern and the rope fed smoothly through the descender: I thought I was flying.

I was becoming keen: soon, obsessive. Another new recruit matched my enthusiasm, Keith Potter: a medical student brought up in the heart of the Mendip caving area. On our last day we undertook what seemed to us a trip of sheer magnificence: a descent of Lancaster Hole followed by a long traverse of the Easegill master cave, all the way to its furthest entrance, Top Sink. A few bends from daylight we climbed Walrus Pot, an 18-metre shaft in the full force of the stream. The water battered our helmets and we gasped for breath, clinging blind to the narrow rungs of the ladder. The water was at freezing point but at the top we basked in the warmth of exhilaration. I was beginning to come round to Simon's idea.

We met each Wednesday in the cellar bar of Brasenose College, and most weekends went caving. Some people remember their student days by parties and punting. For me, the highlights were changing into a wetsuit still damp from the excursion of the previous week by the faint shelter of drystone walls, and trips underground that progressively became harder. I began to love the remoteness of the more challenging caves. On a Monday I would look round at my fellow students in the libraries with a certain smugness. Twenty-four hours earlier they had probably been having lunch in a pub: I had been five hours from daylight at the bottom of a deep pothole.

I knew very little about caving gear, but one day Simon came to see me: "Congratulations. You're the expedition tacklemaster." I had no idea what this meant, but nor did anyone else, and so I pretended to be in control by going to the shed where we kept our equipment and seeing how much rope we had. There wasn't much: a few hundred metres of old-fashioned terylene Marlow, developed not for caving but for yachts, and a couple of lengths of precious American Bluewater. We would obviously need a lot more to push Xitu properly. We looked at our accounts and bought one more reel of the Bluewater, knowing that we still had barely enough.

1979 had been the most successful Oxford expedition to date, but it had not added much to the club's reputation. In the élite circles of the caving bureaucracy responsible for doling out Sports Council grants, we were still seen as effete, southern tyros playing with fire. Simon managed to secure a small grant by promising to collect bugs in the caves, and developed a trap based on raw meat bait. He never caught many bugs, although the baits filled the caves with the distinctive smell of rotting hamburgers.

Fortunately Martin Laverty knew Ben Lyon, the main importer of Petzl equipment through his business, Lyon Ladders. He agreed to give us a hefty discount, and on an Easter visit to Yorkshire we went to his shop in Dent and picked out SRT systems, talking in loud voices about our plans to be the deepest men in Spain to impress Ben and the other customers. He smiled at me benignly as I asked his advice on the best model of descender for negotiating vast unknown shafts. He was also the warden of the Whernside Manor training centre, and a fortnight earlier I had attended an SRT course for absolute beginners. So far I had prusiked up precisely four vertical drops.

Spring gave way to a golden, magic summer. A trip was organised to Otter Hole, a beautiful stalactite cave on the banks of the Wye near Chepstow. Not far from the entrance there is a tidal sump, allowing access to the galleries beyond for only a few hours in each tidal cycle: to reach the end we had to be underground for a full twelve hours, the longest trip any of us had done in Britain. We came well prepared with pork pies, sandwiches, cans of coke, cake and many bars of chocolate, bloating ourselves on the banquet we thought necessary for the trip. John Singleton warned that this sort of thing wasn't on in Spain: "It'll be cooking chocolate if you're lucky."

We were due to leave on July 1, immediately after the end of the third years' final exams. By now our excitement was boundless. On the eve of departure we convened in a curry house for a farewell meal. Simon had got hold of a Spanish guide to the country's deepest caves, and we pored over it, speculating on our chances of making the top 10 or top 50: 500 metres seemed a cert. Only Martin sounded a note of caution. "Xitu's heading for a massive surface depression. It'll be choked."

By noon next day our transport had not arrived. Seven of us were supposed to be travelling overland with most of the tackle in a Volkswagen bus owned by Dudley Page. We waited impatiently at the gear shed: only five hours to go before sailing time. By two we knew we had missed the boat. Half an hour after it left Newhaven Dudley turned up at last in Oxford.

Dudley's van was most impressive, lined entirely with brown synthetic fur. It was, however, prone to faults. It was with some trepidation that we set off for Southampton.

Not far beyond Rouen we suffered the first of a series of breakdowns. We were in a wood and it was raining. It was comfortable if cramped in the bus, but Dudley insisted we had to get out to watch him mend it. Collectively we willed it to get better and set off again, sticking to toll-less non-motorways. At dawn John insisted we should not stop for breakfast: he said it would be good training. By 8 a.m. he had been overruled.

Late that night we snaked along the north coast of Spain, hungry again: those who were making decisions had ruled out dinner. I dozed; after some hours becoming aware that we were going more slowly, lurching about a lot as if we were climbing a steep hill with many bends. Then we stopped. Another break-down: again we had to get out to watch Dudley mend it. "I think there's something wrong with the alternator," he said. I had heard something like that before. It was a black, foggy night, the visibility down to 20 feet. We were on a wet, rocky hillside, in clinging rain: all our waterproofs were packed tightly on the roof rack.

Simon said: "I think we're at Lago Enol. There's only a mile to go." I had almost given up hope that we would ever arrive: his words should have cheered me. Dudley bared high tension cables with his teeth and restarted the van. Five more minutes and we bumped off the end of the road onto what appeared to be a flat, boggy field. Our tents and sleeping bags were also on the roof rack: wet. With Simon I struggled with one of the piles of damp canvas. It was 4 a.m. I stumbled off into the dark and relieved myself, holding a torch in my mouth. When I returned Simon was already ensconced in his sleeping-bag. "Welcome to home for the next six weeks," he said.

After far too brief an interval I awoke. The orange tent was warmer now: it seemed to have dried. There were sounds of clanking enamel mugs and plates outside. We were being urged to get up. I struggled out and gasped. The mist had cleared: the broad green meadow gleamed. It ran down to a lake, beyond which gentle slopes planted with conifers gave way to screes, crags and snowfields, dominated by the towering bulk of two huge peaks. Already people were sorting gear for the walk to Ario. I had never been to the Alps: these were the biggest mountains I had seen. Simon observed my wonder. "Pretty impressive, eh?" He pointed, tracing a high line over ridges towards the far horizon. "Ario is up there." His finger moved round, and came to rest in the direction of a vertical cliff on the opposite side of the Lagos meadow. "The path begins right there."

Over the following three days I got to know that path well, as we slogged up with load after load of rope, tents, stoves, food and finally personal caving equipment. I figured that I would probably get in the way less if I left the rigging of the entrance series pitches to those who knew them, and decided – rightly – that a spell lugging gear would improve my fitness no end. The route began gently, skirting the shore of Lago Ercina, rising slowly to the steep incline I soon came to know as Sod One. Beyond its summit, the lake disappeared from view, replaced by a sterner prospect of tumbling crags and grassy rakes. The hard work of Sod One was wasted on a gentle descent to Las Bobbias, the head of a green blind valley with summer shepherd huts and a cool fountain spurting from a dome-shaped rock. After another up and down was Sod Two: a viciously steep and sweaty climb on muddy scree, with only a short respite before the shorter Sod Three. Still the ground rose, the path following a long dry valley. On its other side bleached bare limestone soared to 2,000-metre peaks, and everywhere dark holes and depressions bespoke the existence of caves.

One last climb gained the valley's head, a sloping plateau – Ario at last. Again, I had been unprepared for the magnificence of the surroundings. Straight ahead, across the Cares Gorge, the towers of the central massif stood in a serrated row like the teeth of a giant animal. On our side, the nearby peak of Jultayu began the main ridge of the Macizo de Cornion, a jagged, diagonal spine. Looking back that first morning, cloud had come from the sea, filling the lower valleys, leaving the massif floating free in the sunlit air. Fifty metres away Xitu's entrance opened in a fold in the ground. We threw a rock in and a sound of startled cawing echoed from below: a mother crow flapped her wings and emerged briefly from the shaft. It seemed unlikely that the birds would be able to put up with the intrusion from cavers for long.

The Ario refuge was ten minutes away across ground with even more cave entrances than the slopes below. Most had been painted with signs and numbers indicating their logging the year before, but we found another which had not, a descending fissure under a small cliff. Before returning to Los Lagos we squirmed in, rigging a ladder on the short pitch we soon encountered. Simon was blasé, but I could hardly believe it: a going new cave on our first walk up the hill! The pitch led to a narrow rift passage, and careless of the projections that were tearing my sweatshirt to shreds I squeezed in. Ten metres further on progress was impossible. I was going to have to learn the hard way that the proportion of entrances which lead to worthwhile systems is depressingly low.

Ario was becoming a colony. Eduardo, a student from Oviedo, was doing the job of warden, and in licentious French he indicated that we could camp next to the water supply – the first spring since Bobbias, ninety minutes' walk away. A cast iron pipe poking from a pile of stones carried a brackish trickle, slowing to a steady drip on dry days. All other liquids save the wine Eduardo sold in plastic bottles were underground. Washing, it was clear, would be an irregular pastime.

We were not an efficient team in the early days of the expedition. Merely to retrace our steps of 1979 down the pitches of the entrance series took three days. Some of the bolts placed in haste the year before needed to be redrilled, and some of those new to Spain were beginning to find out that SRT systems which worked perfectly in trees or gymnasiums were more awkward underground. On the third day I got my chance to enter Xitu at last, on a rigging trip with John and Graham. Each drop led inexorably to the next: a fall from one pitch would have carried one bouncing to the bottom of the entire group. I was itching to get to the real cave beyond, the chambers and cascading streamway. But after leaving the rope rigged on the last shaft, in sight of the passage leading off below, we turned tail and made our way to the entrance. Climbing the long succession of shafts I began to grasp the remoteness and commitment of caving in Spain. We hoped that these pitches would be merely a preliminary to a great underground system. But a rescue even from here would be an undertaking of utmost seriousness: the rift a virtually impassable obstacle for an injured caver.

The division of the ways Simon had referred to began two thirds of the way down, where the stream poured over a series of waterfalls, the Trench Pitches. Beyond, the cave became harder. Many of the pitches were very wet, and the passage dividing them was narrow and full of loose rock. We assumed that this unpleasant route held the key to the deeper reaches of the system. The other route had been only cursorily examined by John and Mike Busheri while the cave was being detackled the previous year. The Trench Pitches doubled back beneath the streamway above: the alternative appeared to be a dry continuation of the previous line. Mike, a chemist from Lancashire known for his orgasmic grunts while negotiating tight passages like the Xitu rift, was vague about what he had found. When he explored it he had been very cold, having waited for several hours at the top of the Trench Pitches for the first detackling party to emerge from the depths. "I think we sort of traversed on ledges above a deep hole. After a while we got to a place where the passage became very wide and the ledges gave out, a sort of bold step. We didn't fancy going any further but it seemed to continue."

On July 6, the day after my first trip, John and Keith designated themselves hard men and decided to push the streamway, taking enough tackle in heavy, PVC bags to reach the 1979 limit and explore the cave beyond. Mike and I were not up to this but wanted to go caving. Simon thought hard: "Well, there are a couple of climbs between the entrance pitches and the streamway which you could put a rope on for safety. And if you have time, look at this famous bold step."

This time, with a little foreknowledge, the entrance series passed quickly. We carried only two short lengths of line, and the threading of rope onto descender and swift abseil descent was beginning to seem familiar. In less than an hour we reached the head of the last pitch where I had stopped the day before. Unlike those above, a short way down it belled out into a sizeable cavern, and I turned up the flame on my carbide lamp to get a better look. Vertical strata of sandy-coloured limestone soared upwards to form a broken arch at the top of the pitch where Mike sat. Behind and below me, a ledge extended towards a beckoning tunnel. Swinging out from the rock with my boots I landed on it: "Rope free!"

Below the ledge the shaft continued for a further 40 metres. Skunk and Jim had pushed on down this route in 1979, but found only an impenetrable fissure. Without an accident of geological serendipity, the cave would have been at an end. It appeared that the entrance shafts, including the last drop below the ledge, were recent creations in geological time. By chance, as the water that formed them cut downwards on its way to impassability, it had cut through the roof and floor of a much older, horizontal passage. Mike joined me on the ledge and we stowed away our SRT gear in bags dangling from our harnesses.

The way led over boulders and a greasy slope, beneath cracked and dry stalactites into a comfortable room: Customs Hall. It had been well named: the anteroom to Xitu's further secrets. Cutting a swathe through its floor was a black, vertical fissure. We held our breath and ceased movement: faintly, from far below, the fissure emitted the sound of a tumbling stream.

To reach it direct would have entailed rigging a long pitch, but to one side a complex maze of dry canyon passages enabled the main drop to be bypassed. Here we rigged our ropes on two vertical sections for use as handlines. The first hardly needed it: a simple chimney climbed by pushing against the opposite walls with back and feet. But the second, even with the rope, remained strenuous and dangerous: an overhanging cliff twenty feet high poised above a further drop. Without a rope at all it would have been reckless: and there had been no rope throughout the 1979 expedition.

The streamway was now close. We popped out of a window a few feet above it and climbed down. The rock changed from golden sand to black marble streaked with white and we charged along, hardly pausing at a short ladder pitch. In one section, the walls were decorated with blood-red stalactites, the result of some chemical impurity. To make progress, we turned sideways, until a short climb up led us into a high chamber with a flat floor – an aven, where it appeared that an inlet pothole entering from the roof had widened the cave. Round the corner the passage narrowed again. We had reached the parting of the ways. Keith and John had gone on ahead and were already somewhere below us, rigging the streamway series, which began most uninvitingly with a waterfall in black, sombre rock. "Well, Mike," I said, "you know the way."

Our advance was more tentative now. Soon the hole between our feet was frighteningly deep. The floor was out of sight and rocks we knocked from our footholds took uneasy seconds to clatter to a halt. We reached an awkward move, between a boulder jammed in the passage and a fragile-looking platform. Stuck to the walls were banks of cemented pebbles, legacy of the time when they had formed the bed of a stream which had long ceased to flow. "Is this the bold step, Mike?" I asked. Mike didn't know, but thought not. We continued.

We had stopped chatting and concentrated hard. There was nothing very difficult about what we were doing, but the silence of the dry cave was oppressive. At last we came to another pit which seemed to fit Mike's description. The rocks we dropped fell free without hitting the sides, suggesting we were above an open shaft. But Mike insisted: "No, this isn't it. We're not there yet." To my horror and amazement he started traversing round the hole on the cemented pebbles, which I had already found to

30

be untrustworthy and friable. "For fuck's sake be careful . . ." He made it to the other side and seemed to be standing on solid rock. I looked around and discovered an easier way to cross the hole, climbing on good limestone.

Surely, I said, that must have been the bold step.

"No, I don't think so. I think it was harder than that, we're not there yet." We examined our surroundings. The fissure had gone: a short flat passage led to a wall of boulders. There was an obvious route through, reached by climbing high and squeezing through a narrow gap between the rocks. On the far side we climbed down again, into a much bigger, winding gallery, with more of the pebbles on both walls and floor.

"Mike, there's nothing below us now. We must be into new stuff."

"Oh I don't know. I think I may have been here before. There might be another bold step round the corner."

It was a beautiful, striding passage of the kind cavers dream about, but Mike had successfully convinced me that we might still be poised above a black drop, the pebbles in the floor merely another unstable cemented bank which might give way at any moment. I could have run along it but instead teetered gingerly, seeking handholds in the wall lest the 'false floor' should collapse and plunge me into the abyss.

We carried on for a few hundred metres. Where was this bloody bold step? I was impatient to get a chance to explore virgin passage. "Look Mike, are you really sure you've been here before?"

"Yes, I think so. There's still a way to go yet."

The passage carried a strong, cold draught: always a good sign underground, suggesting that the cave leads on to something big. A long way from the boulder choke, roof and walls closed in. I was in front, and the only way on was on my belly, squeezing through a gap no more than 10 inches high. The floor was now sand, covered with a brittle, green patina. Still Mike insisted that the bold step lay beyond. After the squeeze the passage stayed low, following an upslope. There were no handholds on the wall here: if this lot gives way we're done for, I thought.

Finally the truth sank in. Beyond the slope, the tunnel descended gently again, larger now, with a floor of indisputable solid rock, broken by shining crystal pools. "Mike, you are a twit. You can't possibly have got this far."

"No, I suppose you're right." Seizing on his mistake, I demanded the right to name the new cave. My heart beat faster as I always thought it should when exploring galleries never seen before: I felt irritated and angry that Mike's poor memory had denied me this pleasure during the preceding section. I had promised my friend Tess to name something after her: to Mike's weak protests I declared the Teresa Series officially open. Had I foreseen the ribaldry which would later accrue from the rest of the expedition and from other cavers for years to come I would have chosen an alternative. But the name stuck.

There was still more: another sandy crawl, some fine, rocky tubes and wide, high rifts. More than half a kilometre from what we now knew to be the bold step, we came to a stop. So far, the passage had been rising and falling but keeping to the same mean level. It was clearly an example of a phreatic cave, that is one formed without airspace under hydraulic pressure, which meant water could cut a path upwards as easily as down.

We came to a halt where its character appeared to change to vadose – a passage formed with airspace above. The cave was still dry, but now it was beginning to descend more emphatically. Once, perhaps several million years before, the Teresa Series had been a long, flooded sump, and here, where the floor fell away in a 10-metre drop, the water would have emerged and begun a new series of cascades. The drop didn't look very hard, but no one knew where we were: a lot further from known territory than we had ever dared to hope. With a little more boldness and experience we would have freeclimbed down but chose to return, the magnitude of our discovery slowly sinking in. Not far from the drop we found a bank of dry sand, dotted with tiny white pebbles. Looking closely, we saw that the pebbles were the shells of albino snails. It was obvious that there had been no water in this spot for a very long time. Our snail corpses must be thousands, perhaps tens of thousands of years old, a realisation that added to a powerful sense of eeriness as we made our way back to the familiar streamway.

John and Keith were just emerging from the Trench Pitches, and at last our excitement found vent. They were not in a mood to listen: their trip had been plagued by bad bolts and Keith dropping a number of essential items down the third pitch. They had been forced to turn back a long way from the 1979 limit. "Dave and Mike babbled incoherently about 'miles' of extension with rifts, shafts, chambers, etc" John wrote dourly in the log. Simon was little more impressed at our account back in the refugio: "Look, the way on is with the water, this is probably just a short side passage." Bets were laid on the real length of our claimed 500-metre extension, with a distance one fifth of that emerging as the consensus view. I wasn't bothered. Soon the doubters could see for themselves.

We were well settled at Ario now. Around the water supply was a circle of six or seven tents, sheltered from the wind by the slopes of Cabeza Forma. There we climbed to a shoulder in the evenings to watch the sun setting into the sea of white cloud that still covered the lower slopes; earlier in the day, we went a little higher and used deep cracks in the bare limestone as one of the world's most spectacular open air lavatories. The centrepiece of the campsite, next to the powerful camping gas stove, was a vast plastic sack of grey-green granules. Dehydrated, unflavoured vegetable protein: the only sponsorship we had managed to con from food manufacturers. John insisted it was very nutritious: against all evidence, he claimed that with enough onions, peppers and tomatoes, it was edible. He even tried it for breakfast: with powdered milk and water, as a cereal. Arguments soon broke out over the polythene bag: "But we are supposed to be on holiday," I said one evening in exasperation at the latest offering: protoveg risotto cooked with short-grain pudding rice set into a salty, solid lump.

John looked horrified. "It's not a holiday, it's an expedition." We were very lucky, he went on: this year we usually had two meals a day. In 1979, with Martin Laverty doing the catering, that had been a rare event.

While John and Keith continued their struggle with the streamway, Mike and I showed Simon our extension and began surveying the Teresa Series. I was shown how to use the compass and clinometer, and Mike read the tape measure between each marked survey station on the wall. Simon did the hard bit, drawing up the notes and making a sketch to fill out the line survey into a proper map of the cave. After forty-one 'legs' we were 300 metres into the new passage and nowhere near our furthest point. Simon began to be impressed.

The climb which had stopped us was very easy indeed. Below, the passage became a rift, and the roof vanished from sight. Holes in the floor afforded a glimpse of deeper galleries below, where pools glistened, reflecting our lights. Another climb, and then a junction: one way led to an aven, the other appeared to be the way on. Time was getting short, and once again we turned round. Mike wrote in the log that night: "Xitu now looks like a much more complex and lengthy system than was expected only a few days ago." In the entrance chamber beyond the rift, Simon heard the plaintive sound of a motherless crow, abandoned in its nest. The disturbance of our passage had driven its parent away. His zoological and maternal instincts got the better of him and he scooped up the bird in his helmet, resolving to look after it in our shared tent.

Overnight, the chilling cloud moved further up the hill, welling up from the gorge and spilling over the fringe of the Ario plateau. Only Colin Nicholls and Mike Boase expressed any enthusiasm for caving next morning, and the rest of us left them to it. As the cloud still crept in, we inched further up the hill, hoping to prolong the sunbathing as long as possible. Mike and Colin left at 1 p.m.: slowly everybody was starting later and later. Usually I got the blame, allegedly taking longer than anyone else to put in contact lenses, brush teeth, check SRT gear and eat another piece of dried out Spanish bread and mysterious green jam. It was becoming clear that any depth gained in Xitu was bound to be achieved in the afternoon.

By 3 o'clock the struggle was lost, and we retreated to tents as drizzle began to fall. An hour later it had turned to steady rain, and the temperature was down many degrees. Simon and I lay on our stomachs, trying desultorily to read and ignore the frequent squawks from our voluble crow. We had put it in an open billycan in the hope that most of its impress-ive lime production would miss the groundsheet. Cooking was no fun that night. Now there was wind as well as rain. I thought of Colin and Mike. Down there it would be wet, the Trench stream swelled in volume. They had not returned by midnight, and we discussed plans of action. The conversation took a course which was to be echoed many times in the years to come.

"They might be in real trouble! The pitches might be impass-able," I said.

"Perhaps we should send an advance rescue party down to look for them immediately," said Keith, "although I'd rather not go myself because my furry suit is still a little damp."

"I ought to stay here to act as controller," Simon said.

"I suppose there's not much we can do if they are trapped by water right now," Keith mused.

We all came to the same conclusion: "Might as well wait to see if they're not back by morning."

The wind beat noisily at the canvas and I snuggled deep inside my sleeping bag. Tomorrow might be a good day to go down to the bar.

I awoke at six, pressed by a cold, heavy weight. Snow. It is not supposed to snow in Spain in July, but it had, and was. We had caught it just in time to prevent the accumulation from crushing the tent. I heaved it off and unzipped the door to peer out into a blizzard. Through the virtual white-out I could see that Colin and Mike's tents had collapsed: they probably weren't back. This time we really would have to go and look for them. I turned back into the tent to pull on as many tee shirts as I could find. The crow was squawking more loudly than usual, and was craning its neck in a highly agitated fashion. "Simon," I said, "I think there is something wrong with this crow." As I got into my only (thin) sweater it retched, sending a powerful stream of green vomit across the top of my sleeping-bag. For five minutes it threw up continuously, spattering walls, floor and Simon's beard. I marvelled that such a tiny thing was capable of holding and regurgitating so much. Then it died. Someone, we later discovered, had fed it a poisonous slug.

With the rescue on the point of leaving, Colin and Mike returned. They were a sorry sight: soaked to the skin and badly exposed. Their trip had been a grim struggle with wet pitches, friable rock and bad bolts: they had reached the 1979 limit, but failed to go further. They had regained the entrance in zero visibility hours earlier and spent the intervening period getting lost in the half-mile distance between Xitu and the campsite. Mike complained of severe depression.

Keith put their ordeal in perspective. "It's a good thing you did get back when you did. If you'd still been lost and we'd missed you and gone down the cave, we'd have been really puzzled not to find you down there."

We moved into the refugio that day and took up residence. It did seem a great deal more sensible to cook on a solid table with solid chairs and benches to sit on, a bright gas lantern at night and beds with mattresses upstairs. The tents stayed up, but were seldom occupied. In a fit of poor commercial sense, Eduardo announced that we could be 'federados'. That meant that sleeping in the refugio cost about 20 pence per person per night. Eduardo had the services of a donkey, which impressed us each afternoon when the shepherds from the huts across the plateau dropped in with their own burro. Eduardo's beast suddenly sprouted a thick, black, four-foot penis, which would, after the invariable rebuff, subside once more to invisibility.

By lunchtime the snow was melting rapidly. Warmed by a few bottles of the burro's burden, a rather sharp vino tinto, we packed and left for Los Lagos. Graham and Keith remained, determined to push into new ground next day. As the rest of us sat in Amador's restaurant above the bar, they were in our thoughts. The menu was limited but well-cooked: trout, steak, menestra stew and fabada, the Asturian delicacy made with beans, chorizo sausage and morcilla black pudding. The range of drinks was broader: barrel-sized ginebras y tonicas, oaky Rioja wines and a long list of slippery digestives: ponche, anís and cuarenta y tres, a brown liqueur served in balloons filled to the brim. Thus emboldened, I took out a harmonica and played the blues. The others put up with it for about five minutes until I realised I had lost my audience. I resolved to keep my talents for underground, as a way of keeping warm while waiting to climb the big pitch which we had now decided must lie around the next corner. Sure it would be wet: there was a lot of water in that streamway. But Colin and Mike, thoroughly recovered, were quite certain: there was a way on below the last pitch, and they had heard the sound of falling water.

Back at Ario the following evening there was an air of expectancy. Keith and Graham were due back, and had lugged down still more tackle, enough to rig half a dozen new pitches. No one was prepared for Keith's glum face when they staggered in towards midnight.

"It's finished. A sump."

Colin and Mike – and the terminus reached in 1979 – had been almost in spitting distance of the end of the cave. One short crawl through boulders led, as Graham put it, "to the plopping sounds of a large sump pool thirty feet down." Black walls plunged uniformly below the surface of the water, thick mud everywhere suggesting that the water backed up a long way in times of high water. We had been 'Ghar Parau-ed' with a vengeance. Ever hopeful, Keith had abseiled into the water and swum delicately around the walls, testing with his feet to see if he could feel any continuation which might 'go' with a short free-dive. But the rock was as vertical below the surface as above: a proper flooded shaft. The old hands recalled the Forcau expedition of 1976: that too had ended with an underwater drop at a very disappointing depth. I tried to inject a cheerful note: "There's still the Teresa Series, don't forget! That might lead to anything." My alternative route was more promising than ever, its long horizontal distance taking the passage well away from the flooded zone and offering every chance of leading to an entirely separate system of shafts. But caving expeditions tend to exhibit a remarkable group psychology, with all participants swinging erratically from euphoria to depression. Today was a depressive day and no mistake.

But the Teresa Series did carry on, although the lack of faith still shown by the team meant that the next two trips were notably unproductive. The first carried no tackle at all, but discovered a pitch. Trevor Neathaway urinated over its edge and christened it Servicio, the Spanish for lavatory. The next group down brought a ladder and descended, but failed to carry additional tackle. A hundred metres further on was another drop. Those hundred metres were enough to lift the prevailing mood of pessimism. The draught was as strong as ever, and blew now along a passage many times the size of the constricted galleries above. To one side, a towering black aven introduced a small stream, although the water sank into a tiny fissure at its base.

The new mood of enthusiasm was not, however, shared by absolutely everyone. A young couple from Southampton owned an all important car which, whilst Dudley's vehicle was in need of yet another repair, was our only transport to the shops at Cangas. It was clear that they were not attuned to the spartan expedition ethos so typified by John's attitude to the protoveg. Eventually, with the cave survey lagging behind the exploration limit, the husband was asked to help on a surveying trip.

"I can't go today," he said, "my wetsuit needs mending."

John examined the item: there were a few microscopic holes around the crutch. Its owner promised to repair it by sticking on a large new patch, and left the thing lying on a rock outside the refugio.

That afternoon it rained. Neoprene won't stick when it's wet, and the wetsuit was getting wetter by the minute. John, irate, picked it up and without a second thought unzipped the couple's tent and flung the cold black rubber suit inside – realising too late his terrible mistake: the wet wetsuit had effected a coitus interruptus. There was a terrified scream as John hurried off. Two days later the couple left, taking their car with them, denying themselves a great place in the annals of potholing history, and forcing the rest of us to rent a SEAT Mirafiore.

It fell to Keith and William to rig the pitch beyond Servicio. It began in an area of loose and shattered rock, and as they searched for hours for a suitable belay in a maze of stacked boulders, the pair felt the insidious effects of Xitu's cold. The air temperature varied between four and seven degrees centigrade: coupled with dampness and a draught, it made the cave feel much colder than those in Britain. William described the first attempt at rigging a descent in his diary:

Inching round a huge rock – 10 feet high, and 6 feet wide – we came to a ledge covered in rocks. There was a horrible takeoff for a ladder pitch. Particularly close to the edge was a rock six feet long, two feet wide and one foot thick. We kicked this over the edge, finding on our return that Trevor had meant using it as a belay point for the ladder. After a bit of effort, we rigged the pitch and Keith set off into the unknown. Some time later, he returned. He was still 25 feet from the floor at the bottom of the ladder. We abandoned the attempt and looked for somewhere to hang a rope from.

They found it at a higher level, where a little round chamber contained an inviting slot in the floor through which rocks fell freely. Keith bolted it and called it The Gap, after the term which Etonian Bill used to describe his year between school and university – most people were happy with 'year off'. William continued:

I was getting amazingly cold, sitting still doing nothing, counting off the hours by the refills of water I had to put in my carbide. When Keith had found the other hang for the pitch, he told me to put the gear away, which I did thankfully, as it was warming. We could just see the floor with our lights, but as we were tired and fed up, amazingly decided not to descend the pitch, as it would have meant putting on SRT gear again. My wetsuit was also rubbing painfully. A slow trip out, as my carbide was burning very low. Self-lining in the entrance series, I had the rope going through my Croll ascender on my chest, and as it was slack pulled it through – it jerked the stinkie off my helmet, leaving me in total darkness in the middle of a pitch.

I was very tired indeed and panting hard when I finally got out. One of the nasty features of this cave is that the rift and the top two ladders require brute strength when one is at one's tiredest. We both got out about 2.30 a.m. My carbide wouldn't stay alight in the wind, and we had a slow walk back. I was walking bow-legged, because my wetsuit was causing me agonies around the groin. I was all for going to bed at once, but Keith had just about persuaded me to eat some food when, as I was starting to change, I heard a scrabbling noise from within my tent. Colin's head shot out and he emptied the entire contents of his stomach onto the grass. I still ate some supper in spite of this. During the night I kept dreaming I was still down the cave and waking up all tense. Not very restful.

Mike Busheri and Graham descended The Gap. The hole in the floor of the chamber dropped into the middle of a cavern of breathtaking dimensions, with a landing after 25 metres on a floor of giant boulders. A short ladder drop followed, and still the floor of the chamber fell away. Graham rigged a rope from a large flake, disobeying all rules about free-hangs and so earning the name of the shaft: Graham's Balls-Up. Out of reach, above an overhanging wall on the far side of the cavern, it appeared that a wide rift passage continued in the line of the Teresa Series above. At the bottom of the pitch, Graham's worst fear was confirmed. He wrote: "The bottom half of the pitch was drippy. At the bottom, the chamber extended a little further. But despite all our efforts, it appeared to choke completely. We pissed off out on the off chance it would still be light when we got out."

John and I did not believe Graham when he returned that night. "Get the bloody thing surveyed, photographed and derigged as soon as possible," he said. To hell with that. Surely, we said, there must be a way through the 'impenetrable' boulder choke. Graham said he had noticed one possibility: a climb up the loose wall at the far end of the chamber had appeared to lead to a hole between the rocks. But he insisted that it was far too dangerous to attempt.

A little after lunchtime on the following day John and I stood at the top of the Balls-Up. The truly appalling rigging convinced us that Graham had already been filled with pessimism before going down – a thin wire with no back-up was no way to attach a rope for an exposed descent of 25 metres. John banged in a couple of bolts. The rope touched the sides in a series of abrasion points all the way down, but at least it was securely anchored. The size of the chamber filled us with awe.

At the bottom we ferreted about in the choke, descending a few blind tunnels in the floor. There was no way through: the trickle watering Graham's Balls-Up disappeared through microscopic cracks. Everything was made of boulders: roof, walls and floor. In British caves, the passage of potholers has tended to stabilise such areas of collapse. Here, huge rocks were balanced on impacted mud. A climb up to a possible way on looked loose, but there were no other options.

Seized with determination, I scrambled up without telling John, who was still furtling in the interstices below. The climb was easy, the only risk being pebbles and sand on its capacious holds. At the top, I clambered over a watershed into a rift. Solid rock again. I held my breath. It looked as if the choke had succumbed without a fight. Seven metres further I poked my head through a window in the wall. "Aaarghh!!! Ni ni ni!!!" I later wrote in the log, "a wide shaft with roaring water at the bottom!" I called to John euphorically, and he joined me at once. We cursed that we had brought no tackle, lobbing boulders into the pit. They echoed back, suggesting that Xitu was about to resume the dimensions of the Gap.

We munched a piece of cooking chocolate and glowed. We had not been underground long, and resolved to make our exit as fast as possible in order to return next day. Back at the climb John went first.

There was a scrunching sound, a strangled yelp, and John was tipping backwards, head first. He bounced once at the bottom of the climb and slid on, down to the bottom of the boulder pile: in all, a fall of more than seven metres. His light was out. Leaning out from the lip of the climb, I saw him staggering blindly, trying to find somewhere to sit down. There was blood on his face.

My emotions flipped from joy to terror. I climbed down delicately, thinking, "Please God, let him be OK." I reached him and dabbed at his face: relief and gratitude flooded in. He was shaken, but largely unhurt: he had a small cut near his nose which was producing an impressive amount of gore, diluted with sweat, but his helmet had saved him from more serious injury. We sat on the boulders and recovered our breath, and then a light appeared on the rope on the Balls-Up. William. His distinctive tones echoed down to us: "I say, is this the master cave?" We took out the tension of the preceding minutes and slandered him mercilessly.

John's accident on the climb – which had now been named after his birthplace, The Pilling Slip – led him to take the uncharacteristic action of asking for a day off. Kev Senior and his fiancée Kathy had just turned up from Southampton, greeted warmly by everyone. John had phoned him from Cangas the day before his departure:

"Hello, it's John here. I'm in Spain."

"How are you?"

"It's sumped about five metres deeper than last year."

"What? What did you say?"

"But it's still going. We found a route over the Trench Pitches. Listen. Not much time. We've run out of porridge. Can you bring some out? We can't buy any anywhere in Spain."

"Yes, I suppose so. How much do you need?"

"As much as you can carry."

Next day Kev and Kathy struggled towards the Brittany Ferries terminal with bulging rucksacks and a hold-all full of oats. A few minutes after his arrival at Ario, I had signed Kev up for pushing next day. He recorded events in his diary:

Dave obviously enjoys showing me the Teresa Series. I feel like a tourist, on a guided tour.

The Gap stuns me. Dave is a tiny patch of light among the boulders far below. I catch up with him above the climb where John fell off. The rocks we throw down make ambiguous noises as they come to rest. Dave wants to go first: keen. I am happy to let him as he thrutches through the hole to the top of the pitch, the rope belayed to some stalagmites. I look down after him but can't see him, because he has moved away along a ledge.

"Are you down?"

The reply comes back in short bursts. He is obviously preoccupied.

"No. There's a big ledge but the pitch continues. I'm going to have to put a bolt in. You can't come down. It's too loose everywhere and I want to stay on the rope."

The tiny sound of hammer blows filter up as I wait and wait and wait. I think Dave is taking an incredibly long time over this bolt. I could put a bolt in much faster than this. I occupy myself checking my gear and flexing muscles to keep warm. I remember my dream of discovering a big lake in Xitu, but we are much more likely to find a pile of boulders than a lake. The hammering has stopped!

"Kev! I'm going down. Hey, it's a lovely pitch . . . Kev, it's fucking enormous. Rope free! You're not going to believe this but there's a lake at the bottom."

About time, I think. A lake, though. I want to see this.

It was late in the afternoon of my twenty-first birthday, and now the fear had gone. Twenty minutes later we reached that little chamber described at the start of chapter one and dropped our rocks, listening to them land after five or six seconds. Kev again:

Addicted to the silence of the falling rocks, we select another each and traverse out along the rift to see if we can get an even longer fall. Dave throws his out but the interval is still no more than five and a half seconds. He points to the slot below us, where we sit braced across with our backs and feet.

"How far is it down there?"

"Only about 15 metres, I think. The lip of the main pitch must be in front of us somewhere." I drop my rock to prove the point. It hits something very soon and makes no more sound until . . . boooommmmm!!!

"Oh God. We're over the pitch here as well." We brace ourselves more firmly and traverse very carefully back to the boulder chamber. We have been sitting nonchalantly over 500 feet of nothing. In fact the boulders we have been picking up from the floor of this chamber are just a blockage in a narrow part of the shaft. We decide not to remove any more rocks from the floor. To think only two days ago the cave was believed to be finished. The hard bit is only now beginning.

We 'wake up' outside, under stars. A breeze blows away the stale smells of carbide and the sardines we have been munching underground. We want to run but are far too tired, so settle for a brisk walk back to the refugio. Dave sings an inane lyric to a tune by a group called Tuxedo Moon. It has two notes and goes: "Two hundred metres (pause) in one pitch . . . thousand metres . . . in one cave." I join in with this tuneless rubbish as we crash up the stairs into a bedroom filled with sleeping cavers. It is six a.m. but Dave wastes no time: "We've found a fucking enormous pitch. Six seconds!" "Oh God," says John, sleepily. "Shit," says someone else. We descend for a breakfast of cold hash and a bottle of wine. Breakfast first, then a wash; then at last, disturbed sleep.

3

The Big Shaft Men

On a series of subsequent trips, the scale of the physical and psychological barrier which the big pitch posed became apparent. The first part was easy: 15 metres of rope hung from two bolts took us to a spacious ledge. But that was only 15 metres: beyond, the vast black pit yawned, chilled by an icy wind. For some way below the ledge, the wall sloped gently outwards, making it impossible to rig a rope free of the walls. Abrasion points guarded by rope protectors, rubber sleeves sealed with velcro tape, were all very well on short drops like Graham's Balls-Up. But to use them on a shaft that might be 100 metres deep was out of the question. You could never be sure that the rope protectors were in the right place, and one person climbing a pitch of this length would be easily enough to sever the line. Different parties tried several angles of attack, but failed to make such impact. On one excursion, Graham and I poured fluorescein dye into the stream at the top of the pitch, and watched everything turn vivid green – the idea was to put charcoal dye detectors in a series of springs around the Cares Gorge to discover where the water came out. We penduled and dangled in the green cascade, and at last found a tiny ledge ten metres below the first where we placed two bolts, one in the floor of the ledge itself. I proved that even then it would be necessary to rebelay a little further down by dropping the bolt hammer when the task was finished. Like everything else, it hit the jutting wall before plunging free with a sickening whistle.

Down at Lagos, Amador was impressed. "Pozu del Xitu is now 500 metres deep or more," he told the baffled drinkers gathered in his bar, "and these English have found one of the deepest shafts in the Picos." "Hombres!" came the ritual response. Cider bottles were thrust upon us, as we tried and failed to perform the Asturian ritual of pouring the local scrumpy into unusually thin glasses from a great height without spilling a drop. Gradually it was dawning on us that Xitu might be very deep indeed.

43

The SIE, a Catalan group from Barcelona, had arrived at Ario, to renew their campaign in Cabez Muxa. This year, they were determined to reach the bottom of their entrance series shaft that made ours look puny – El Gran Abisu, 247 metres deep, albeit with ledges. But they too were impressed. We had stuck the original 1979 survey of Xitu on the wall by the refugio stairs, adding pieces of graph paper as each new discovery made it expand. Already, we were several steps down, with a huge question mark below the big pitch ripe for removal.

Skunk's advent from Birmingham finally put on end to the unproductive, wittering terror that had marked our attempts on the shaft thus far. He marched up the hill with Keith to retrieve our longest rope from Pozu Vayeya, a surface pothole Keith had been dabbling in on his days off. The rope was a monster: 200 metres of new, 11mm Bluewater III. Next day, the pair spent half an hour laboriously plaiting it into an eight strand chain – it was about twice as much as the maximum capacity of any of the tackle bags. Pausing to gather Skippy and John, they posed for photographs and set off for the entrance.

As John was to remark later, it took only four hours to reach the top of the pitch with the giant rope, but another three to untangle it, crouched uncomfortably on the freezing, wet and windy ledge. At about midnight, John and Skippy had had enough, and left the work to the hard men. They used my bolts on the micro ledge and continued down to the jutting rub point, where they dangled free in space to place two more. One gets used to spinning above very large drops with nothing to attach oneself to the walls, but the first time, it is intimidating and strenuous. At last Skunk was ready to descend. There was still an awesome black pit but now it had a rope running down it: just another pitch, he said. Three hundred feet below Keith he touched land again. A big bouldery ledge, with the stream landing splashily to one side. But it was only a balcony in the shaft. A few paces from the bottom of the rope, the drop continued, stones falling for another two seconds. "Actually," Skunk said next morning on his return from what had turned out to be a 21 hour trip, "it's quite boring."

He christened the shaft Flat Iron, not after the famous landmark on the Eiger nordwand, but through a circuitous piece of reasoning. Everyone had told him how fucking enormous the pitch was, which made it Fe – the chemical symbol for iron. But the descent kept close to an uninspiring muddy wall, so it was Flat. As a steelworker, he found that satisfying.

Kev and I were very grateful to Skunk: he had set us up for

what promised to be a trip as good as our last. And so it proved. The last drop from the balcony, another 30 metres, landed in the biggest chamber yet. At the back, atop a high boulder slope, was a black space we didn't bother investigating; instead, we found a way down through a maze of blocks into further chambers in dark, unreflective rock. We descended steadily, the depth clocking up. In one cavern, an array of old, white stalactites festooned the roof. From there we climbed down into the finest stream passage we had ever seen. The volume of water was considerable, and we stepped delicately around swirling pools in a corridor two to three metres wide, the roof far out of sight. There were extraordinary helectite formations, horizontal stalactite deposits like strings of spaghetti 30 centimetres long, and at one point a circular, dark green pothole in the stream, filled with water that looked about seven metres deep. The rock was amber-orange now, and still we advanced, down cascades, beneath a drenching inlet, traversing over a section of deep canal. at last the roar of another waterfall grew louder as we rounded a series of bends, and we stood once more at the top of a pitch.

We had left the tackle at the bottom of Flat Iron, but had no hesitation at retracing our steps to fetch it. The pitch looked easy to rig: no need for bolts, with large natural flakes offering what appeared to be a free but damp descent. We got lost on our way back, and again on returning to the shaft. "Bags I first" said Kev. Grudgingly I concurred. Kev's light slowly diminished. Another pitch lay immediately beyond.

Martin, meanwhile, had been gathering up his dye detectors. Next morning, he demonstrated the technique: to 'activate' the charcoal left in balls of nylon tights with alcohol. If the dye had passed out of the spring where they had been left, the theory went, the solution would turn green. The results seemed unequivocal and depressing. The detectors left at the bottom of the gorge by the valley system Cueva Culiembro stayed clear. But those collected from a small spring at the Canal de Trea, a precipitous gully joining Ario with the Cares, turned green as pea soup. The spring was only 700 metres below Xitu's entrance: if the test were accurate, that was the maximum depth we could hope to achieve. Once 700 metres had seemed an impossible goal. But now, we were all not very secretly hoping that Xitu would pass the kilometre mark – the first British-explored cave to do so. Martin's experience carried weight, and gloom returned. Only Keith and Skunk seemed unaffected: "Let's just have a bloody look, eh?" they said.

My reaction to all this was to go cave-hunting in the sun with

Dave Thwaites. If Xitu were about to end, as Martin's test suggested, we would have to find another hole to explore. Simon pointed us in the direction of the Vega Aliseda, a vale high above the Ario plateau, below the main ridge of rocky peaks. I was tired from my efforts the previous afternoon and evening, and took little notice of our exact path. I had also forgotten the compass, with which we had planned to take sightings on peaks in order to fix the position of any promising entrances. After several hours, we had found very little. We had climbed a long way, over difficult terrain, but all the shafts were blocked with snow or scree close to the surface. We had run out of water, and today was a day of unremitting heat. By the time we toiled up yet another slope of boulder scree, I was exhausted.

But at the top, just below what I believed to be the main ridge of the massif, a snow patch provided a welcome drink. Behind it was a cave – not another vertical shaft, but a proper, walk-in, horizontal passage. We squeezed past the snow plug, alert again, and by the light of a single torch walked down a sandy slope. Soon a pitch blocked our way, but on the opposite side from where we stood a small stream spattered into the drop. Both of us were aware of the potential: a cave high above Ario, perhaps as much as 2000 metres above sea level, with a stream. "Dave," I said, "this really could be the deepest cave in the world." It was a shame about the compass, but being so close to the ridge, the hole should be easy to find again. We painted a sign above the snow at the entrance, arbitrarily designating the region Area 6: 'OUCC 1980 1/6.' Clambering onto the ridge, a magnificent view of the rocky triangle of Pena Santa de Enol rose above a new field of bleak limestone pitted with shafts. There was one almost at the top of the ridge, a circular tube ten metres across. It sounded deep, and we called it 2/6. One day, I thought, these caves would provide OUCC with some happy times.

Unlike British limestone, the rock in the Picos contains large quantities of razor-sharp authigenic quartz needles, and the sand through which one often had to crawl in Xitu would have made a good grinding paste. We all wore rubber gloves to protect our hands, but many of us were developing painful septic sores on the fingers caused by the needles working their way under the skin – the 'Ario Festers'. This highly abrasive material was also taking a heavy toll on the equipment. On some of the heavily-used abseils in the entrance series, each descent was marked by the extrusion of a grey sludge from our descenders – ground up aluminium. The ropes were also wearing out. The sheath of the penultimate rope before Customs Hall was disintegrating: bits of nylon flying off every time it was used. We should have replaced it, but now we were running alarmingly short of gear. Every length of rope available had already been carried deep into the cave, ready for pushing, but it amounted to no more than a couple of bags full. The manufacturers claimed that even the bare core of the ropes had a breaking strain above 3000 kilos: crossing our fingers, we tried to believe them and left the worn line in place.

Keith and Skunk went down the pitch discovered by Kev and named it and its wet predecessor the Samaritans, after Skunk's act of generosity in providing Kev and me with such a pleasant trip two days before. Beyond, the cave was much less hospitable: a tortuous, awkward and narrow route over stalactite blockages in a winding rift. At the end, four steep climbs, the Marble Steps, brought a widening of the passage. But the stream was now a powerful torrent exceeding all but the wettest of British caves in volume, and it was impossible to keep dry. The entrance rift and the other narrow sections had long ago worn away most of the waterproofing from their oversuits, and opened up many tears which, like the rest of the team, they tried with increasing futility to repair with patches and glue.

Keith wrote up their trip in the log: "We didn't give a shit about getting wet. We came to the edge of the last climb, a drop of about 30 feet. I said we ought to tackle this with a rope. Skunk agreed, and then we both half climbed, half slid down without one, right in the middle of the stream. We were intoxicated by our discoveries – it was superb. Every corner we rounded we feared the end, but it continued, and we were stopped not by the end of the cave, as the others at camp predicted, but by a pitch. It's about 45 feet deep, and there's little in the way of belays. We were both dying to rig and descend it, but a sober appreciation of the situation made us agree to return. We were both thoroughly wet, we'd spent a long time at the head of the previous pitch, and the only food below Flat Iron was half a bar of choc in Skunk's prusik bag. (All my chocolate had fallen out through the holes in my bag.) At the entrance, I couldn't believe it: daylight yet again. Another 21 hour trip."

Slowly, the pyschological limits of what was considered a reasonable trip and time to spend underground were being extended. Once, a journey to the top of Flat Iron had seemed long and serious. Now, after the marathon prusik up that shaft, in all 138 metres, it seemed as if one was 'nearly out' – four hours from the entrance, in itself a quite respectable caving trip in Britain.

As exploration progressed, Martin's theory was beginning to appear less convincing. The depth reached at the top of the undescended shaft must be, we thought, close to 700 metres, and there was no sign that an end was imminent. It was also clear that the lower reaches of the cave carried rather more water than that emerging in the spring in the Canal de Trea. The obvious explanation was that the dye test result had, for some reason, been false. Martin chose another, more tortuous analysis. "Maybe the water falling down the big pitch doesn't flow on into the rest of the cave," he said. "Maybe some or all of it goes off in the direction of that black space no one's looked at at the back of the chamber below it, and then comes out at Trea."

That chamber, easily the biggest in the system – so big that sometimes it took a while to find the end of the Flat Iron rope before climbing out – was now known as Eton Palais, after a spirited rendition from William of his old school Boating Song during a surveying trip with John. Measuring the pitch had been time-consuming and difficult. Our longest tape measure was only 30 metres, much shorter than the shaft, and they had been forced to resort to string. William recorded their antics in his diary:

I overtook John on the big ledge, making a survey station there. Next, I went down to the mid-air bolts on the rub point. It's quite interesting making notes, hanging from bolts with nothing to grab hold of. I tied one end of the string to one of the bolts and abseiled down the main pitch, paying out the string as I went. After some distance, I ran out of string, and had to tie a second ball on, which in its turn also ran out. I tried to tie a third ball on, but it got tangled, so I broke it and tied the end of the tape on as I could see the floor so presumably I was less than 30 metres above it. Reached the floor after what had seemed like ages to John and he abseiled down, getting the string tangled round the rope as he did so. I reckon we must have spent the next four hours untangling the string as both our lights ran out of carbide. We talked, sang, and finally just untangled, or more exactly, I held the string while John untangled. In the end we cut it. I'd got very cold, although I'd been artificially shaking to stop myself getting exposure.

Climbing up, William continued on above the ledge while John began the ascent of the main pitch. "This was a big mistake. The rope I was on dislodged a couple of large rocks which whizzed horribly close to John four or five seconds later. 'Below, my God, below, BELOW' I cried." Not that there was anything John could have done if the rocks had not missed him.

Rigging the pitch beyond the Marble Steps was as difficult as Keith had predicted. At about 2 a.m. on August 1st, Graham finished the job, with two bolts in poor rock. Although only 20 metres deep, it was the wettest shaft yet – 'Dampturation'. Not only did Xitu's stream tumble on top of the caver, there was a very large inlet crashing down from a huge aven above; one of the largest inlets anywhere in the cave. At the bottom, Graham wrote, they set off along a wide passage into virgin territory:

Our spirits were aroused with exploration fever, as always on arrival at the sharp end. We strode out boldly, hoping that we were about to enjoy a long stretch of this grand streamway, but it suddenly took a sharp turn to the left and down a steep slope: another pitch. Keith eagerly scrambled down to the edge to estimate the size of the shaft, but the noise of the water obscured the sound of the rocks he dropped. "Could you go up the passage and get a bigger one?" he asked.

There was only one rock that would do; so large that I couldn't lift it. Instead I rolled it gingerly to the top of the slope above Keith. He told me to roll it down to the small ledge where he sat, but as soon as I had eased the thing over, the boulder began trundling towards him with unstoppable acceleration. It hit the ledge, bounced up and flew towards Keith's chest. It was all he could do to jump up onto small handholds as the block whizzed beneath him and over the lip, to be engulfed in the darkness. The two of us were frozen, exchanging horrified glances as we realised that we still hadn't heard it land. Finally there was a distant boom of its impact on the floor of the shaft. Keith smiled, and so did I. The depth of this pitch made Xitu without doubt the deepest cave ever explored by a British group.

The two traversed above the divide where the water poured down, to reach a balcony ledge looking out into the impressive shaft. They had two ropes left, neither long enough to reach the bottom: they tied them together, and Keith tried to remember the awkward procedure needed to pass a knot during an abseil. His Petzl bobbin descender was worn away by the quartz, and he had had to borrow Martin's rack device for this trip. This too was now etched with deep grooves, so he borrowed Graham's descender, promising to tie it on the end of the rope for Graham to pull up and follow. The line of the rope ran down a right angle buttress in the wall, and hence the name they chose: Pythagoras Pitch. Graham went on:

Sometime later there was a distant call from below, indicating he had reached the bottom. Looking down, I could see his light moving and flickering in what was obviously another enormous chamber. Spurred on by the intoxication of discovery, he neglected to tie my descender on the end of the rope. He chimneyed down past two large waterfalls, and on via a loose boulder slope. Eventually he reached a stream passage again, and followed it a long way past numerous cascades, finally arriving at another pitch, where he turned back.

To me, this seemed an eternity, stranded as I was in a wetsuit at the top of Pythagoras. I fell asleep for a while, which only made me still colder. An exuberant Keith returned to a subdued reception. He insisted I shouldn't wait for him on the way out, as moving independently would speed up the eight hour journey to the surface. Finding a way back through unfamiliar passages kept giving me the nagging doubt that I was going up a blind inlet, and I tried to suppress the feeling of being lost, even though I could rarely remember where I was going. Starting off on the 200 foot Samaritan pitches, my light went out. Carbide lamps do not function when doused by water tumbling 200 feet. My electric back-up wasn't working, so I was plunged into darkness. To add to this minor trauma, my foot ropewalker was jamming on the rope and I couldn't see why. Being in total darkness does not mean you are without sensations: swinging on the end of a 200 foot rope alternately bashing against an unseen wall and then beneath the full force of the waterfall made me a little unwell. I suppressed panic by swearing at my ropewalker. Eventually it came free and I carried on in the dark. I knew when I was at the top because the water was coming at me horizontally, not vertically. There I was able to relight my lamp and carry on.

After nearly 24 hours in wetsuits, Graham and Keith were suffering from agonising groin sores when they regained the surface at last. Keith emerged, clutching his genitalia, just as John and I appeared over the hill from Los Lagos. He bent down and kissed the rock: "Xitu, I love you."

Little now remained but hard work. We had only one length of rope left, and that had to be cut from the end of the line rigged into Eton Palais. Dutifully, on another trip well over 20 hours, John and I carried it to the limit reached by Keith. I was surprised and impressed by the passage beyond Pythagoras: it was one of the most difficult in the cave, but Keith had explored it alone. A section of meandering corridor with helectites like bonsai trees led to an overhanging, smooth drop of twelve feet. Descending was easy, but a large flake that refused to detach itself when we hit it with a hammer made climbing up again wet and strenuous. Near the top, with the stream pouring in through his open collar, John stuck on his harness, suspended painfully and aquatically. I rescued him with a strong pull from above, but the ordeal gave him haemorrhoids. The climb was christened PAFS Pot – Piles Arising From Suspension.

Below was a pool deeper than any yet encountered. The stream flowed now in a vicious diagonal rift, sharp projections tearing at what little was left of our oversuits. A chamber beyond led to Keith's pitch, which we rigged badly from jammed chock-stones. Another 20 metre descent; and a short length of more comfortable passage; we stood at the top of yet another drop. It looked quite big, 40 metres or more. We had used every scrap of rope we had, including the strapping used on Dudley's roof-rack. It was the end for the season.

There remained surveying, photography and detackling. Kev, Simon and Keith polished off the former all the way from the Samaritans to the limit in one 24 hour extravaganza, keeping going with the aid of hot soup. It was midnight before they began their labour, starting at the bottom: a nightshift, as Kev remarked. He described the trip:

We decide to try and measure the undescended last pitch so I climb down to a ledge which will allow me to lower the tape without it catching. I tie my rack on the end because it will make a good clatter when it hits the bottom, then slowly lower it down the hole. Carefully I haul it back up.

There's a risk of it catching and if it does I lose my descender and some of the tape but it comes up OK. I start rewinding the tape back into its case but suddenly the winder comes away in my hand. This is bad enough but then the spindle in the tape case falls out and disappears down the pitch. "Oh well. We'll just have to carry the tape in loops over our shoulders," I suggest. I mark where I am sitting with a paper tissue under some stones. This will be our first station on the survey and the tape is stretched between me and Keith, who is at station two. "Two point eight metres," he says. He starts to take a compass bearing. It's taking him ages. What's he doing? Eventually, "nine five degrees." Another long pause while he gets out and reads the 'clino. "Come on," I think to myself, "at this rate we'll be down here all week." It's getting to Simon too. "Is there something wrong with the instruments?" he asks. "Well I can't see the dial very well," says Keith. "Hang on . . . which scale should I be reading?" We struggle on and build up a rhythm at last. The tape snags and we lose ten centimetres off the end. A little later it snags again and now we have to subtract a metre from each measurement.

There are only a few legs to go now, but Simon has run out of paper. The only sheet left is muddy and soaking. He tries to dry it out over the flame of his light. This is quite simply ridiculous. Here we are, more than 600 metres down, 10 hours from the surface, drying tracing paper over a carbide light so we can measure a few more metres of passage. It's so stupid I begin to feel really good for the first time on this trip.

It's six am, and the job is finished. The survey notes are safely cached in a bag and we're huddled round a gaz stove waiting for the soup to boil. If I had to choose between ensuring that Simon, Keith, myself or the survey notes got safely out of the cave at the moment I think I might just go for the notes.

The surveyors gathered at the top of the entrance series and met Skunk and me just before the rift, on the way down. Our trip, in which we removed the ropes and hauled them up as far as Eton Palais, was even longer: 28 hours. On the way in, Skunk took our only photographs of the deeper regions of the cave, coaxing his increasingly chilly model while he shot off three rolls of film. After turning round, the trip became steadily more arduous, as we collected rope after rope, prusiking up the shafts with bags dangling from our harnesses. But I was beginning to feel more at ease deep within the cave. Below the big pitch, Xitu had a dark, exhilarating splendour, a grandeur which only we and our few friends had seen. The effort of the trip was its own reward, and we seemed – like the rest of the expedition – to be working instinctively as a team. The days when Simon had had to draw up detailed 'masterplans' of who should be doing what and when had long gone: decisions were being taken automatically, without need for leadership or discussion. We had attained that rare level of oneness described by Doug Scott as the apotheosis of Himalayan climbing: what we were doing was right, felt right. The caving was the finest we had ever done or were ever likely to do, but the way in which we were doing it gave it an almost spiritual, transcendental satisfaction.

Reaching the upper streamway above the Trench Pitches at teatime on the second day, we met Martin and a party on the way in to continue with the derig. We were exhausted, but their tidings restored our vigour: the wall survey had almost reached the floor of the refugio, and according to rough calculations, Xitu was 910 metres deep – number 20 in the world. And it was still going, 'Rape B'Rape' Pitch – its maidenhead breached by rope and tape, according to the peculiar workings of Keith's system of nomenclature – the first of many shafts left for 1981. Back in England, we found that Simon had done his sums wrong: the furthest point reached was actually only 829 metres below the surface, while the passage length was some four kilometres. But that still made us second deepest in Spain, the deepest in the Picos and the deepest ever British team.

Nevertheless, none of us was going to rest easy until the last pitch was detackled, and the last trip had made its exit from the cave. I felt sharply aware of the cave's continuing dangers, now that we were pulling out and concentration was less intense: it was with some relief that I replaced the chewed-up rope in the entrance series with one retrieved from further down. But there were no mishaps. On August 8, the last bags were ferried through the rift into daylight. We headed for Amador's for a feast.

We ate and drank long into the small hours. Amador provided champagne on hearing of Kev and Kathy's impending marriage: just another beverage to add to the complex and evil melange of alcoholic fluids blending inside our stomachs. At 3 a.m., ignoring the large number of family tents pitched at the Lakes for the fine holiday weekend, we headed back to camp, armed with brandy and liqueurs, for a raucous session of blues, caving songs and anything to which at least one person knew the words. At five thirty, the last revellers finally bedded down, heads reeling.

An hour and a half later we were woken by the painful and deafening sound of the Spanish equivalent of Terry Wogan blaring from what sounded like a public address system. We had scarcely absorbed the shock before our tents began to shake, and then to collapse. A posse of the other campsite residents, enraged by our antics during the night, were wreaking an awful revenge. I emerged from my sleeping-bag in my underpants: there were about 40 of them, and they looked mean. "Silencio!" I tried weakly. It was not a good line. The fattest and ugliest of the assembled matriarchs, backed by several strong and ugly sons, slapped her face in derision: "Silencio? Silencio? Silencio la noche!" I couldn't catch the rest, but "los coños Ingleses" stood out.

We were a long way from the nearest British consul.

4

El Puritan and Beyond

DAVID After Xitu, home and Oxford seemed unbearably flat. Fitness faded. With advancing Autumn, the previously distant threat of finals loomed very large. On my wall in a flat I rented for an incredibly low sum from Magdalen, the survey of Xitu, now drawn neatly and printed on a vast sheet of AO size paper, had pride of place. As the months passed, I would often break off from study and turn my chair to meditate on the map of the cave and its continuing challenge.

In September, most of us travelled to Nottingham for the annual conference of the British Cave Research Association. Simon's lecture with slides was the highlight of the two-day show, and he had to give it twice, flagged in the programme under the impressive, simple rubric: "Pozu del Xitu – 829 metres." When we had left for Spain we were caving unknowns, meriting only a small grant from the Sports Council subcommittee in charge of donations to expeditions. Suddenly, we had arrived. Our heads swelled.

Early in the academic year we chose a committee for the return visit in 1981. It was obvious that this expedition would be on a much bigger scale than anything OUCC had organised before, and already we were getting requests from old members and other cavers with a stronger or weaker connection with the club to come. Everyone knew that Xitu was almost certain to become the first British discovery deeper than the magic 1,000 metre level.

The sudden fame and great promise of the cave, further broadcast in a series of articles in caving publications, made me uneasy that another team might try to 'pirate' it. To arrive in Spain again to find another group already in the system, or worse still, to reach new ground and find a tell-tale line of bolts, was a dismaying prospect. After a chance meeting in the barn used as a changing room for Swildon's Hole in the Mendips just before Christmas my worries became almost obsessional. Some cavers from Sheffield University told us that one of their number, Steve Worthington, a well-known figure in caving circles, had gone to Xitu in September with the intention of pushing it solo. He had been using the 'cordelette' technique, whereby a complicated system involving a lot of nylon string means that the main rope does not need to be left in place on the pitches, but can be carried on down the cave, to be hauled up in place from the bottom of each shaft using the string on the way out. The net result is that much less gear needs to be carried. Worthington, our informant told us, hadn't got far: from the description, it sounded like no further than the bottom of the entrance series. But I wondered if he intended to try again. He had already been solo to the bottom of the Gouffre Berger in France, the first cave deeper than one kilometre and still a classic. Xitu, according to Martin, who had also done the Berger, was much harder. But if not Steve Worthington, I thought, what was there to stop some Poles, or Catalans or French? The rest of the team tried, unsuccessfully, to allay my fears.

Slowly, the organisation proceeded. Raising money, food and equipment was extremely easy this time. In charge was the only person with any sense of order – John Singleton, the leader for 1981 by acclaim and default.

RICHARD John wasn't only organised in himself, he was good at organising everybody else and cajoling them into helping. We were planning an underground camp, somewhere near the limit of the known cave, so that more teams could reach the bottom in comfort and, therefore, safety. More rope and ladders and karabiners and tapes and wires and bolts and hammocks and thick sleeping-bags were bought than any of us had thought possible. One thing was certain: this time, we would not be stopped by lack of tackle. What wasn't being used in Xitu could be used for pushing the other caves which we knew existed in the Xitu region – Dave's find on the ridge was top of the list.

Jim Shepherd turned up one evening with a computer-printed guide to all the SRT rigging throughout the cave, planned so that newcomers would know what to expect. Like me and the other Oxford cavers who had missed the 1980 expedition, he was fired with enthusiasm by the stories being told and retold in the stone-vaulted cellar of Brasenose.

A crucial figure in our plans was Nick White. Together with his wife, Alison, he had been caving regularly with the club for some time. The epitome of the scatter-brained scientist, tall, intense, bespectacled with a wild thatch of blond hair, he was working on new methods of radio-carbon dating, and his big ambition was to get hold of a piece of the Turin shroud. His great asset was that he knew about cars.

For a while Nick and Alison had lived in a double-decker bus in the car park of an Oxford supermarket in order to save money to buy a house. Its eventual purchase meant selling the bus, whose big-end bearings had long since gone. Nick couldn't get hold of any new ones, so built a fire with some bricks around a pile of coal and cast them in the car park, oblivious to the puzzled glances of the shoppers wheeling their loaded trolleys past him.

John told Nick to buy a vehicle. He chose a Land-Rover, built twenty years before. We heaved up the engine outside the club tackle hut in deep snow, as George Hostford, Nick's mechanical assistant, lay underneath to change the clutch. George was already acquiring a reputation for being hard. He shovelled in a quantity of fresh snow beneath the cab so that he had 'something soft' to lie on as he worked. Nervously, I wondered how I was going to keep up with people like this underground.

Nick insured the Land-Rover on the policy for his own Morris Minor and drew up a list of drivers, as at the last moment he was unable to come too. But he gave us lessons on the hills around Oxford, showing us how to double-declutch in the lower gears. George welded together a huge roof rack, which was loaded to a height of several feet with gear. More was loaded in the back, until there was almost no room at all for those travelling out by road. The passengers had to lie with their noses against the roof, on top of 2 kilometres of rope.

As we drove through France next day Keith let out a sad sigh. "Well, this is the last OUCC expedition to Spain I suppose. It's a shame really."

I was stunned: I was hoping this would be the first of many expeditions for me, and I thought Keith was even keener than I was. He went on: "We shall bottom Xitu this year, and I doubt we'll find another cave at Ario, as we've already looked pretty hard." I told him he was surely wrong, and there were still many caves yet to find in Spain. But he continued prophetically: "Even if there is another expedition, I shan't be going on it."

In the misty dawn we pulled off the road onto the broad meadow at Los Lagos to a couple of small tents, the only ones on the huge field. A thin voice emerged from one of them.

"I say!" William's unmistakable Etonian accent. "Are you from Oxford?" Skunk responded with his usual friendly greeting:

"Get up you lazy sods." Dave stuck his head out from the other tent. He looked serious.

"Richard, it's worse than I thought. The cave *has* been pirated. There's a team in it already!"

"Who are they?" asked Skunk.

"Estonians," said Dave, "and some Letts. One or two Uzbeks in their party as well, I believe." A cock crowed from the top of a large, semi-permanent structure made of a big green tarpaulin at one corner of the meadow.

"What's that?" I asked William.

"That's the bar. You'll enjoy this expedition." Brandy for breakfast was a new concept for me, but one that I had obviously got to come to terms with. We came back from the bar to create a vast pile of equipment where the neat flat lawn had been. The tents, of course, were at the bottom.

John had given the expedition vanguard the job of setting up camp and moving as much gear as possible up to Ario. We were to rig the cave as well, but this was supposed to be a bonus. It was assumed we would not go far. Some of us, particularly Dave, Skunk and Keith, took this as a challenge. We had about ten days before John and scores of others joined us. If we took things gently, we might achieve very little. On the other hand, it was possible, Dave said, if we went at it, to rig the entire cave and push on into new passage. Skunk didn't say much about this, which was a sign he agreed. Dave insisted that we should rig the whole of the entrance series next day. Everyone was sceptical: it meant carrying an awful lot of stuff up the hill and there surely wasn't time. It had taken nearly a week the previous year. Dave was adamant and asked for a companion. I volunteered, to dark looks from the others. This wasn't Yorkshire, they muttered, but Spain.

Soon enough, sweltering under a huge rucksack, I discovered what they meant. The walk up to Xitu made the walks in Yorkshire look like a turn around the block. With the lakes out of sight we marched along through a broken wilderness of nothing, each rise bringing into view another one just ahead. The pointed peaks remained as distant as ever, as did Dave, who had left me far behind.

"I usually sing to myself," he shouted back, "to set the pace."

I was terribly, terribly unfit. In Oxford I had rather foolishly bought an extra-specially large rucksack, into which I should be able to fit everything I needed to go caving. I was paying heavily for this mistake, because my extra-specially large rucksack was now crammed full of an extra-specially large load of ladders and ropes. I was carrying very much more than any other member of the expedition would, and comforted myself with this thought as I plodded along slowly behind Dave, whose rucksack obviously weighed next to nothing.

I caught up with him eventually at Las Bobbias, a small spring, where I threw off the terrible weight. As I drank the lovely mountain water, Dave revealed to me in the gentlest possible way that the last hour's walk represented the first, and easiest third of the walk up to Ario.

"You haven't anything to eat, Richard, have you?" he asked tentatively.

I told him that I had been relying on him. We had still eaten nothing all day.

"Not to worry," Dave reassured me, "we shall be able to eat at the refugio."

Dave hadn't been pulling my leg about the rest of the walk. The way became steeper and rockier, and there were some galling sections of descent.

By the time the refugio came into sight, in the lovely alp of Ario, I was no longer exhausted, for the tiredness had seemed to vanish again some way through the third hour of the walk, and I was completely resigned to the rhythmic plod and my heavy pack. Nevertheless I was famished. We met Eduardo, the guardian of the mountain refuge, and he was pleased to see us.

He had been warned of the arrival of our expedition, he said, and was looking forward to our siege of Xitu. He didn't seem to hold much regard for mere walkers, who were only on 'holiday', and not into dangerous sports. He himself, he told us proudly, was proficient at 'le ski extreme', where one skied off-piste down excessively steep drops at very high speed. Dave asked him if he had anything he could let us have to eat.

Eduardo apologised for being nearly out of food. He did have, he said, a couple of cans of something which was apparently 'tipico Asturiana', and called 'Callos'. He got them, then left to look for his horse, which had been wandering loose in the meadows outside.

We opened these tins and tipped them into one of the re-fugio's greasy dishes to heat up – it was a gaudy red stew containing quite a few white blobs of indeterminate ancestry; they were rubbery and spongy-looking. It smelled horrible, but Dave grabbed a spoon and plunged it into the bubbling mess. My stomach rumbled uncontrollably.

A few moments after taking a mouthful of this stew, a look of horror came over Dave's face and he rushed over to the window and spat it out.

"Try it, Richard, it's . . . lovely."

It was the foulest thing I have ever tasted. Callos turned out to be pig's lung stew, famous for its incredibly hot sauce, which managed to make the lungs even more vile than if they had not been cooked at all. With Eduardo outside, we took the opportunity to chuck the whole lot behind a rock, where the refugio's dog jumped on it with a whine of delight. After three mouthfuls it stopped eating, coughed violently, then scurried off. The Callos was still steaming incriminatingly when Eduardo returned. He glanced at it, and smiled to himself.

Dave and I were now desperate for food, having had our appetites whetted by the thought of the stew, but the only food was at Los Lagos. We had no option but to go, and ran back down the mountain with our empty packs flapping on our backs. After a massive meal at the base camp, we packed our bags with food and still more caving equipment, and walked back up the path in the dying sun. The sunset was remarkable, tinging the tips of the highest peaks in some improbable shades of scarlet and crimson. At the refugio, now worn right out, we made another large meal and climbed into the uncomfortable bunks which sagged so badly in the middle that for the rest of the expedition I slept outside on the grass.

Eduardo had again decided to make us all 'federados' on special reduced rates. Lying in the dormitory, a disturbing thought crossed my mind, for I had watched rather too many spaghetti westerns, and I knew that 'federados' were the cannon-fodder Mexican soldiers who were mercilessly slain by the dozen towards the end of the second reel. I had bad dreams.

My apprehensions were fuelled further by the amount of gear that we sorted out the next morning. This year we were planning to rig every one of Xitu's entrance pitches with electron ladders *and* with ropes, so that they would be set for the heavy traffic ahead. This meant that even with Eduardo carrying for us we could hardly manage to get the gear to the entrance in one trip. How could there be a cave, I wondered, that required this amount of tackle just for its *entrance* series? We had bag after bag of rope, and tangled bundles of ladders which dragged along the ground behind us. We had to take this monster pile of gear through the Xitu entrance rift, the rift that I had heard so much about in the Brasenose College Bar, the rift in which one chap had been stuck for two hours, the rift that made Xitu so serious.

The idea was for Dave to go through first. I was to follow with as much gear as I could manage, and we would make trip after trip until all the stuff was through. I reckoned that we could manage it in four trips: in fact it took six.

"Follow me then," said Dave, and disappeared into the darkness with the first couple of tackle bags; down the first pitch to the start of the rift. As I dragged some ladders behind me, I fought to control my worry. This was my first caving trip outside Britain. Just how hard *was* Xitu going to be?

Almost straight away there was a curse from Dave. It wasn't the normal sort of swearing that you hear underground, the sort that cavers use when a minor problem arises, such as ripping one's suit, dropping a bag down a hole or falling up to one's neck in icy water, it was an abrupt 'Oh No!' in a quiet icy tone. Something horrible had happened, and I crawled forward as quickly as possible to see what it was. There, on the floor of the chamber below, Dave was on his hands and knees with his nose pressed against the rock floor, not moving. He looked hurt.

"What . . . what's happened, Dave?" I asked, expecting the worst.

"I've lost my bloody contact lens, dammit!"

"Thank God it's only that; I thought it was something terrible."

"It *is* terrible! I shall be wearing glasses in all the photos from now on."

Half an hour later, wearing the glasses, Dave led me through the rift. The heavy bags and awkward bundles jammed repeatedly below us – drop one and you never get it back. One of the landmarks was a forlorn karabiner winking up from the narrowest part of the floor. I couldn't turn my head around to see ahead, and my ears rubbed on either side of the smooth limestone walls. Soon, soaked through with our own perspiration, we sat on the pile of gear on the far side of the rift and watched our breath curling in great wafts as we paused to cool off.

These trips solved the rift for me. I got to know its every bulge and subtle change of shape. I knew every place where you could get a toe-hold, or use an arm-jam to stop yourself from sliding into the funnelling walls. The rift was Xitu's gate: get through it easily and you started your trip feeling fresh, or emerged on the surface not too close to desperation. I never had trouble with it again.

Some people had epics in that rift, with vast amounts of sweat and energy used to go only a few yards. Later on in the expedition Chris Danilewicz, a geology student who had just joined the army, got stuck for more than an hour. He slipped down in the central part and was thoroughly jammed, trying time and again to free himself whilst his four companions waited patiently on the far side for him to get out. The rift was far too narrow and difficult for them to have helped him, and eventually, cold and impatient, they realised this. As the stuck man wasn't in any *real* danger they might as well get out and begin making supper. Furthermore, his jammed body was just the thing they needed to make their own trip through simple – they could walk over the top of him! It is said to this day that he has them down on his personal hit list.

Beyond the rift we continued the descent, the volume of tackle slowly diminishing as Dave and I used it up. We rigged the pitches with self-lining ascents in mind, where one abseils down the rope and climbs back up on the ladder, with an ascender clipped onto the rope as a safety device. It was a good method, and quick, but there was always the danger that cavers who were tired after a long trip would be over-confident and wouldn't bother with the ascender, which could be fiddly and took time to arrange on the rope. Later in the expedition one chap was knocked right off a ladder by a stone falling spontaneously from the roof. He dangled 20 metres above the floor from his self-liner, which for the first time he had taken the trouble to use.

Dave and I finished our trip by rigging the last of the twelve pitches which led to Xitu's first stream. Worn out, but elated, we regained the surface just as the last flickers of the sunset were leaving the highest peaks, twelve hours after we entered the cave. Tomorrow, we both agreed, someone else could carry on with the rigging.

At the refugio there was only William, who had gone to bed, in his pyjamas as usual, and Keith. Keith was stirring a large stew, which looked delicious.

"Try it," said Keith, "it's fabada, 'tipico Asturiana'." Thankfully, it was quite unlike Callos.

"Tell whoever else is going down tomorrow that they've to rig to the Gap at least," Dave said between mouthfuls of beans.

"There's no one ready to cave tomorrow," Keith replied. Apparently the rest of the expedition vanguard had done a series of carries in the midday sun, and were now all suffering from heatstroke. Kev Senior had arrived and was fit, but had had a swim in Lago Enol and lost his glasses underwater – he was now blind as a bat. Dave had two gulps of wine then changed his mind.

61

"Right! *We'll* rig to the Gap." I lowered my aching body into a chair and inwardly groaned.

DAVID After we had made this foray with William the following day, the pace of the expedition quickened. Jan, Keith, Skunk and Skippy, all now recovered from the heat, piled tackle at the furthest point we had rigged, then carried on downwards in a series of trips. Keith and Skunk spent a long time re-rigging Flat Iron Shaft, making it safer by 'gardening' it of loose stones.

Belayed from their new take-off at the big muddy ledge where the main shaft began, they happily dangled in space and knocked small scree and large blocks down the booming pitch. Some of the bigger blocks had seemed firmly part of the cave wall, but on closer inspection Keith and Skunk were finding that they were merely stuck on with a layer of dried mud. One such boulder turned out to be the 'chossy ledge' of 1980. Driven into it, of course, were the two bolts on which we had abseiled 100 metres.

They emerged late in the evening of July 11, just seven days from our departure from Oxford. There was enough tackle stockpiled at the bottom of Flat Iron to rig the rest of the known cave, they said. Anyone who went down next day with another bag or two could, if they were prepared to spend long enough underground, push on into new territory. Richard and I looked at each other. It was our turn.

Next day dawned cold and foggy, a clinging drizzle reducing the visible world to an unappealing radius of about ten yards. The entrance pitches were wet, and by the time we reached the Teresa Series the prospect of doing a trip on the epic scale required to advance beyond the 1980 limit seemed remote. The ebbing of enthusiasm was unspoken but shared.

"Well, this is it." We were at Flat Iron. The shaft had lost little of its power to intimidate. I sat in the small chamber below the last climb down and smoked a cigarette, hiding from the terrifying inflation of magnitude lurking through the slot beneath my feet. I at least had been there before. Richard had never been down a pitch remotely as large, and he checked and rechecked his gear, obsessively making sure the screwgate on the karabiner linking his descender to his harness was tight. In a few weeks' time, this shaft would come to seem commonplace, but now it needed an effort of will, a conscious, slow effort of fear-control to stand up and clip onto that rope.

"See you soon. It's not that bad."

A small era later Richard joined me on the platform above the last drop into Eton Palais. I had now worked myself into an angry lather of frustration: "Jesus fuck shit Christ!"

Still trembling, relieved in the extreme to have bottomed the pitch, Richard looked at me, bewildered.

"The tackle! I can't find the bleeding tackle!"

To this day, I do not know what happened. Skunk and Keith had told us that all the rope we needed and more was here, on this ledge. We could not find it, and vainly Richard joined me in hunting under every boulder. With the gear we had brought down ourselves, we had only enough to rig into Eton Palais and the first of the Samaritan pitches. When faced with a long, overnight trip into unknown passages I had felt unenthusiastic, unsure whether I was ready at such an early stage of the expedition. Now that that prospect was gone, I was inconsolable.

Glumly we fixed the rope into the chamber and resolved to poke about as much as we could. We found the place where the water falling down Flat Iron arrived in the Palais, and followed its tortuous course through the chamber's boulder floor, hoping to ascertain whether it really did flow off somewhere to emerge at Trea. The evidence of our eyes was unequivocal. It passed through the cavern straight into the streamway below. Martin's dye test – and the elaborate, improbable theory which he had based upon it – was false.

At Samaritan One we rigged the pitch more sensibly than it had been in 1980, reducing the wet section to the last few metres. We stood on the ledge above its sister and cast down a few rocks. The draught was very strong, the blackness enthralling. "You know what we've done," I said. "We haven't just fucked up our own trip but made it virtually certain that Skunk and Keith will get a long way into new stuff." Richard mournfully agreed. Teamwork was all very well but some ideals are best in moderation.

Our only accessible lead was back in Eton Palais. From the Flat Iron rope, it was possible to pick out what looked like a passage on the far side of the chamber, much further round than the streamway. The walls of the cave appeared to taper in, but not to close down altogether. Trudging up the loose slope, we confirmed that there was a passage, a slot about a metre wide. Soon the only way on was down. The stream was no longer audible. Postulating an alternative shaft system, or a new high level passage like the Teresa Series that might one day turn out to be the real way on, our depression lifted.

Richard led the first climb down. I had noticed that he had

taken a long time on it, and had said very little. After a few moves, on brittle flakes above what looked like a long drop to one side, I was more voluble: "How the hell did you do this? It needs a bloody rope!" Richard's response was neither too mocking, nor too alarmed. "This *is* a bit bloody . . ."

We were in a circular room, 15 metres below the start of the climb. The floor below the ledge on which we stood plunged down in a further drop which was obviously not freeclimbable. Everything was loose. A few days earlier, interested to test the liberalisation of Spanish culture since the death of Franco, we had purchased a gynaecological text cum girlie magazine called *El Puritan*. This was the name we decided to give to the new series of passages.

"And this," Richard said, "shall be the Sala de la Disciplina Inglese."

Our log-book entry after surfacing described what was to come:

Now El Puritan bends decisively to the right. Two further exposed climbs in another chamber, the Sala de la Ropa Interiore, the second of which has a very nasty exposed mantelshelf traverse move, lead into a passage, a high, brittle rift of considerable age, the Galería de las Mujeres Perversas. Progress is variously walking on jammed boulders, crawling and climbing until a very nasty climb at a T junction where I (Dave) nearly went to the bottom of the rift, about 40 feet, with a large boulder that had been the main handhold.

I have never been so close to being killed before or since. With the main drop directly below me, I had lowered myself over the edge, intending to reach a ledge 2 metres down on the right with my feet. I was clasping with both hands to the firm edge of what I thought was simply a ridge of rock in the floor of the passage above.

I was fully committed when I realised that the ridge was a boulder pinned only with dry, dusty mud. It was moving. As it slid, so I began to slide into the hole beneath.

Richard saved me with a hand under one armpit. I grabbed his arm and my legs dangled. The boulder moved down my body and fell free, reaching the bottom with a booming retort. I scrabbled for land.

Our lights were now dim. Sorting out the series of climbs had used up all the water in our carbide generators, and their gas output was greatly reduced. At the slightest knock, they went out. We had electric back-ups, but both of us had not troubled to bring spare batteries, and this alternative light source was running low as well. We knew that if we lost the light altogether, we could be in serious trouble: no one knew we had any intention of venturing this way, and we were far out of earshot of Eton Palais. We had to hurry, yet the climbs, illuminated feebly, were more difficult than they had been on the way in. By the time we reached the safety of the Palais and its water supply, we were both in a shaken, nervous state. El Puritan was going. But it was far and away the most frightening and unattractive piece of cave we ever found in Spain.

Hours later we tiptoed into the dormitory in the refugio, the dawn sun breaking on the peaks but still far from the grassy Ario depression. Keith stirred and opened one eye:

"You haven't been long. What time is it – 7.30?"

"7.15. We couldn't find the tackle."

He looked at me with disbelief. "You couldn't find the tackle? But it's on the ledge, you stupid berks!"

Later that day the character of the expedition changed. John arrived, purple beneath his mountainous rucksack. With our leader were Graham, and eight others. The days of being a cosy, close-knit advance party were gone.

John was all for establishing an underground camp immediately. He argued that the cave was almost certain to be several hundred metres deeper, and that any further pushing would be highly dangerous. There was tension in the air that night in the gaslit common room of the refugio as the argument went back and forth. Keith and Skunk put it forcefully that having worked so hard to be in a position to begin new exploration – something no one had expected so soon – they deserved one crack at it. John put the counter-argument just as strongly. Even to reach the top of Rape B'Ràpe pitch, the limit of 1980, would be a serious undertaking, involving the rigging of five pitches and the carrying of a massive weight of tackle. In the end, with some grumbling, John gave in. He urged Skunk and Keith not to spend more than twenty-four hours underground lest fatigue lead them into carelessness and danger.

Having won their point, the two pushers took it easy next day. They rose late, and took a long time over breakfast. William and Skippy left to have a look at 3/5, a promising entrance found in 1979 which the survey showed to be very close to the line of Xitu, suggesting that the cave might provide an easier entrance. Graham went down Xitu to tinker with the rigging in the upper

65

part of the cave. John descended with Jan and Mark Godden to survey William's Bit, the long muddy passage William had discovered the previous year branching off the Teresa Series. Still Skunk and Keith sat chatting in the refugio, smoking endless Winstons and chewing bread and tinned pâté. Keith spent a long time trimming the ends of yet more cigarettes so that they fitted in his waterproof case. To fond and envious farewells, they left at last at two.

An hour or two later they met John and his party, who were already on the way out. Again John admonished them not to take longer than twenty-four hours and they promised that if they went over that limit, it wouldn't be by much.

William and Skippy emerged with a promising report on 3/5. It was never going to be an easier entrance to Xitu: much of the cave was constricted, and formed in crumbly rock. But it was still going nearly 100 metres down, and would repay further visits. According to the survey, it was near the great black aven above the Gap. If it did connect there, it would make a magnificent entry to the main cave.

The following morning, July 16, was cloudless and warm. We took our breakfast out onto the grass and wallowed in the sunshine. John, Richard and I decided to take some rope and look at the unexplored pit beneath the 'bold step' at the beginning of the Teresa Series. With any luck we should meet Skunk and Keith on the way out and could give them a hand if they were tired. It seemed strange that they had already been underground for a night and the best part of a day, and were going to be underground a long while yet.

Leaving at ten, we were down for about ten hours. The trip was very efficient, and after reaching a first ledge 25 metres down we rigged five further pitches, all dry and spacious. Drawing us on was the sound of a considerable volume of water.

To rig the last drop into what appeared to be a chamber containing a deep pool, we stood on a calcite bridge across the shaft. John and Richard bolted furiously while I played a wailing blues harmonica, spurring them to complete the work more quickly than might otherwise have been the case. I was just getting into the theme from the Old Grey Whistle Test, when John handed me a rope.

"For fuck's sake get on down. We can't take any more."

A nice free abseil of 20 metres then wet feet. I recognised the place instantly. We were in Chopper Chamber, having found merely an alternative – albeit a pleasanter one – to the Trench pitches route.

There was no sign of Keith and Skunk on the way out. Graham, Hywel and Mark had gone down to the big pitch with some camping gear, and they had not seen them either. By the time we were all changed and sitting in the refugio ready to start dinner it was 9 p.m. The two pushers had been gone thirty-one hours.

Richard, typically, looked on the bright side: "Well it does mean the cave probably hasn't sumped."

I feared the worst: "What if one of them is hurt? What would the other do – stay with him and wait or come out for help? What time should we plan a rescue?"

John grumbled about what he seemed to regard as a challenge to his leadership: "I told them very clearly about the time. They know exactly what they're supposed to do."

As the evening wore on, our uneasiness grew. It seemed unlikely that it would have taken Skunk and Keith more than twelve hours to rig the remaining pitches up to Rape B'Rape. Given that they must have expected it to take eight or nine hours to reach the surface from there, it was hard to come up with an innocuous explanation for their lateness. By midnight we had finished the last of the pungent red wine Eduardo sold in plastic bottles. Eduardo had gone to bed, so we couldn't purchase any more. Richard expressed the consensus which had emerged by default. "We'll wait 'till morning then. And if they're not out then move fast . . ."

It was hard to sleep in the crowded dormitory at first. Two fears occupied my mind: that they had finished the cave, or that one of them was hurt. But at last sleep came. At 3 a.m. I jerked awake. They had arrived. I asked Keith what had happened. Almost incoherent with exhaustion, he was fighting with his sleeping bag, trying to get into bed, and complaining of a sore groin. He said only one thing that related to his experiences of the past thirty-seven hours.

"Xitu isn't giving up easily."

A few hours later on the force of that remark became apparent. On their way out, Skunk had bashed and badly bruised his elbow. Later, clipping onto the rope at the bottom of Samaritan One, Keith had flicked it, pulling it out of the water, hoping to avoid a soaking. It had caught behind a projection and then, when he was already on the way up, come free. He had been sent penduluming into the rock with great speed, and took the full impact on his right knee. By the time he reached the top of the pitch it was badly swollen. From this point on, their exit was extremely slow. Keith was able to use his leg only by gritting his teeth. Most of the time, he was forced to prusik up the ropes on one foot. The long horizontal passages between the big pitch and the entrance series took him eight hours to negotiate, instead of the usual two. All the time the pair had battled against exhaustion. They had long run out of cigarettes and food.

Yet their trip had been an outstanding performance. From the bottom of Flat Iron they had carried five tackle bags between them. It was not until 6 a.m. that they reached the head of Rape B'Rape. Keith wrote the trip up soon after regaining consciousness on the morning of their return:

> This was the trip we'd been looking forward to for nigh on a year . . . after rigging the pitch we breakfasted on a few squares of chocolate and a very welcome fag and at 7.15 a.m., 16¼ hours after setting off we started the big push to the bottom of Xitu. A nice section of long, winding marbled streamway with a few short climbs saw us to a three-metre scramble down to an attractive greenish lake of unknown depth. We traversed round the right-hand wall.

Beyond, Keith wrote, the stream cascaded down a narrow slot which looked impossible to rig on rope:

> Not to be defeated I espied a small hole between large boulders jammed overhead in the rift. Balancing precariously on a rock I lunged upwards, copped hold of a flake and heaved myself up, laboriously working my way through the vertical squeeze. Emerging into a small chamber I looked around and a few feet away saw a much larger hole heading back into the rift I'd just come out of.
>
> There followed a period of profound blasphemy. Ahead of me the floor dropped and disappeared and I found myself in the roof of the rift, with the stream 100 feet below. I rigged the pitch with natural belays. This drop is to be known as Flyer Pot, because we found it after 18 hours underground, and an 18-hour shift at British Steel is known as a flyer.

At the foot of the pitch the stream roared away down a series of steep climbs, the last bypassed by an exposed path along the right wall – The Traverse of Truth.

> After 50 feet or so we dropped into a tight, sharp rift which rips Petzl suits to shreds – ask Skunk. Several hundred feet of this suit-shagging, body-shagging, morale-shagging passage

are followed by a small chamber. The river disappears down a four-inch slot and we climbed up, to a perch 25 feet above the re-emerging stream, which we rejoined after a rather unsafe climb down. This leads to a wet, overhanging 10-metre pitch which will require bolting. It appears to land on a ledge, beyond which is a 15-foot drop to another ledge, and then we thought we could make out a further short pitch beyond. At 11.30 Thursday morning we began our 15 hour ascent, emerging to a beautiful moonlit night at half past two Friday morning.

Keith ended his entry in the log with a recommended list of tackle for 37-hour pushing trips:

Four times normal cigarette supply; ammo can of either valium or librium; cyanide capsule (only to be used in extremis); spare limbs to replace those belted against rock walls; spare boots, light, undersuit, oversuit, SRT gear, knackers; replacement crutch, to be used when the first one is chafed by furry suit and harness out of existence; replacement brain, to be used when first one is worn out of existence by lack of sleep.

The new passages sounded serious. But the depth of the cave must now, we knew, be approaching 1,000 metres with no sign of the end. Meanwhile the epic qualities of Keith and Skunk's adventure had removed any argument about the need to camp.

5

La Galería Amador

RICHARD "I think we've got everything actually." It was Graham speaking. John's master plan put Graham in charge of organising the camp, but unable to keep out of it, he checked off everything Graham had done. Dave took no notice of either of them and packed things which weren't on the list. Confusion reigned.

"Let's take another rope . . . look, there's room in this one if we repack it," said Dave.

"Noooo . . ." moaned Graham and rushed over to prevent Dave from pulling all the carefully documented tins and bog rolls from the tackle bag. Everything was wrapped in bin-liners and sealed, and two further bin-liners placed inside the PVC tackle bags. We hoped that the important items like sleeping bags might thus stay dry.

While Graham and Dave argued in one corner of the refugio, Skippy tried getting in one of the special furry sleeping bags and thence into one of the single point suspension hammocks, hung from a hook in a beam. The bags and hammocks had been bought on the cheap without anyone trying them out. Skippy tried once, and tried again. He fell onto the floor. "Be all right underground," said John.

Skippy and I were the last in the refugio dining room. He produced a bottle of ponche. "Look, help me get this inside this bedding roll . . . hold it still while I push it in."

He forced the bottle in with his foot, then stuffed the whole inside back into one of the bags. There was an encouraging glug when the bag was rocked.

There were four of us: myself, Skippy, Dave and John, going to set up the world's deepest underground camp. The Xitu rift was a terrible prospect next morning with two heavy tackle bags each, made more awful by John, whose method is to beat a cave into submission, rather than the preferred technique of trying to glide through it with minimum effort. In the confined space he reached behind him and lifted a bulging bag over his head. "God he's strong," I thought. He handed it to me.

"Take this, Richard." As he spoke a hissing came from deep within the bag, and the air in the rift began to smell more and more of butane. Graham. Ever cost-conscious, he had given us a half-used butane stove to take 800 metres down a pothole, and had merely switched the thing off with an easily-dislodged tap. I felt for my carbide flame and singed my hand as I put it out. "John," I said, "you and I are stuck in a squeeze with a bomb. I prevail on you to put your flame out with all possible despatch." By the time we emerged from the rift, we had headaches from the camping stove, which had finally run out. Fortunately we had spare cylinders.

We moved slowly. It was many hours later that we reached the mantelshelf, the ten-metre wet climb at the end of the Marble Steps. Dave wished to put a ladder there, feeling that an unprotected freeclimb which often required standing on each other's shoulders represented an unacceptable risk at such depth. He leaned across the drop from a slippery ledge and put a bolt in. It was suddenly very cold. Only Dave was warm, banging away at the hard, black rock. He gave the bolt a final tap to drive it firmly home and the whole section of wall sheared away, bolt and all. He cursed and began again in a different place, while the rest of us, soaked from Dampturation and the other Steps, felt the creeping symptoms of hypothermia.

Eventually Dave managed to rig the ladder. It hung directly in the water. As we gripped the rungs with numb fingers the stream tipped itself down the inside of our sleeves, finding an icy home in the armpits and points south. John stayed at the top of the pitch, his movements even less graceful and sure than usual, passing down the precious bags which alone held the prospect of warmth – dry thermal underwear, gloves and balaclavas. Against advice, he tried lowering two at once by their drawstrings, and before they could be grasped from below dropped them. They fell with a splash and a thud into the pool below: shallow enough to cushion the impact, deep enough to cover them with water.

"Oh no," Skippy whispered, "the ponche."

We shook ourselves like wet dogs and carried on. Our next problem was to decide exactly where to camp. Back in Oxford, John had suggested the chamber above the stream by Choss Chock pitch, the last rigged in 1980. This was one of the few dry places in Xitu's lower reaches, but it suffered from having neither an accessible water supply nor a flat floor. No one had yet suggested an alternative.

In the end the choice made itself: we stopped at the first place that looked as if it would serve at all. It was at the foot of Pythagoras, where the stream ran along a boulder-strewn passage for a short distance. One wall was clean overhanging rock, the other a series of boulders stacked on top of each other like cinema seats for as far as the eye could see. We began to unpack while Skippy organised a cup of tea.

"Right," said John, "the next thing to do is to rig the hammocks." He took the bolt kit and drove a bolt into the overhanging wall at head height. "That should do," he said. He clipped the hammock to the bolt; it looked like a giant knotted handkerchief. He lowered his ample bum into the hammock and found himself sitting on the floor. More bolts were placed, higher up. Eventually the hammocks looked quite good. "Dinner's ready," said Skippy. We had already been underground for fourteen hours. It was 3.30 a.m.

DAVID One of the results of the confusion surrounding the packing now presented itself. Skippy had noticed it first, and having done so had missed out the proposed cup of tea and gone on to beef stroganoff. There was only one cup, and a very small cup at that. There were no plates, no knives and no forks. The camp kitchen was far from ideal, perched on the loose boulders. Keeping the little stove upright was a frustrating and time-consuming chore. Skippy had already dropped one of the spoons down a crevice between the rocks. He made Richard retrieve it by moving a good part of the floor before we were allowed to sit in a circle round the pot and eat, each of us watching eagle-eyed to make sure that no one got more than his fair share.

Yet slowly the place was becoming more homely. We had packed a lot of our supplies in empty porridge tins, which came with handy sealing plastic lids. Now we put them on ledges around the campsite and used them as candleholders. Their silvery insides made good reflectors, and with the addition of the light from our carbide lamps the rocky cavern seemed bright and cheerful. Its homeliness was emphasised after making a dark, cold, stumbling trip downstream for a pee before bed. I had not bothered to take a caving lamp with me and on its own a single candle cast an unreliable and shadowy light. When I returned the others were levering themselves into their hammocks. I was the biggest, followed by John. He was having great difficulty, and I watched him for hints. It looked impossibly uncomfortable to me, but once in John insisted that he had never been more cosy.

For the next half hour, while the others pestered me to hurry up and extinguish the last candles, I struggled with the unyielding fabric. I was just about able to lie in the damn thing with my sleeping bag undone as far as my waist, but as soon as I tried to lever my shoulders inside the thick fibre pile bag and do the zip up I popped out of the hammock at one end or the other. If this happened at the top, it meant my head and neck were unsupported. If it was my feet which objected, the hammock developed a downhill slope, and soon I was sliding steadily towards the floor. Finally I gave up in disgust and took the hammock off the wall altogether. I laid it on the least steep slope I could find and used it as a groundsheet. That way, I woke up only once, when I started slipping downslope towards the stream, initiating a small landslide in the process.

RICHARD My hammock was so tight that my jaw couldn't open on its own, which at least precluded snoring. The only position possible was lying on my back with my arms crossed like Tutankhamun. I slept for no more than a few minutes at a time, dreaming at one point that I was being eaten alive by a snake.

Far too soon the alarm went off, a cheap clock which wound down as it rang, becoming more and more feeble. The stream gurgled softly and there was no other noise. I opened my eyes and experienced the continuing absolute blackness of a cave. I could have been anywhere. Dave, lying more comfortably and in easy reach of his helmet, switched on his electric lamp. John found a torch and looked at his watch, forgetting the time he had set the alarm. It was five o'clock.

"Morning or evening?" Skippy asked.

"Evening."

Already, we had begun to slip around the clock, without day and night to regulate the rhythms of sleep and wakefulness.

Breakfast was simple: the same as dinner with the addition of porridge. No one felt like talking much. Then Skippy said he had a surprise. The ponche. The bottle was undamaged, and he had kept it hidden before we had gone to bed. A shot each was of such great psychological value that not even John was prepared to complain. Dressed in our dry thermal underwear, we got on with the chores, rinsing pans, filling lamps with carbide, tidying up. Finally the evil moment of putting on our wet furry suits could no longer be postponed. Stripping off in the bitter cold –

the air temperature at camp was about 4 degrees centigrade – we stood naked on the rocks and tried to bear the shock of the icy fibre pile on bare skin. Screaming made it seem easier, and one by one we uttered bloodcurdling cries. I noticed Dave was missing. Minutes later he bounded back looking unaccountably pleased with himself.

DAVID To my amazement, the others seemed prepared to spend three days underground without relieving themselves. I had given careful thought to the matter, and after breakfast went to put my ideas into action. A little way downstream I had noticed a dry chamber, reached by a short, unlikely-looking climb. It was sheltered from the draught, and placing a candle tin in front of me I pulled down my thermal bottoms and crapped into a plastic bag.

It was most important that no turds should make their way into the stream. Not only would we be using it for drinking water below the camp, but the presumed destination of the Xitu water, the Rio Cares, provided the main supply for a number of villages along its banks. My chamber, though, fulfilled all requirements. I carefully sealed the plastic bag and half buried it in a recess. I returned to camp, and someone came up with the name for our new underground lavatory: the Galería Amador, after the estimable bar and restaurant owner at Los Lagos, whose more conventional facilities had been of great value to successive expeditions.

RICHARD The day's caving from the camp was to be, at John's suggestion, quite light. He and Dave were to try to find a bypass to the rift which had so wrecked Keith and Skunk's gear, while Skippy and I were to start the survey of the passage below Rape B'Rape.

I was astonished at how difficult the cave became beyond the camp. British caves were usually easier the deeper one went, as the streams grew bigger with inlets and the passages correspondingly wider. In Xitu, progress at this depth was through narrow rifts, and past ever-deeper pools, which required increasingly more difficult traverses on ledges below water level. Slowly my boots and leggings filled with water. Passing tackle made it more difficult still. I was terrified of slipping: the result would have been total immersion in a pool just above freezing.

After Dave and John had descended Rape B'Rape, I abseiled

down with the end of the tape measure. A few metres down was a ledge, with a large projection from which the rope was rebelayed. "Let's take the first leg down to here," I said. I took off my helmet and put it on the belay, so that Skippy could get a fix on my light to read the compass and clinometer. As I put my helmet on the rock, it wobbled.

"Hell fire, the belay's loose!"

"Push it over the edge then," said Skippy, "it'll make a bosting bang."

Carefully I hauled up the rope and removed it from the belay. Leaning against the wall I heaved the television-sized boulder away from its moorings, two tiny blobs of calcite, with my feet. Skippy clapped. There was a sickening pause, and then a mighty crack as the boulder hit the floor 35 metres below and disintegrated. A long way down the passage, John and Dave heard the sound and hurried back, fearing that it had been the noise of a falling body.

We were already impressed by the work carried out by Skunk and Keith. Immediately below the pitch, the passage formed a glorious, clean-washed corridor in green, marbled rock. Negotiating the deep lake, we reached the next section of rift, and the upward squeezes leading to the next pitch. Like Keith, I failed to notice the easier of the two holes, and grunted my way up strenuously, legs waving in the air. "Tell you what," I said, "this is much easier without anything tied to your waist. Put both our SRT bags into the tackle bag, and pass that through to me." He did so, and climbed up.

On the other side of the climb the steep rift was cut into narrow ledges, and the way on was clearly to traverse along past the slot where the stream poured down to the wider pitch head. I moved along to give Skippy room and parked the bag on one of the ledges, in front of me. It sat here, then started to topple. I made a lunging dive which succeeded only in putting out my light. In the dark I felt the bag fall past my feet into the hole below. There was a pause, and muffled crashes a long way down.

"Oh bugger."

"That's really great," said Skippy. "Here we are in one of the world's deepest potholes and you drop our SRT gear, food, spare carbide, and everything else down a pitch. How are we going to get out of the cave now?"

I considered the logistics of ascending more than 800 meters with two SRT systems between four.

Skippy still had his descender clipped to his harness, and said he would descend the pitch to see if he could find the gear. He climbed over me, still cursing, and abseiled down.

The bottom of the pitch did not, alas, communicate with the hole the bags had fallen down. The stream cascaded down its slot, then poured out of an arm sized fissure at the bottom of the shaft. The bag was through that fissure. Skippy shouted up the bad news. He couldn't ascend now, and I couldn't go down. All I had was a length of thick cord round my neck which I used to attach my carbide generator. Skippy did have a scalpel blade, and yelled up that if I dropped the cord he would cut it to make a pair of prusik loops.

"Just . . . tying . . . the . . . knots." He shouted, letting the echo die away after each word. After a while he shouted again. "Climb . . . ing."

For a long time I sat shivering, watching the patterns made on the wall of the shaft by Skippy's light. At last he reached the top, and we began a further wait for the other two.

DAVID Climbing up above the stream we did manage to find a bypass of sorts which avoided the far rift, Fernie's Delight after what it did to the suits made by the company owned by the veteran French caver, Fernand Petzl. I marvelled at the determination of Keith and Skunk in coming this way before: the lower route was not only tight but waist deep in water. I felt remote and deep, even with an underground camp to return to, and into territory that had already been explored.

The bypass, though dry, was still awkward. It ended in a climb just above the undescended pitch reached by Skunk and Keith.

Bolting the pitch, and attempting to find a line of descent that avoided the waterspout pouring over the lip, took a long time. At last the rope was fixed, but it was late by now. John and I agreed that I would descend, and briefly examine what lay beyond, while he stayed at the top.

I clipped on and walked over the edge. Once again I felt the rush of exhilaration, exploration fever, always at its most intense when abseiling a new shaft. We had chosen the line well, and I passed the two ledges that Keith had seen without needing to rebelay. Fifteen metres below I unclipped and traversed over the source of the peculiar belching noise that we noticed from the top: it was a deep pool which filled and then discharged its contents in regular pulses. The walls were light-coloured marble, and rounding a corner I felt a strong, droplet-laden breeze. The passage plunged down in a series of waterfalls which looked freeclimbable: but without a companion, I turned back. Xitu was going still, and the next section suggested that at last we might be out of the area of the tight rifts.

Two hours later, at the top of the Flyer, we met up with an exposed and miserable Richard and Skippy. The wisdom of not pressing on was now justified, tantalising as leaving the beautiful streamway had been.

RICHARD By the time Dave and John arrived, Skippy and I were both very cold. We had been playing 'I Spy' to try and pass the time, only there hadn't been much to look at:

"I spy with my little eyes something beginning with R."

"Rock."

"Yep. Your turn."

"I spy with my little eye something beginning with G, B, H, D, W, R, T, O, A."

"Er . . . don't know."

"Great Big Hole Down Which Richard Threw Our Ascenders."

Dave lent me his SRT gear, and Skippy rigged the rope that had been hanging down the Flyer and hurled it down the small dark hole. The belay consisted of a knob of rock around which Skippy wrapped the rope again and again, finally sitting on the knob himself. From the dark pit came the sound of a great crashing of water . . . I was already cold, and was now about to get very wet.

As I abseiled into the shattered shaft, I had to go down at an angle, walking with boots against the falling water. Far below I saw the yellow bag, apparently unharmed. I soon reached it, and was greatly relieved to find that it had survived the hundred-foot drop intact. I began to prusik up again through the torrential crashing spray.

I couldn't look up into the spray, and I had failed to notice that on my diagonal descent the rope had snared towards the top, making it hang in a dog-leg. Suddenly it unsnared, and I was thrown to the floor, landing in a heap but with the rope still stretching up above me. What had happened I had no idea, but it occurred to me that maybe one of Skippy's loops had slipped off his belay. I tried shouting, but the roar of the stream was deafening, and even my whistle blasts were drowned by the waterfall. I gave the rope a huge tug, and it seemed sound – if the belay was going to fail there was only one way to find out, and so I continued upwards through the falling water. My right wrist had been smashed by the impact, and I was forced to climb one-handed. We had dinner that 'night' of dried meat and rice which were not fully re-hydrated. Once again we crammed ourselves into the appalling hammocks and tried to sleep.

When the alarm went off, John announced that it was eight o'clock in the evening, but we had no idea whether he was pulling our legs or not. As we got out of our beds and into our freezing clothes, heavy with water, I vowed never to camp in a cave ever again, especially this one.

My wrist was a great problem now. Over 'night' it had swollen up and was virtually useless. I couldn't put on my wellies, and I couldn't lean on my right hand without it giving way. I couldn't even pick up a bag. To strengthen it I bound it up with nylon belay tape. Trivial as this injury was, it reminded me just how remote the campsite was, 800 metres underground.

Dave and I left first, with a short length of rope in case I needed assistance on the climbs. We reached the surface at 9 a.m. the next day. We had gone down on a Sunday, and now it was a Wednesday. We blinked in the daylight at the absurdly vivid colours, released at last from the monotony of brown and grey-green rock.

DAVID While we savoured the pleasures of camping under-ground, the expedition grew still bigger. Those who had just arrived carried out a series of acclimatising trips in the upper reaches of Xitu. William, Trevor and new recruit Hywel Watkins investigated a passage leading off the Teresa Series, and found a chamber and a passage for 200 metres beyond, which ended in a beautiful crystal grotto, dominated by a huge, pure white stalag-mite formation, the Snowcastle. Layer upon layer of stalactite daggers hung from the roof. On the walls, crystals sparkled, and there were dazzling arrays of helectites. As they advanced, the three explorers crushed more pristine crystal formations on the floor.

Others went into El Puritan. It became clear that all the various holes in the floor led, by more or less devious routes, back into the main stream. The high level rift still went on, but it seemed certain that this too would eventually rejoin the normal route. Richard and I had been terrified for nothing.

Jim had arrived with John Forder, a caving instructor at the Whernside Manor outdoor pursuits centre in Yorkshire. John had been a member of several Oxford expeditions in the 1970s, but he was little known to the current team. On his first trip, used to the perfection expected at the Manor, he refused to descend Servicio pitch, saying that the belay was too dangerous.

He disliked it because it was rigged to natural projections in the rock, instead of bolts. Had we but known it, the mild frisson this caused among the expedition anticipated the most hotly contested debate within caving of the 1980s: to bolt or not to bolt.

This debate had not yet assumed its later pretentious, 'ethical' overtones, but as I listened to people discussing John's decision and subsequent action – to go down and place three bolts in the pitch where there had been none – I couldn't help thinking that if he didn't like Servicio, he should wait till he got nearer the bottom. Dampturation, in particular, was a pitch that was not, to say the least, rigged according to the textbooks. But all too often in Xitu, the nature of the rock left no choice as to the method of rigging a pitch. In 1980, when we had gaily climbed ladders without lifelines above large drops, we had taken stupid and needless risks. In 1981, I felt, we had reduced the danger a great deal. It rankled when we discovered on our return that John Forder had informed friends in Yorkshire that we had been reckless, and lucky to escape without a serious accident.

There was also intense activity on the surface, as a series of parties examined some of the entrances noted in 1979 and 1980 in more detail. Some, like 28/5, a deep shaft on the slopes of Jultayu, which had seemed so promising at first, proved to be blocked with ice at a hundred metres. The most exciting prospect for developing a new system to explore after Xitu was finished remained Ridge Cave, the high entrance I had dis-covered the previous year with Dave Thwaites. John set off one morning with two others and what I had thought were precise instructions, but despite fine weather, he had been unable to find it.

The next camping trip was planned to begin on July 25, three days after the first group's return. There was every chance that this would be the first British caving team to push a pothole deeper than one kilometre. John held long discussions about who should go. All those on the first camp were out, with the exception of Richard, who had soon to go back to England. Skunk, with his experience and endurance, picked himself. Graham had put a great deal into exploring Xitu and was another obvious choice, while Jan, though new to Spain, was going well and deserved a chance. That left Keith as someone who in any normal circumstances should be one of those taking part.

But a day before the camp was due to leave, Keith could hardly walk. Since his thirty-five-hour epic, his knee had stayed swollen, red and filled with fluid. It was so painful that he had not even been able to walk to Los Lagos to carry food or visit the bar, and he had spent the week since his accident miserably immobilised at the refugio. "I might as well go home," he said. "It's much worse being here and not being able to go caving."

The situation called for desperate remedies, and one was proposed by Eduardo. He knew an old mountain shepherds' trick for reducing inflammation, he said. It would be painful, but had been known to work.

Eduardo disappeared into the kitchen. The smell of vinegar wafted out. He returned with a poultice, made, he said, of boiling vinegar and salt. Gritting his teeth Keith extended his leg and Eduardo slapped the poultice onto his livid knee.

"Aaaargh . . . arrrr . . . errrg . . . arrr." There was no doubting the pain Keith was in. His face had gone grey, and his eyes seemed sightless as he tried to keep the poultice on. Finally he could take no more and flung it away, still gasping.

Our medical officer, Richard, had assumed that the swelling and inflammation were caused simply by the impact of Keith's knee against the wall of the cave. But that afternoon, to his and Keith's amazement, the knee began to point. A dot of white appeared among the redness. It had been an abscess all along. Richard remembered one of the cardinal rules of his trade: "The good surgeon never lets the sun set on undrained pus." By teatime, Keith's knee was ripe for puncture, and a pint of poison spilled out. It began to return to its normal size and colour. By evening, Keith was walking with only a slight limp. Next day even that was gone. He dressed the knee and ran up the hill behind the refugio. The treatment had worked. He joined the camping party. As the group of five made their way to the cave a mist rolled in from the gorge, obscuring them and everything. When I saw them again, I thought, Xitu really would be one of the deepest caves in the world.

RICHARD We arrived at the camp, a haven of relative comfort, and put on a brew of tea. The plan was for Skunk and me to press on down the cave and to push the passage to the next pitch; not a long trip, because we had already been going for some five hours by this time. The five of us sat in a circle and slurped. By the time I had finished my tea I was already starting to shiver – although Xitu was a few degrees above freezing the permanent wetness gave the air a bone-chilling quality which seeped right through. It would be much warmer to be moving, so Skunk and I set off.

There was little doubt in either of our minds that this pushing trip would be the one that would crack Xitu. If it really *was* going to be deeper than 1,000 metres we would soon know, for the limit of exploration was roughly 900 metres down, if you added together the pitch lengths since the limit of the 1980 survey. Unlike on a mountain, we could neither triangulate nor use an altimeter to calculate the depth.

It didn't seem to take us long to get through the known cave to the limit of exploration at Chunder Pot, the 15-metre wet pitch that only Dave had descended. At the bottom of the pitch were two yellow tackle bags containing the rigging gear. These were the same bags that Dave and I had brought into the cave only two weeks before, and they had been slowly moved down the cave by each successive rigging party like two oversize batons in a relay race. We took one each, and then walked along the broad passage and around the next bend following Xitu's stream into a passage no one had seen before.

"What is it, Skunk? A pitch, or a climb?" My voice was lost in the crash of the stream as it launched out over the lip of the drop down which Skunk was peering, in an attempt to see through the spray. By way of an answer he picked up the two bags and threw them out into the darkness. They landed with a thud a few feet below. It was a climb, perhaps ten feet.

In a British cave you would jump down a climb like this and get soaked to the skin, just for the hell of it; we preferred to stay dry. We were going to have to wear our furry suits for many hours yet, and again tomorrow, maybe even the day after that. Instead of lowering down on the big handholds which jutted out of the swirling water, we bridged out over the drop on the crumbly rock that had so often let me down before in Xitu.

The spray from the climb had put my carbide flame out, but it easily re-lit to flood the cascade in the warm carbide light. The short waterfall looked for all the world like part of Swildon's Hole in the Mendips, one of the most enjoyable passages in any cave in Britain, and, just like Swildon's, there was another sporting cascade around the next bend. Instead of passing the 1,000-metre mark with another dull shaft, Xitu was taking us there down a wonderfully exciting passage, just the sort of thing that had made me take up caving in the first place. Cascade followed cascade until after perhaps fifteen of them we arrived at a drop which was too steep and too big for a free-climb. We looked around for a way of rigging a rope, but the rock was the useless crumbly stuff again. It was time to eat.

"Richard," said Skunk as he unwrapped the chocolate, "if the top of Chunder Pot is at −900 metres, then I reckon that you and I are the first Brits ever to get below 1,000 metres of depth." He bit off a chunk of the rock-hard cooking chocolate.

I chewed mine, which precluded any conversation, so tried instead to imagine what a kilometre of rock looked like . . . half a mile's worth of limestone that had been scrunched into place by the titanic forces that were moving Africa northwards, and being slowly eroded by this stream. The down-climbing had made my wrist injury start to bother me again, and I noticed Skunk was rubbing his damaged elbow.

At the very first cascade on the way back, I was soaked. Climbing first I found I was forced to use a crucial hold which lay right in the stream, and the icy water poured down the sleeve of my suits demolishing the dry warmth I had cherished for so long.

"Give us a light down here, mate!" came a pleading voice from behind me. Skunk only now revealed that his electric head light wasn't going. It needed resoldering. In the wet cascades we couldn't keep our carbide flames going, so we had only one light between us – my feeble lamp with its dying battery. The yellow glow barely made it down to Skunk as he came up, and it was fading visibly. I thought about the kilometre of rock again, then told myself that, in fact, this was just Swildon's, not Spain . . . and this double-think made things easier, and more fun. Climbing the cascades involved several drenchings, as the whole of Xitu's stream shot past inches from my face, but the buzz of passing the 'Classic Numbers' below 1,000 metres kept me warm inside.

Keith was waiting up for us when we got back to camp, wet and worn out. It was 10 a.m., some eighteen hours after we went down, and it was time for a bed, a meal. 'Tomorrow' Keith and Jan were to see what Xitu had in store for us next. Now it didn't matter so much. Xitu had made the grade, one of the deepest caves in the world, the deepest cave in the Picos de Europa. Any extra depth was going to be just a bonus.

Next 'day' Keith was raring to go. Until now, it had taken three hours and more from first awakening at the underground camp before anyone was ready to leave. This time, Keith had tea ready minutes after emerging from his sleeping bag, and soon he and Jan were off. Skunk, Graham and I rose more leisurely, before leaving to continue the survey. After a long trip we returned, and began to prepare supper.

Keith and Jan had not come back. We were already in bed when they returned with their news: Keith ebullient, Jan more tired and subdued. They had rigged two short pitches and descended further climbs, until they reached a point where the stream flowed down a crack too narrow to follow. But there was a high level passage, full of jammed and broken boulders, and here they had crawled about, getting lost more than once, at last finding a way back to the enlarged stream passage below. There was a difficult climb here which Jan had been unwilling to try, but Keith jumped down, ascending it later with considerable difficulty. He enthused about what followed:

"It gets really big. Really big. Then I came to a huge pool: very deep and no obvious way round. But I could see passage beyond and hear water flowing. We need wetsuits or a boat."

We slept and woke again, shedding our warm sleeping bags and getting dressed, a process which became no more pleasant with experience. I remembered my vow not to camp again. Yet here I was. Leaving Jan and Keith asleep, we moved off downstream, our breath curling upwards in huge clouds of steam.

Keith had done a good job with the pitches, rigging from tiny flakes – the only option available. We found our way through the complex boulder area, an awkward series of climbs, crawls and squeezes. I couldn't believe how difficult it was, more than 1,000 metres down. We had expected a huge master cave, but instead were required to slide and stretch between jammed blocks which threatened to tumble and crush the insignificants who had disturbed the peace of the centuries.

At last we emerged into a horizontal streamway. We had bypassed Keith's last climb, although we had no idea how or where. We marched along, the cave flat now, at first in a narrow, slanting fissure, and then in a majestic borehole, floored with shingle over which the stream flowed in silence. It was the largest passage we had found in Xitu, but all too soon it came to an end at Keith's pool. It was much bigger than we had imagined: 30 metres or more to the other side, where the walls plunged sheer into the water. It was clear with a perfect, turquoise transparency, and we could see that the lake was very deep indeed.

Above was something that left me in little doubt that this was Xitu's end: something which we had not seen properly since the entrance rift, six kilometres away. The roof. It arched up to form a dome above the slightly fluorescent water, and we could see that it contained no further ways on.

"We've got to check the far side," said Skunk, but we all knew that Keith must have heard an echo when he described the sound of falling water beyond. With three lights, we got a much better view than Keith could have done. There was nothing on the far side of the lake, but Skunk still traversed round on tiny holds. Twice he fell in, sending waves which rebounded across the still surface from the opposite walls. Eventually he rejoined us, and we sat and ate some chocolate. We were in one of the remotest spots on earth. No helicopter could winch us to safety if something went wrong; nobody could be lowered to us on a rope. Nature had hidden this lake in the most secret of places, littering the way down with obstacles which had taxed us to our limits.

Skunk broke my reverie. "Bloody Judson."

"Sorry?" Like me, Graham didn't understand.

"So much for bloody Judson."

Dave Judson, we remembered, was the man who had come up to Ario and written it in print.

He must have walked right past Xitu's entrance, before dismissing the region as too shattered to contain a deep cave, and going off to Iran and Ghar Parau.

"That was a bustin' mistake," Skunk said.

We got up to begin our journey back to camp. I picked up a small stone from the edge of the sump, just a pebble like any other. Perhaps on my mantelpiece it would remind me of this beautiful, secret spot. I changed my mind and flung it as far as I could into the water, sending ripples which disturbed the still surface for a few moments more.

Moving quickly, it took us seven hours to reach the camp from the bottom of the cave. Keith and Jan were still in their hammocks, having been in bed for more than twenty-four hours. Lying in their warm sleeping-bags, they had been unable to face getting up, even after Jan had somehow torn his hammock and been tipped onto the floor. Keith got up and cooked dinner as we undressed. They decided to leave for the surface.

"Just tell John we've bottomed the cave and by the way we didn't do any surveying because we overslept for twenty-four hours and would he mind mending this hammock," said Graham.

Keith scowled, and ran after Jan. They were both angry with themselves for having lain in so spectacularly.

Ages later, I pulled myself up out of the entrance to Xitu. Not having any idea of the time, I was overjoyed to find a glorious summer afternoon. We had been three nights underground, although we had spent only two periods asleep. The sunshine was blinding, and we squinted as we lay exhausted on the grass. The colours of the sky and hills were as vivid as if we had been given sight for the first time. I gazed down at the entrance. Single-handed yachtsmen could look out across the ocean and

think, "I've crossed that." Back at base camp, Himalayan moun-
taineers could look at the peak above them which they had just
conquered. Xitu was an opening in the rock among hundreds of
others, all alike. For all the world it was as if it didn't exist. We
went off for a cup of tea.

DAVID I had mixed feelings at the news of Xitu's end, disappointment that the great adventure was over tempered by a conviction that the survey, when complete, would put Xitu well over
1,100 metres below the surface. For the moment, the expedition
was overflowing with able-bodied cavers wanting a chance to
visit the sump and stay at the underground camp, while those
that had already been down searched the hills around for a new
cave. One promising site was 12/5, called 'Cueva del Near Miss'.
It was an obscure hole at the lip of a cliff which dropped in two
pitches to some very nice formations. Where it ended the cave
narrowed to a slot no more than four or five inches wide, but
stones dropped through this rattled on down a massive, open
space to hit the floor some seconds below. Colin Nicholls tried to
break through by jumping up and down on the sides of the slot
until he realised that if it were to suddenly enlarge he would fall
to his death. Cueva del Near Miss was forgotten about.

The other cave we had marked as having potential was Ridge
Cave, but as no one could find it again, myself included, most
people thought I was making it up. Elsewhere, much of the
impetus behind new exploration was provided by Keith. He
spent several trips bolting down the wall of Sima Catalina, a vast
shaft he had found in the high country between Ario and the
peaks. After several pitches, none of which were separated by
anything one could call a ledge, Keith reached a hole down
which stones fell free for eight seconds. He cajoled Skippy and
me to go back with him armed with three ropes. Knotted
together these totalled 180 metres in length. Skippy described
the trip:

Because Keith had pushed most of the cave so far, we un-
selfishly insisted that he descend it first. It became apparent
that he was getting a little psyched up over this, and after
spending an hour on the tiny ledge rigging the drop with
secondary, tertiary and quaternary back-ups, he spent
another half hour checking things while we stood shivering,
passing helpful comments like "for Christ's sake hurry up!"
and "I don't think this rope's going to be long enough."
At last he clipped his rack on the rope, but this was only a

prelude to another 15 minutes of alterations and adjustments. By now we were blue with cold, and after threatening to castrate Keith and throw him down if he didn't get on with it, he was finally ready.

We agreed a complex whistle code so we would know what was happening: one blast for the first knot, two for the second, three for I'm at the bottom, follow me, four for I'm at the bottom, don't follow me, etc, etc. Keith disappeared slowly into the void. We couldn't see much from our precarious position on the ledge, and shivered for another 15 long minutes. "ARE . . . YOU . . . O . . . K . . . ?" The reply came faintly: "YEEEESS!!" Well, what the bloody hell are you pissing about for, we thought.

At long last came one blast on the whistle. Ten minutes later, two quieter blasts. We waited eagerly for another 10 minutes. By this time he had been on the rope for 35 minutes. I was shivering so violently that I nearly fell down the pitch twice. We discussed what might have gone wrong. Finally Dave peered down the shaft, and with a shout more devastating than curried beans, bellowed down the abyss: "IS . . . THE . . . ROPE . . . LONG . . . ENOUGH?" Back came a very faint reply, tinged with a note of paranoia: "NOOOOO!"

Dave and I looked at each other. "Serve the sod right for making us wait so long," he said. "Glad we let him down first," I said.

We waited patiently while Keith prusiked back up to communication distance. Managing to stop before the end of the bottom rope, he said he had dropped something down the pitch and estimated a further 70 metres to the bottom. He didn't say what it was he had dropped. We got quite excited now. The total depth of the shaft must be over 300 metres! Must be one of the deepest in Europe! I prusiked out, desperate to warm up after doing three hours' hypothermia research on that ledge. Dave and Keith followed quickly, knowing we had left some food at the entrance, and having no trust in my integrity.

We rushed back to Ario in a euphoric state. The first person we met there was Eduardo, who appeared most impressed with our breathless account. Then a look of recognition came into his eyes. He asked us to point out the entrance of Sima Catalina on the map. He rummaged in a cupboard and produced a survey made a year earlier by the SIE. Alas, our new discovery had already been explored. It was really Pozu Jou Tras la Jayada, and ended in an impenetrable choke 315 metres down. That meant Keith had been about 50 metres from the floor. As to the lack of evidence of the SIE descent, we assumed that they must have made their way down the opposite wall of the great shaft.

Finding a second Xitu was proving more difficult than we had imagined. Almost at the end of the expedition, when the detackling of Xitu was already underway, it was Keith who again came up with the most promising lead yet. Pozu Optimistu, Optimist's Pot, was found – and often lost – on the hill above the refugio, Cabeza Forma. There were no known caves up there, and the entrance was considerably higher than Xitu's, suggesting the potential for greater depth. When the time came to return to Britain, there had been only a few, preliminary trips into the cave, but Keith was convinced of its worth: it had 'infinite possibilities' and was 'extremely promising', according to his write-up in the log.

As August wore on, the expedition returned to more manageable size, and teamwork improved as the massive project of removing more than a kilometre of rope, an underground camp and other items from Xitu began. After an initial camping trip to de-rig the bottom, the work was carried out from the surface, and culminated in a pile of twenty-one heavy bags being hauled up the entrance series. The completed survey was computed and Xitu's depth worked out: 1,139 metres, or 1,148 including the plumbing of the sump by a weighted tape measure. Its length was more than six kilometres: easily the deepest cave then known in the Picos, and the deepest ever explored by a British team.

Martin had met a very experienced caver called Dick Willis whilst he was on an expedition to the great tropical systems of Borneo, and now Dick organised a proper dye-test. Fluorescein dye dumped into the Xitu sump was collected by charcoal lumps suspended in pieces of ladies' tights hanging in the resurgences. This test had the great advantage of having control samples for comparisons, and unlike the misleading experiment of 1980, came to an undeniable and obvious conclusion: that the water from Xitu came out at a powerful spring in the Cares Gorge.

Above the resurgence a group of Swiss cavers had, some years before, discovered a beautiful stalactite cave which intersected the underground stream not far inside the mountain. Like Xitu, Cueva Culiembro ended in a sump, and the two pools, Xitu's and Culiembro's, were separated by little more than a kilometre, but were also 150 metres apart vertically, suggesting that what cave there must be between them must be open, with airspace.

One day, after a long drive from Los Lagos and a long walk along the gorge, we drank gin and tonics in the small bar in Cain, 1,200 metres directly below Ario. Maybe in the future, we mused, cave divers might find a way through. To dive from the Xitu end would be a logistical nightmare. Culiembro though, had that much more potential . . . only not for us.

Fit but tired, I carried a pack down from Ario to the lakes for the last time on a day of hazy sunshine. I didn't know what I was going to do next: I had considered staying in Oxford for research but the prospects afterwards seemed uncertain. I hurried along the path without giving the view a second look. At the col I turned briefly and saw Xitu, just an innocent fold in the ground. There was no time for contemplation: I had a bus to catch. I marched on down: surely, I thought, I would not be passing this way again.

6

Only Another Five Hours' Hammering

DAVID And so, to some acclaim from the caving world, we went our separate ways. Of the 1980–1 hard core – the 'hombres' as we were beginning to refer to ourselves with tongues only half in cheek – several were staying in Oxford. Keith still had another year to go before finishing the pre-clinical part of his medical training. John, Graham and William began research projects. Richard started learning how to be a proper doctor at the John Radcliffe hospital. I went home to my parents in London, and threw myself into journalism, first as a freelance and then as a staff reporter at the magazine *Time Out*. Skunk went back to Birmingham and developed a serious illness that was never satisfactorily diagnosed until it cleared up as mysteriously as it had begun nearly three years later. Martin moved to Cardiff and began work at British Telecom, and Skippy began to train as a doctor too in Birmingham.

For the best part of three months I was out of touch with the club altogether. I had had enough of caving for a while: the arguments and tensions of the latter part of the 1981 expedition seemed fresher in my mind than the thrill of Xitu and I devoted all my energy to a new kind of discovery, digging out the news.

The way things worked at *Time Out* Mondays were always the busiest day of the week, before the magazine went off to the printers. Often I would be in the office until after midnight finishing off stories. My phone rang at about 7.30 in the evening of Monday, November 16. A piece of paper was in my typewriter on which I was about to begin my main article for the week, and the sound of the telephone bell came as an annoying distraction.

It was John. He came straight to the point. He had already conveyed this message several times that evening. "Dave, I'm afraid I've got bad news. Keith's dead. He was killed diving at Wookey Hole on Saturday. The funeral's later this week."

I stammered out the obvious questions: how, when, most of all the one nobody could ever answer, why?

John knew very little: even today, no one really does. Keith had been with several experienced divers in the far reaches of Wookey Hole, the cave from which flows the River Axe near Wells in the lee of the Mendip Hills. The first part of the cave, as far as the ninth chamber, is open to tourists and lit by permanent electric lighting, but beyond, it is accessible only to divers – who have still not probed all its secrets.

Keith had been attempting to dive the sump between the ninth and nineteenth chambers, a long but now well-worn way which he had successfully negotiated before. There are two routes through the sump, and Keith set off first through the lower, deeper passage, leaving Martyn Farr – one of the best cave divers in the country – to follow along the shallower, but more difficult route.

When Farr reached the end of the sump Keith was lying – in sight of airspace, at the very end of the flooded section – in ten feet of water, motionless, with his airtank mouthpiece floating free. Farr immediately dived to retrieve him, and soon joined by others, began a desperate attempt at artificial respiration which lasted vainly for nearly an hour.

What might have happened? Some thought that perhaps Keith passed out from cold: his wetsuit, his friends would remember with a grimace, was not always in the best condition, although he was wearing two wetsuits when he died. Rob Parker, another experienced diver who was on that ill-fated trip, suggested that Keith may have swum too fast uphill from the 'elbow' of the sump at seventy feet depth, and found himself unable to take in enough air to feed this strenuous exertion: then, maybe, instead of resting he decided to 'go for it', thinking himself (rightly) to be almost at the end of the sump but without enough air in his lungs to make it. There will only ever be theories.

And we had lost a friend, an hombre, a comrade without whose skill and daring we might never have reached the bottom of Xitu. Keith was an overwhelming person: for a very long time after his death, sometimes even now, we would speak of him as if he was alive, telling stories about him: not consciously as a way of remembering him, but simply because he had played such a central role in everything we had done that it was impossible to talk about Spain or caving without bringing him into the conversation.

Without his death, we might never have gone back to the Picos. His own presence on the next expedition had been doubtful: after Xitu, he said, he didn't think deep vertical caves could ever have the same allure, and he had, he said, 'found the way on' – with air tanks on his belt. His losing that way stopped the rest of the team's accelerating drift apart. At his funeral in Wedmore, not five miles from where he died, we were together again, and after the Catholic priest had intoned what seemed to me a maddening ritual untruth about how lucky Keith was to get to heaven early, we sat with his parents, drinking whisky in celebration at our own survival and toasting the man that he had been. A few weeks later we had a dinner in Oxford. Graham would lead another trip. El Joon '82, a small reconnaissance, was on.

RICHARD "Above all we need a van," Graham said. At this stage in the late Spring this lack was keenly felt. The most obvious thing to do was to invite some mug who already owned one. George had a Land-Rover, but the most important bits of it were often wrapped in old newspaper on his kitchen table. The only place it was going was perhaps his living room table, and then only if he cleared the Maxi away. Nick White was a good bet: good old Nick, without him there would never have been transport in '81. Perhaps he guessed the way our minds were working. He emigrated to America. We wrote to Kenning's van hire. Six weeks later came the reply: Mr Kenning, to whom we had made our request, had never made loans of this nature and anyway, he had been dead for some months. Word seemed to have got round.

Paul Cooper, a medic and climber on his first trip to Spain, suggested thinking big. "Let's buy one. How much cash have we got?" Graham knew: "About three pounds." We went to the pub, to be joined by Tom Houghton, yet another medic.

Sitting in the Rose and Crown John took a sip of his beer: "Barclays!" he exclaimed.

"I thought this was Ind Coope," mumbled Tom.

"No – this is the answer. Borrow the money, buy a van, and sell it when we come back." But who would want to buy a van after it had been used by cavers for six weeks? Nick White? No, he had emigrated to America. We agreed to solve that problem when we returned. I went over to the phonebox and called the bank. They would see us next day at 11 a.m. "It'll mean getting up early then," said Tom. Paul was trying to be practical: "Let's all go looking really smart, to impress the manager how sensible we are." I looked around the room. There wasn't anyone there a mother would willingly leave alone with her baby.

The following morning we were ushered into the manager's office by a pale girl. She pressed herself against the wall as we passed. The manager rose to greet us, but instead of shaking his hand, John rolled our huge survey of Xitu out onto his desk. It smelled more than a little of stale beer. "This is the cave," John said, not letting the manager speak. "We camped here and explored it right down to this sump. It's mainly vadose, but there's a bit of high-level phreas here, and here." He stabbed the map with his finger as he spoke. Graham had got out a file and opened it, spilling photos out onto the desk, pushing them under the manager's nose. The latter had gone pale too and was gripping the top of the table tightly.

"I went caving once . . ." he gave a slight shiver.

"Oh, that's great," said John. "We're off to the Mendips this Saturday. Fancy coming? Ever done any free-diving, I can lend you my old wetsuit though it is a bit leaky . . ."

The manager looked up, ashen. "How much do you want?" he said, reaching for his pen.

Oxford University itself sold us its old van: a yellow Ford Transit that had taken various clubs all over the United Kingdom. It had been abused by students but well looked after between outings by one of the 'bulldogs'. In the 1960s these university policemen were the terror of rioting undergraduates. Now that the rules had been loosened they took out their frustrations on the Transit's engine.

It turned out to be the all-time great expedition vehicle, differing markedly from all its predecessors and successors by starting, travelling along and stopping when, and only when, requested. Graham fitted his 'ghetto-blaster' stereo cassette into the front and on the appointed day, Friday July 9, we set off to the heavy beat of rock and roll. Laden with two kilometres of rope, food, tents, caving gear and several cavers, thirty hours after departure we lurched once more onto the grassy Los Lagos campsite. The mountains, fringed by glinting snowfields, were as calm as the windless surface of the lake.

"The first thing we must do," said Graham, "is . . ."

"Go and have a drink at Amador's" came the immediate reply. Graham found himself standing in the field alone, and raced off after us. Catching up by the entrance to the bar he told us breathlessly that on no account should we mention the Falklands. The task force had recaptured the islands only eight weeks before, and the Spanish had been warm in their support for their Argentine co-linguists.

The rotund, twinkling Amador hadn't changed at all. "Hombres!" he exclaimed.

"Hombre!" I took his hand. He got out some glasses and

poured ponches, the local liqueur. None of us had had time to change money but this is never a problem in Amador's. For his regulars, los Ingleses, it was always possible to defer payment until mañana. Beaming, Amador explained to the others in the bar who these foreigners were. One turned to Graham, furrowing his brow, and dredged out some schoolboy English:

"What you theeng of Heneral Belgrano?" Graham choked on his drink, but before he could think of a reply, the Spaniard continued: "When you geeve back Hibraltar? You like Juan Carlos? Lady Diana ees beautiful. I have been in Tunbridge Wells."

The whole bar fell into laughter, and the Spaniard's pals clapped him on the back. More ponches were ordered. Amador waved aside our feeble attempts to explain about the cash: "Mañana, mañana."

Once installed again at Los Lagos our plan was to set up two further camps, at Ario and later, after making a series of forays from the Ario refugio, somewhere in the high country beyond.

The pasture of Ario lies at the head of a long dry valley running up from Los Lagos, followed for most of its length by the sweaty path only too familiar to Oxford speleologists. Xitu, of course, is where the valley rises to meet the plateau's edge, near the viewpoint or mirador which affords a panorama of the surrounding hills. Looking towards the main ridge of the massif from here, at first the land slopes down, into a confusing area of depressions, blocked shafts and interconnecting ridges, the Joos de la Cistra. Beyond it rises again towards a wall of high peaks: Jultayu, Cuvicente, La Robliza and La Verdellengua. It was among these peaks that our first goal, El Joon, lay. The Joon, a deep, scooped depression, is entered by a high pass, the Boca del Joon. To get there was a long walk across difficult country. In high alpine limestone like the Picos no one valley or natural feature can be followed for long. Without surface drainage to guide and shape the landforms, valleys have no outlets, while most ridges tend to end in sheer cliffs. Alvaro, the new warden at Ario, said he would show us the way. It seemed to be an excellent idea.

Alvaro had been a keen and expert climber until a serious fall left him wrecked. He was a short, powerful man with curly hair and long arms. Bulging muscles tugged at his T-shirt, which covered a scarred body. His left leg bent sideways at the knee, the bones knitted badly after his accident, so that as he walked he would lope along at great speed. His broken English was almost a parody of an accent, and lurching by my side he told me what had happened to him. His pidgin gave the story a simple horror.

"I have very luck. In Macizo Central I make climb – very difficult. Is winter. After finish climb, I descend and felled three hundred metres. I lie in snow for four hours before found, but all the time I . . ." and he made a sign to indicate that he had been unconscious. He had, he said, broken both legs in several places, and had had operations on his shoulder, left knee and his right elbow. It was a remarkable testimony to his endurance and his determination that he had got himself back into such fine shape: eighteen months after his fall he was itching to begin climbing again and could now easily do pull-ups on his middle fingers alone.

Alvaro knew the mountains well, and his skill made the walk to El Joon much easier. Our problem was that we had been molly-coddled on Ordnance Survey maps, which generally showed mountains as up and valleys as down, and marked rivers only where there were any. Spanish maps didn't bother with such dull traditions as this, and so required some imagination to interpret. Alvaro had no difficulty at this, and could often even point out on the map where we were! He seemed quite at ease with the fact that the map showed a depression where there was in fact an obvious mountain, and that the thousand foot cliff wasn't shown at all. Navigating in the mist with this map would be impossible for us – so we decided to build a line of cairns across the wasteland of the Joos de la Cistra. Stuck in bad conditions in El Joon, all we would have to do would be to locate the start of the cairns and then follow them back to food and a warm bed.

Slogging uphill the first landmark was Pozu Jou Tras la Jayada, the 300-metre-deep abyss abortively explored by Keith in 1981 and before by the SIE. Close up, the entrance was a terrifying, jagged rent in the earth. Fifty metres away, among the grassy boulderslopes and clumps of startling alpine flowers this gateway to hell was invisible.

Further up the mountain was la Jayada itself: a huge open cave that could be seen from the Xitu mirador and further still. It amounted to a very large rock arch spanning a snow-field, and here, an hour's stiff walk from Ario, we set a tent, leaving it filled with tackle as a base to 'bash' the nearby shafts. It was only a few minutes now to the Boca del Joon and a curving desert valley, bounded on all sides by dizzy, jagged peaks, the Joon proper, lay just below. No matter what the name of the expedition, one glance at the floor of the Joon – snow and jumbled scree –

showed there were no prospects of finding a cave. Alvaro and I poked around for a while and set off down our line of cairns in the dying rays of another Picos sunset. Even if the Joon appeared to have limited potential, many of the slopes nearby looked promising in the extreme.

The next two weeks were blessed with superb weather. High in the mountains the sun blazed down from a clear sky, hot and clean in the sparkling air. Below us, on all sides, was a thick layer of cloud which covered the Costa Verde and usually Los Lagos: it was easy to imagine, walking among the rocks and flowers in search of entrances, that the rest of the world no longer existed. Day after day we walked the slopes to check each open pothole to see if it led to a cave system. There were dozens of openings everywhere. Most were blocked with ice or rubble not far from the surface, but of these many required a preliminary descent on rope or ladder to check that there were no ways on.

There was much to make up for our initial lack of success. Large square-winged Egyptian vultures circled the cliffs in the rising thermals, and also small thrushlike birds known locally as Perdices. Sometimes the silence was broken by a falling rock, and there would be a flurry of movement high on a cliff face – shy rebeccos, the chamois of the Picos. These small deer, though the timidest of creatures, would gaze at the cavers from a vantage point on the skyline, baffled no doubt as we grunted and sweated along with our heavy packs. They were incredibly agile, racing along the crags with enviable ease. Only once did I see one slip. As George and I rested on a small col, a pair of the delicate animals raced away from us up an apparently sheer face. Above them, the rock looked a severe proposition for a roped human, but as they stood abruptly motionless on a ledge there were perhaps seven hundred feet of precipice beneath their hooves.

The female charged at the rock, her four legs slipping briefly on the last, smoothest steps. She got to the top and looked back at her mate, as if to say, "How about that? Your turn now." He launched himself up the cliff but on the smoothest part he began to slip helplessly. Still running for all he was worth, he slid backwards down the blank wall toward the huge drop below. All at once he leapt off and spun round in the air, landing so as to face down the crag. Half falling, half running, he raced down until he regained the tiny ledge and stopped dead, resting for a few seconds. After another failed attempt and similar jump and retreat he gave up, picking a longer and less steep route across the face while his mate waited on the summit above. How dare we think ourselves masters of the caves we explore, I thought. The rope and ironmongery in my pack seemed all the heavier as I slung it on my back and began a slow trudge up the mountain-side. The graceful rebeccos had long since disappeared.

We divided the mountains into sectors, each with an appropriate letter from A, given to the area round Jultayu, swinging north to F, the highest and most remote region at the back of La Verdellengua. Soon the log-book was covered in people's jottings on the entrances explored. Needless to say, no one found Dave's increasingly mythical Ridge Cave. There also remained Pozu del Optimistu: this, for the time being, thanks to Jan's dire warnings, we left well alone. Finally, after much slog, we decided to pursue C4.

Paul and I found the shakehole, and thought at first it was blocked, but a small black space required further inspection. A 10-metre ladder climb led to another drop of similar length, although at the bottom our electric lamps showed what looked like an impenetrable rubble floor. I suggested leaving it at that, but Paul insisted on finishing the job properly, tying another ladder to a dubious flake: "There you are. You can go down now."

Over the centuries, the entrance to C4 had acted as a giant funnel for frost-shattered rock, which had tumbled down to make a great pile of underground scree. The ladder lay against the scree and for most of the way down seemed to be the only solid barrier preventing the whole lot from caving in on top of me. Only a few rungs down I could see that the way on at the bottom was hopeless, filled with razor-sharp boulders on every side. Yet just below the pitch head, set in one wall, was a square window into a much larger shaft. Stones fell down a long way before hitting anything.

Somewhat ecstatically we raced back to the store tent to grab a 100-metre rope. Soon we had it rigged: we crawled through the window and into the shaft, reaching the bottom via a series of difficult changeover manoeuvres in mid-air.

The chamber below had no outlet. There was, however, an overhanging wall some 8 metres up one side, with another window through which stones vanished when thrown up from the bottom. How to gain the window? Alvaro! He had done some aid climbing, and a little caving. We grabbed him when we got back to the refugio that night:

"You can do it, Alvaro! Come with us and make a great breakthrough tomorrow."

"I bring it. Is necessary it."

"It?"

"I bring it. We have when finish cave."

Alvaro's SRT gear was rather individual . . . it was his climbing gear. For ascending he used two jumars with étrier stirrups attached to them by very thin pieces of cord. For descending he used a figure-of-eight, the simplest type of descender available – fine for climbing, but not suitable for use underground. They are difficult to control and twist the rope into tight kinks as you go. Worse, they have to be removed from one's harness before they can be attached to the rope, so there's always the chance of dropping them. We decided to put Alvaro in the middle of the party.

At the flying rebelay, 20 metres above the floor of the first big pitch, Alvaro stood in his étriers and removed his figure-of-eight, putting it on the rope below the rebelay. Then, using his gorilla-like strength, he gripped the rope and pulled up on one arm to detach the jumar and his étriers, and lowered himself onto his descender so that he could carry on abseiling. The only problem was, he had forgotten to *re*-attach the figure-of-eight to his harness.

"Plis!" came the cry.

Paul raced down the rope to the rebelay and peered down the shaft. Alvaro was standing in his étriers again, having managed to clip them into his figure of eight via a safety cord. He couldn't go back up to sort them out because the figure of eight was now out of his reach; nor was the safety cord clipped to his own harness – he was clinging to the étriers for dear life. The figure-of-eight couldn't even let him go downwards, because the rope had twisted over the top of it, stranding Alvaro in a very exposed perch.

From the belay, Paul could just reach the figure-of-eight, but Alvaro's weight loading it made it impossible for him to unlock the loop of rope. The only solution was for Paul to lower to Alvaro a loop of rope attached to the belay, from which the jibbering warden could dangle whilst Paul freed his descender, which Alvaro then thankfully pulled down to him, and used to reach the bottom of the shaft.

Up ahead, John and I had found a third window in the wall of the cave, which led to another big pitch – Alvaro's skills as an aid-climber would no longer be needed – possibly just as well, as he was still shaking. We decided to take him out, and he was very pleased to see the daylight again. His eyes lit up:

"Ah!" he exclaimed. "Now is time for *it*! I have *it* in my bag." With this he reached down into his bag and produced ham, sausage and a tube of gooey evaporated milk which he squirted into our mouths in turn. "Is good it, eh?"

We reckoned to do our own aid-climbing in future.

C4 was a disappointment, though. The new pitch was 35 metres deep, but very difficult to rig. The problem was that the rock at the top was loose and dangerous, flaking away in great chunks and making loud booming noises from the floor far below. At the foot of the pitch was a large hall, but with no way out. The cave had finished, like the others we had found, only 120 metres below the surface. Optimistu, the revolting cave by Ario, was our only choice left.

DAVID Pozu Optimistu was the deepest cave in the world. I was sure of it. Before the expedition left, I could talk of little else. Occasionally Graham would protest: "But Dave, we want to get up into the high peaks this year, and Optimistu really doesn't sound very nice . . ." But I would have none of it. It was also Keith's last cave in Spain, pushed by him and whoever else he could commandeer in the tail end of the 1981 expedition. I felt that I owed a duty to Keith's memory to explore this cave.

The entrance was high on Cabeza Forma, a rocky hill rising above the path between Xitu and the refugio. There were no other known caves on this hill, and the additional height gave it a depth potential well in excess of Xitu's. Arriving in Spain, to be met by chance by a shopping party in Cangas – I was deeply impressed by their suntans and their powerful smell, discernible even from the other side of the town's little plaza – I made plans to make a start on Optimistu immediately. The entrance had been located but was very difficult to find, Richard warned. But that same evening I was up at Ario with George, with whom I had driven out, raring to go.

We were lucky: the next morning dawned warm and clear. About a kilometre from the refugio as the crow flies, it took only two hours of stumbling under the weight of several hundred metres of rope – always a good idea to think deep, after all – to find the entrance. It breathed depth, I thought to myself. A great black cleft, entered on a 30-metre rope; at the bottom, a slanting mossy cavern, dominated by an enormous pile of snow.

I knew from Keith's description that the way on was very obscure. We found it, almost buried under stones, below one wall: a low, flat-out crawl, leading to a bizarre little tube, barely big enough to enter, corkscrewing down. It was time to take a deep breath: impossible to see what lay below beyond my body filling the descending passage. I had to let myself go, trusting to Keith's account in the 1981 log that the tube did not suddenly open out into a large shaft. Soon I was reassured. It slowly enlarged and gave way to an easy climb down the wall of a big, dry and exceedingly pleasant corridor. "George!" I yelled, "this place is absolutely brilliant . . ."

For some reason, most caves that are, according to the pot-holer's definition, 'nice', begin that way and usually remain it. Equally, those that are not – filled with loose rocks, tight, in the habit of making their explorers dunk their ears, nose and throats in cold grey mud – announce their hostility at the outset. We have been very lucky in Spain. Nearly all the systems discovered over the years have been very nice indeed. They may have had their dangers and difficulties, but such struggles as they have entailed have been fought according to Queensberry rules.

Optimistu's true nature dawned slowly. It became slightly nasty, then really rather awful, then unremittingly horrendous and then lethal only by degrees. Its bare statistics – 102 metres deep, 254 long at its miserable finale – give no hint of the desperation involved in reaching the end. My nice dry corridor gave way to a shaft, blind at the bottom, traversed over on a series of sloping, loose and slippery ledges. By now I was already having doubts: the next section, a slimy, tortuous fissure, confirmed them. There followed a dangerous, missile-prone pitch into a big, steeply sloping gallery.

The floor here was made of boulders; so too the roof and walls. Between the boulders were many black spaces, and occasionally one would step on a crumbling foothold and slip: as one re-covered, clasping the largest available piece of rock, one would hear the clatter of the former foothold as it tumbled down the black space before coming to rest with an echoey thud 30 metres down. (Subsequent investigations confirmed that all possible routes at this lower level were blocked.) After a final nerve-wracking 45-degree descent along the edge of a big flake, with only balance handholds along the nearby wall, a solid floor was reached again.

There was worse to come: a tiny hole, the Oubliette, leading straight into the side of a shaft, 15 metres deep from the point of entry. There was no way one could squeeze through the hole wearing a bulky descender. We forced our bodies through backwards, pushing out over empty space until the widest part of the chest and shoulders was through: then a rapid scrabble to clip rope into descender, descender into harness, before the strain on the left arm hanging from the knot on the belay became too much. On the second trip we fixed a ladder here, improving matters considerably.

When I get to Spain I always feel a great rush of enthusiasm which takes a few trips to wear off: every year it's the same. Despite all the above I remained keen to carry on. We still had not reached the last, undescended pitch found by Keith the year before, an essential target for the first day. It didn't seem too bad at the bottom of the Oubliette. A passage in clean rock, with a little water should we need a drink. A dead end. Still pulling three bulky tackle bags between us we glumly submitted to the alternative, a low tunnel at boot level. Keith had mentioned this crawl but surely it couldn't be *that* bad?

It was a measure of my beginning of expedition keenness that even at the other end my first worry was that this passage – Unclean, Unclean as it came to be called – would be a tiresome and time-consuming obstacle when Optimistu was further along the way to being the deepest cave etc. The first 10 metres or so weren't extreme: the next five times that length were. The sludge, cold, grit-laden, viscous, was many inches deep. At different levels in the fissure were broad flakes, forcing one to press deeply into the filthy trench beneath them. Everything caught. The last part was the worst, contorting, unremittingly strenuous, appalling with the infuriating yellow tackle bags. Again it emerged onto a pitch, but a traverse led to a small ledge from which to belay. Even the roof was covered with mud here. We were still keen but it seemed wise to leave it for that day.

Overnight we became keener still, and Tom joined us for a foray into the unknown. Things were bound to improve soon: we decided to take even more tackle into the cave – it would be a pity to waste the trip. Several hours on, the pitch was rigged and I abseiled down 15 metres. My heart leapt. The mud had gone: I was in a spacious stream canyon strongly reminiscent of Xitu. "George, Tom," I cried, "I think we're on the verge of a really significant discovery." Sometimes people do actually talk like that. Round the next bend was total defeat. It took a long time to explore the numerous levels in the canyon but all were far too tight. It seemed only fair to take out the three big bags of extra tackle and we turned round for a long, hard ascent.

Outside, thirteen hours after we had gone in – it hardly seemed possible that such a short cave had taken so long – the 1 a.m. hillside was as gloomy as our moods. It seemed to take an age to dekit, with Tom quite exhausted: setting off into heavy drizzle and impenetrable fog we were soon lost. After an hour of climbing, descending and complete failure to hold to a straight line Tom suggested stopping for the night. Still caked in the mud from Unclean, Unclean, George and I demurred, but Tom just sat down. If he stayed there he would soon be out of earshot. When we needed it most the Ario path at last betrayed itself: a sandy runnel across a featureless meadow. Expecting to find a silent, sleeping refugio we stumbled towards the hut, puzzled by the light still shining from the ground floor. Inside there was chaos.

RICHARD Alvaro had unexpectedly lowered the price of beer to almost normal from its top-of-mountain premium, and helped by brandy and Coca-Cola a wild session ensued. Only that day Alvaro had guided his horse up the mountain with a new load of drinks, and by the time Dave appeared, grey-faced with mud and fatigue, the mountain of cans on the table betrayed the dismal truth – we had drunk the lot. The lone Spanish walker staying at Ario had a hard time of it, as one by one the victims of the free market economy lurched across to the door, the born again fabada falling out to the eagerly awaiting goats. William was especially bad. Later, with everyone tucked up in the dormitory upstairs, his terrified yelp suddenly rent the night air:
"Help, help! Am I being sick out of the window or over the edge of my bed?"

DAVID Under a cold, wan sun next morning, with storm-promising clouds on the horizon beyond the gorge, the casualties of the evening's revelry began to face up to the miserable truth that after nearly four weeks, El Joon '82 had not produced a decent cave. Our leader was in the worst state, and in no shape to make the suggestions needed to lift the growing despondency. He crouched on all fours on the grass by the fuente, softly groaning. Richard examined him tenderly, peering with disbelief into the acid-ravaged battlefield of Graham's throat. "This man has a prolapsed uvula," he announced. Paul and Tom, the other medics, rushed to view this unusual clinical event. Graham felt no better at all. It was to be several days before he returned to his normal, unobtrusive self.

As the hope of finding a new deep pothole receded, the clouds moved in. By afternoon it was raining steadily. Wrapped in waterproofs, Martin and I made a half-hearted foray to look for a cave which Martin had decided ought to exist under the dry valley below the Ario path. We found nothing. People laid plans for a series of trips to the beach. Our Picos days looked like being about to end with a sad, frustrated whimper.

That evening, as Richard and I made one or two members of

the team blench by drinking a small amount of beer (Alvaro had been to the shops once more), we discussed the only course left open. One of the areas marked off on the map, 'F', the most remote and inaccessible, had still not been examined conclusively. There was one entrance up there, Richard said, which might go: it had already been rigged down a big pitch onto a pile of snow and there appeared to be a way on. It would mean setting up a new camp high in the hills, a longer hike from base camp. Back in England – convinced that we need look no further than Pozu Optimistu – I had argued vociferously that it would never be practical to explore the really distant parts of the mountains without a helicopter for supplies. Now I enthusiastically agreed with Richard's suggestion of setting off next day. A new phase of exploration was about to begin.

The cloud had gone again next day, and enlisting the help of Martin Laverty and Martin Hicks, a talented cave photographer who had met his namesake in South Wales, we set off for area 'F'. Our walk took us up over a col into the Vega Aliseda, a grassy valley closed at each end, and then up a further steep slope to a pause in the gradient below the peak of Punta Gregoriana. Here, about 1,950 metres above sea level, was an arid, rocky desert, with neither vegetation nor water. Below a small cliff, between an ice sheet and some big boulder screes, was a shakehole of impressive proportions. At one end, below the cliff, it dropped into a black void, vertical, blade-like strata seeming to emphasise the possibilities that this place held for a deep cave system. Opposite the cliff, the shakehole was floored by a steep slope of stones down which we walked to peer into the shaft. The whole was like a giant scoop taken out of the mountainside.

A small stream was running off the big ice sheet on the nearby slope, and we filled our water containers above the point where it disappeared into the ground. Ten minutes below the cave entrance in the opposite direction we had spotted the only flat patch of grass for a very long way. At first sight hardly bigger than a snooker table, we were to find ways of cramming tents here into every corner.

RICHARD Dave and I pitched the tents while the Martins went off for a closer look at the cave entrance. When they returned Laverty spoke first: "I don't think it'll go. There's lots of evidence of glacial action and some big erratics, and the beds looked slumped . . ." The rest of his geo-speak was lost, because Dave was whooping and jumping for joy:

"That's fantastic! He's always wrong! He said Xitu would end and it didn't; he said Xitu would come out at Trea and it didn't; he said Optimistu would probably go and it didn't . . ."

Manfully, Martin agreed. He said, as he had always done, that the only way to find out what really happened underground was to go and look. The others bade us farewell and set off down the hillside in the late afternoon sun, leaving Dave and me alone. From our camp, the bare and ragged limestone mountains fell away into the bed of cloud far below, a white carpet stretching to the shoreline 30 miles away. On one side, the peaks of the Sierra de Cuera, a lower range between the Picos and the coast, rose up from the cloud like islands in a sea, beginning to go pink in the dying sun. Our perch felt higher and wilder than Ario, with its busy refuge. That extra altitude must yield a still deeper cave, we felt sure.

Rousing ourselves from our reverie we decided to begin exploration that evening. The name I had originally given the cave on finding it had now stuck – FU56. The Spanish authorities would want another name after a local feature, we knew, and eventually the official title became Pozu Jorcada Blanca, corresponding to a rocky col above the entrance. But meanwhile FU56 seemed highly appropriate. The previous year, we had been sure that Xitu was the deepest cave in Spain, and its camp the deepest ever set underground. It was only on returning to Britain that we discovered the truth: BU56, a French/Spanish exploration in the Pyrenees, was deeper on both counts.

DAVID The first pitch from the bottom of the scree slope was a twisting, awkward descent of some 30 metres. Now, as in the first, brief foray a week or so before, we rigged it on electron ladder without a lifeline – dangerous and scary. For much of the way, one wall of the shaft was lined with slowly melting ice, chilling our fingers to the bone when the ladder rungs pressed against it. Twenty metres down we landed on a broad, sloping platform made of snow, carrying on through a descending body-sized tube, the conduit for the not inconsiderable volume of water from the melting icebergs above. Suddenly it opened out into a vertical rift, floored with unstable stones, falling rapidly to the head of a large shaft. The position was exposed: the floor was too loose to stand on and we wedged ourselves in gingerly, without a belay, as I banged in a chilly bolt in one wall. Threading a tape round a large spike at the shaft's lip, we soon had the requisite two points of anchor. Before letting down the rope, we dropped stones. The soft, almost inaudible sound of their landing suggested both depth and more snow at the bottom.

It did not do to look at the ceiling here. It was made of very large blocks, balanced, it seemed from beneath them, on soft, dry mud. I pointed this out to Richard as he eased his weight onto the rope to begin his descent into the unknown. "Piss off, Dave. I'm busy."

He slid down in uncharacteristic silence, thinking of the blocks no doubt. Soon enough the familiar cry: "Rope free!" I joined him. He seemed to be having second thoughts. He was not at the bottom at all, but crouched in an alcove formed by a ledge no more than half a metre wide a long way from safety. The rope was too short. Richard lobbed a few more pebbles over the edge. Shining our electric lamps downwards, we could see a dull white patch. There wasn't far to go but the further reaches of FU56 would have to wait until next day.

RICHARD Heavily laden with the sausage-shaped tackle bags we set off on a fine morning, the weight of the gear hanging on donkey's dicks from our waists adding to the hazards of entrance pitch. We tied on a longer rope at the top of the shaft below the loose boulders. Dave went down first and soon confirmed that he had reached the bottom: on a pile of snow, as it transpired, but only a small one. The way on was not blocked.

We were in a chamber the size of a drawing room. Stepping over a deep pit at one end, we reached a further drop almost immediately. Another bolt and a short descent; at the base, a further drop of 12 metres. Dave rigged it in no time at all from large flakes. The cave was going swimmingly.

Our hopes were quickly dashed. Beyond the last drop the cave continued as a tiny, winding slit, far too small even to enter. We stared in miserable disbelief. This was just how the other caves had ended – but this time we weren't even 100 metres below the surface. Dave crawled in – well, wedged his head and one shoulder inside – the widest part of the passage. There was a long series of grunts, and his feet inched forwards into the tiny hole. He backed out again. "Let's eat the chocolate," said Dave, "then I'll have a go at widening the passage with the bolt hammer – you can't really see but it might widen past the first bend. Meanwhile you have a go at looking for a bypass." He began banging – I wasn't letting him at the food just yet – while I climbed the short pitch with bags of tackle.

Halfway up the pitch above, there was an inlet on the wall opposite the one we had come in by. I tried climbing up, but the rock was very unstable and overhanging. Instead, I tried prusiking up until I was level with the hole in the wall, and swinging across. This wouldn't do . . . I had to be a little higher. I took a few more steps, began to pendule and gained the passage without difficulty. Getting off the rope, I tied it carefully to a boulder, lest it should swing back to the vertical, leaving me stranded.

I was in an inlet, long abandoned by its stream, running upward from the junction with the pitch where I had swung across. And yet . . . suddenly, only a few metres on, it reversed gradient and began to run downwards, further into the cave. It was an easy scramble along the passage, ducking under the old flake, to the top of another pitch! What was more exciting was that I could hear Dave's remorseless hammering coming *up* the pitch from below, not behind me. I cried out: "Dave! I've found a bypass." He was as excited as I and made haste to join me. I met him at the pendule junction and we collected the tackle.

"Er, Richard, the head of this pitch is only four inches wide." I looked down at the shaft properly for the first time. He was right. But it looked as if the constriction was only really narrow right at the top. We were in luck. It was made of calcite, calcium carbonate first dissolved out of the limestone by the water which formed the cave and then redeposited. Calcite – the stuff from which stalactites and stalagmites are made – is very weak rock. It took only a few blows with the hammer before our constriction was flaking off and falling down the pitch in satisfying chunks. The electric excitement of discovery held us fast and we hit harder and harder.

"That's it. We can manage that all right." The top of the pitch was still tight, and rather unusual, involving forcing oneself through the narrow gap from a comfortable sitting position. We called it The Chair. It was broken by a ledge, and in all turned out to be 18 metres deep, watered by a splashy trickle. It dropped us into a room with a sandy floor, with a large passage leading off. To my chagrin, I found that this passage ascended, rapidly becoming too narrow to force – it was the very fissure Dave had been trying to hammer. He came racing up behind me, having just completed the descent of The Chair. "How big is the next pitch?" he asked. There was no next pitch. The Chair water joined the inlet and seeped away through sand. It was the end of the cave.

DAVID "Might as well eat the chocolate and piss off out," I said. Then I noticed the pile of boulders sloping up above my head.

105

We had already found a way on by climbing up a little in this cave – could it be the same here? Scrabbling up, showering Richard with loose, muddy debris, I reached the top of the pile. Curving away left there seemed to be the start of a narrow rift passage. I crawled over to a gap no more than a foot wide. Through it, I could see the passage continued, but a big flake – made this time of solid rock, not calcite, barred the way. After a few token hammer blows, the position seemed hopeless again. "It's no good. There's no room to get a decent swing. I'm coming down."

RICHARD As Dave backed out, one of the boulders he was lying on rocked gently. It became clear that the pile was very loosely packed. We began pulling at the unstable blocks, at first the small ones, cautiously, then, with a new frenzy we pulled at much larger boulders which had originally seemed to be part of the cave walls. They rolled down the slope and buried our tackle bags. In ten minutes the hole was big enough to enter. Without the rocks, we passed easily below the flake which Dave had tried feebly to hammer, and the passage led off, a winding fissure with white, smooth walls. As we crawled in, they reflected our carbide flames, filling the passage with bright light.

The passage was of a type which French cavers call a meander, a narrow corridor winding both in plan and cross section. Movement in it was strenuous. As in the Xitu rift, we had to support ourselves without a floor in the widest part, and it was so narrow that it was impossible to face ahead. We thrutched sideways, looking over one shoulder, unable to turn our bodies or our heads.

DAVID Richard was trying to find a route high up, near the roof, and I struggled along six feet below him. At a particularly fierce bend, the curses from above indicated that his level had come to an end. Mine too looked impassable. The only chance seemed to be to drop down into a wider space at boot level and pray that if it didn't go I could climb back up.

Without holds, I went for it and slid down five feet. My wellingtons came to rest on a ledge, and using the extra leverage thus gained I made it round the bend. I shouted with delight: "It goes! Come on down!" My last words echoed and re-echoed. Not much further – all easy going along the ledge – I was at the lip of a big shaft, booming and honking like a crazy foghorn and listening to the glorious reverberations coming back from below. My conversation with Richard – "get the tackle-ackle-ackle . . .

don't forget the chocolate-olate-olate" – resounded mightily, the first human voice the cave had ever heard.

By the time Richard returned through the rift – then and henceforth the Meander of the Argonauts – I had a bolt nearly in. Lassoing a projection on the opposite wall, I rigged a 'y' belay, sharing the load between the anchors – an excellent, almost universally applicable technique which was, however, new to OUCC at the time. The pitch below was ample reward for the struggle through the rift. No more than half a metre wide at the top, where the fissure came to an end, it belled out immediately. The rope hung perfectly in the centre of the shaft. A powerful draught was rising from below, breaking up the stream into soaking droplets.

At the base, a flat platform 18 metres from the top, the water gathered itself and flowed into a narrow chute. As Richard hurried to join me, I climbed down the steeply descending canyon to reach a last ledge. I rolled a portable TV-sized rock from its perch on the left wall and it fell free for two or three seconds. The sound of gunfire rattled up the shaft, suggesting the rock had broken up; and the fragments continued, each new booming impact deeper and more muffled than the one before. Richard was beside me again and we repeated the exhilarating process. The cave was a goer. At last we were beneath the awkward zone 100 metres down, and our rocks were falling perhaps 100 metres more. "OK," he said. "Now we can eat the chocolate."

RICHARD We had discovered the entrance series into a properly developed stream cave. In the days that followed, Pozu Jorcada Blanca fulfilled its promise. Below the limit of our first exploration, three further pitches – the Mistral shafts, after their icy wind – took us to a further difficult horizontal section.

We reached Rift 2 by means of a traverse over a 10-metre drop – at floor level, the passage was far too narrow, but across the traverse, Walk on the Wild Side, we gained access to a meander every bit as bad as the first. It would have been virtually impossible to have rescued anyone on a stretcher from beyond it.

It led to another fine pitch – a 15-metre drop in a waterfall landing in a pool of water with green marble on the floor and walls, strongly reminiscent of the deeper parts of Xitu. George, Paul and Tom explored the streamway beyond, rigging four wet drops on ladders. Eventually, after a final short descent, the stream flowed through a slit in the floor of the narrow, straight

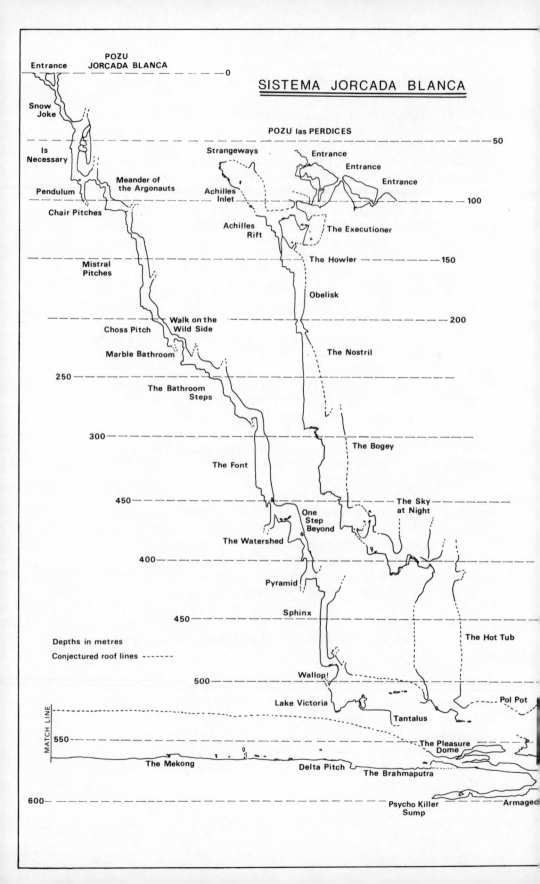

passage. Crawling ahead, they found themselves once more sitting at the top of a large shaft.

The Font was possibly the most impressive pitch any of us had seen. A perfectly circular tube 55 metres deep, the walls were made of grey and yellow marble, washed constantly and made more reflective by the drizzly falling stream. From the top, Tom watched George abseil down for the first time, surrounded by a ring of light, a small figure dangling beneath him. Abruptly, the ring became a disc as George reached the floor far below.

The bottom of the Font presented another difficulty. The stream, which had grown larger as it made its way through the cave, crashed down a narrow slit 20 metres deep and then disappeared through an impassable slot. A minute rift led off horizontally above. Perhaps it might be passed, but it would be hard going, with projections on the walls making it narrower still.

John heard the news when the pushers returned about break-fast time. "Right. We'll go down and force a way through with a hammer."

With Martin Hicks and William (the thin men), he left soon afterwards to push the cave further. It was now 370 metres deep. The vertical slit below the Font ended in a small chamber, from where John and Martin made forays into the rift, trying to hammer at the flakes and projections blocking the way. They could see that the passage enlarged ahead of them, probably ending in a vertical drop, and they rolled a chock stone along the rift above their heads – attaching a ladder to this gave them a means of getting to and from the hammering position and something to grip while carrying out the exhausting, frustrating work. Lying flat out, in a passage that squashed from all sides, they made feeble taps with the hammer at full reach. It was slow progress.

William was a long way behind them. His electric light had bust, and his carbide flame was refusing to stay lit for very long. He cursed in his inimitable way and called on ahead.

"I say, chaps, where's the way on?" No reply, just the sound of frenetic hammering from far below.

He got to the rope and slid down the cleft as his light failed again, this time for good. Now in utter blackness he cautiously abseiled on, feeling for a possible floor with his toes. He came to an abrupt halt, swinging in the dark and bouncing against the wall. What could be wrong? He felt his descender and found . . . yes, it was a rope-protector jammed in it. Unable to see, and out of earshot of the other two maniacal hammerers, he had to

109

change over, move up, disentangle the rope protector, re-position it above him, change over to abseiling, lower his weight onto the locked-off rack, detach his ascenders and clip them to his waist, re-position the rope protector and finally after an age, get ready to abseil again.

He moved only two feet before, in the dark, he stopped again unexpectedly. There was a second rope-protector immediately below the first and he had abseiled onto it.

The three of them staggered out of the cave the next morning with John subdued but breezy. "It'll only take another five hours' hammering," he said. Dave questioned him closely from the warmth of his sleeping-bag. Could normal sized people get through? Was there any chance of a bypass. Yes, said John, perhaps there was. Before dozing off again, Dave vowed to find it.

DAVID By the time I woke up properly, the weather was at its vilest. Breakfast, swaddled in waterproofs under the makeshift plastic tarpaulin at one corner of the campsite, did little to inspire any of us with enthusiasm for going underground. The tired hammerers said they would make their way down to Los Lagos to join the rest of the expedition for a meal at Amador's. Richard and I looked at each other glumly. It had been quite a few days since either of us had eaten a large hot meal, much less sampled any interesting Riojas, during which time we had put in two surveying trips. But time was running out. We had to get this cave as deep as we could. As we changed into our damp furry suits, hardly able to see beyond the rim of the tiny camp, William volunteered to stay in his sleeping-bag until we returned in case we got into trouble.

Reaching the entrance, our spirits sank still further. We felt sated with caving, and the conditions did nothing to revive our appetites. The cliff above the first pitch was carrying a stream from the heavy and continuing downpour. Correctly we ex-pected to get wetter still as we descended. We carried two heavy bags of tackle. Vainly I tried to summon up my conviction that an easy bypass to the hammer rift would exist and be discovered immediately.

By the time we reached the end of the Meander of the Argonauts the emerging consensus between us found ex-pression. "Richard, this cave is awash. Let's jack." Without another word we dumped the tackle and turned tail.

The weather was no better after our short trip. The afternoon was wearing on, and the stupidity of having gone down at all –

instead of making for the conviviality of Los Lagos – bore on us heavily. Changed back into chilly surface clothes, we looked at our watches. "We should just make it if we set off now," said Richard, "but to save time let's go across country on a compass bearing." Knowing no better, William and I agreed.

Richard's plan was to cut out the big dog-leg of the normal route by way of the Ario path. From the map, it looked as if nearly half the distance of the walk would be saved. Thinking hard of steaming plates of stew we set off into the mist.

We were soon stumbling in a bewildering maze of depressions, rises and descents. Even if we had wanted to, we would have been unable to find the relative haven of Top Camp again, and we clung to the bearing for dear life. Time and again we began steep downslopes: this at last must be the climb down to Lagos, I thought. But pausing for a spot of awkward boulder scrambling at the bottom, the bearing took us inexorably up again. William had ricked his knee and was going very slowly. Increasingly anxious, aware that the others would be well into their meal while darkness was approaching, Richard and I hurried ahead through the veil of rain. From a long way behind, invisible, William made urgent pleas for us to wait. When he caught up, he showed the first signs of exposure.

At last the bearing brought us to somewhere we knew – Las Bobbias, no more than two miles from where we should have been. I told Richard and William to follow me along the path while I ran ahead in the twilight to tell the restaurant to save us some food. I dashed off, pleased and surprised at my remaining energy and fitness. Splat. I went headlong in the mud, grazing my ear on a rock, pulling thigh muscles and adding filth to my drenched clothing. Yet we all made it. Richard and I munched our way through most of the menu: soup, menestra stew, trout, steak, cheese, crème caramel. William was served with his soup. Splat. He closed his eyes and slipped, unconscious, his forehead on the rim of the bowl and the soup spilling across the table.

RICHARD The bypass to the final rift did exist. Dave and I found it two days after our difficult walk to Lagos. It was a classic piece of Picos cave formation.

At one time, the water from the Font had flowed off at quite a shallow angle into a wide passage. With the centuries, it had found a weakness in the rock and cut down in a new, thinner slot – Stead's Braille Blunder and the impassable rift beyond. As in many other cases – perhaps rainfall had once been higher – the old way was big enough for cavers, and the new was not.

Dave was waiting on the small ledge at the top of the blunder while I went down to investigate and noticed a black space in the opposite direction, to his right, about a metre away. John had muttered something about there being a possibility here and after a short climb Dave had confirmed it. One Step Beyond was the bypass we were looking for. The rock was loose, muddy and brittle: difficult to bolt and untrustworthy as a source of natural belays. But it was big.

Three pitches led into a strange chamber, flat-floored and square. It had smooth vertical walls and was silent, sound-absorbing: as oppressive in its way as the row from the crashing waterfalls further up the cave. It had almost no water at all and we called it the Valley of the Kings. Pitches led off from it in opposite directions. To the right was Pyramid Pitch: a short climb down into a triangular passage with thousands of tetrahedral pendants in the roof and walls. A further drop lay beyond and we dropped the usual booming rocks, guessing its depth at about 30 metres. To the left was the Sphinx. This gaping black chasm, into which we peered from a slippery ledge covered in fine, ochre mud, was even more sound absorbent than the chamber. Our stones landed with the muffled, choked sound of thunder many miles away. The unreflecting mud made it very gloomy. The whole area of the cave was also numbingly cold, chilled by the silent, yet powerful draught which was itself a sure sign of greater depth.

DAVID We both felt unaccountably uneasy, and relieved to make the decision to leave these pitches for another party. FU56 had, without anyone noticing, become a serious undertaking. Our trip had lasted for more than twenty hours. From the Valley of the Kings, it took at least five hours of steady effort to reach the surface: the hard slog and natural grandeur of the shafts punctuated by the struggles – harder on the way up – in the rifts. The big decision each time was whether or not to remove one's gear. Taking off the encumbrances of chest harness, chest ascender and other bits and pieces was time-consuming, and the process had to be reversed at once on the other side of the meanders. But leaving it all on increased the risk of getting stuck, of wasting energy in a futile battle with solid rock.

RICHARD As the depth of the cave increased, so too did the logistical problems. After a twenty hour trip, cavers were good for nothing but eating, sleeping and lying in the sun. Ferrying loads from Los Lagos was a three to four hour walk. Moving

112

Colin Nicholls in the Xitu streamway near the Samaritan pitches.

Helectite formations in Xitu's Snowcastle series.

The first Samaritan pitch, where Xitu began to go deep.

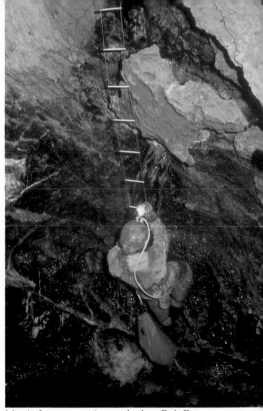

Hywel Jones regards the 138-metre Flat Iron pitch.

Martin Laverty getting soaked on Pafs Pot, 850 metres down.

Home from home, the Xitu camp.

Looking up the blackness of Flat Iron shaft.

David Rose in the narrow section before the Marble Steps.

Phil Rose attempts to emerge from a pitch head in 3/5.

The Culiembro streamway near the final sump.

The Classic Numbers, hard wet free climbs 1000 metres down.

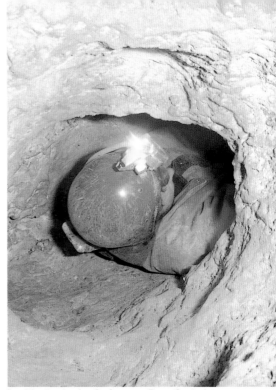

Fred Wickham enjoys the Perdices entrance series.

Jan Huning in the Corkscrew, Pozu Optimistu.

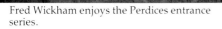

Jan forcing his way through the Oubliette, Optimistu.

Camshaft, Pozu la Cistra.

Richard Gregson taking survey readings in the Meander of the Argonauts, FU56.

Andy Riley traversing near Obelix pitch in Perdices.

In the lower reaches of Pozu la Cistra.

Looking out to daylight from Ridge Cave.

Dinosaur Beach, the first great cavern in Ridge Cave.

Nicola Dollimore in Cueva Culiembro.

Another view of the Snowcastle in Xitu.

rope, belays, food and carbide up the hill was a major task, and we were down to just ten active expedition members. With ten days left before we were due to leave, Jan advanced the proposition that it was time to halt exploration and detackle.

Worn out by our long trip Dave began to get angry. He said that now was the time for an all-out assault and rather over-stating his case – not for the first time – he claimed we could double the depth and de-rig if everyone were to pull their weight. Jan, who had just arrived from doing a strenuous carry, was particularly annoyed at this, and maintained that it would be irresponsible to push the cave a metre further. Dave was due to leave a few days before the end, he said – and wouldn't that just be so convenient as a way of missing the de-rig?

As we went off to fetch some water, Jan confided in me.

"Richard, this cave scares me. It's all right for you – you've explored most of it, but for those of us who haven't got used to it, it's pretty serious."

He was right, it was. The pace of the expedition had excluded some of the team for no other reason than their failure to be in the right place at the right time. Not everyone relished a twenty-four-hour trip down a tight, cold pothole. A compromise was reached the next day. One last trip to photograph, descend the Sphinx, complete the survey and begin the derig. When no one was watching, Dave slipped a spare rope into the bag with the survey gear.

Fit now after the exertions of the previous days and weeks, Dave, George and I slid almost effortlessly down the cave. George had with him his huge photographic ammo can (it was slightly smaller than the Xitu fibreglass version, but still as big as a comfortable stool). He also had his big prusik bag and even bigger tripod. As he came down the Font, we watched from below; he looked like some monstrous live bait with fishing weights dangling below. The things clanged together as they swung below him from his donkey's dick, but this clutter didn't slow him down in the slightest. George cycled 20 miles each day to work and 20 miles back, fuelled by a break-fast of dry wheat – at lunchtimes he went for five-mile runs. Twenty-four-hour caving trips were quite a relaxing weekend for him.

He unpacked in the Valley of the Kings. His idea was to photograph me on the first ever descent of the Sphinx, and handed me a flashgun and a mouthful of bulbs. The pitch was rigged with 'lightweight' rope – 9 mm in diameter instead of the usuall 11 mm. It was tied to a huge projection which jutted out over the drop, and to get onto the rope meant squeezing down between the edge of the shaft and the rock lump whilst tied on; the unnerving 62 metres of nothingness directly below. I remembered Ben Lyon's words as we bought the rope off him. He folded our cheque up and said, "Now don't be going and killing yourselves will you?"

As I loaded the rope, about the thickness of my little finger, it visibly narrowed. I am always scared that the rope will break. It's not enough to know that its specifications prove it would support the weight of several London taxis. What would I think about in the moments before hitting the floor? Would they be seconds of peace or of panic?

I began to abseil. It was no help to my nerves when George said: "OK. Hold it. Turn your light off, Richard, and when I say 'now' fire your flash gun."

I had gone about seven metres, and when I stopped, bouncing gently on the rope, there was a lot of empty space between my heels.

"NOW!"

There was a succession of flashes as George, Dave and I all let off the guns we were holding. For a split second the chasm below was brightly lit. It seemed to be a pleasant tube. I hung there while the process was repeated. Fifty feet further on George called for more shots, and twice more again.

At the bottom the crackling from my PVC suit and the clanks as I undid my descender from the rope hid a thrilling discovery. The pitch became quiet again as my shout of 'rope free' echoed into the distance and a new sound became noticeable – the very faint rumble of a great volume of rushing water.

"What's it like?" shouted Dave, impatient.

"I can hear the stream!" We could hear each other perfectly at either end of the 62-metre shaft – its second unusual acoustic property. There were cheers from above me. We were surveying as we went, and as they came down George and Dave measured the pitch. Together we walked over to the hole in the wall which was producing the noise.

There was another, 30-metre pitch – we were all pleased now about Dave's extra rope. For 1982 this would be a one-off, and George rigged the pitch as quickly as he could. There were many severe rub points near the top but rather than place a bolt he installed a safe, but preposterous rebelay on one wall – a tape round a flake that meant the changeover was carried out at an angle of 45 degrees, a manoeuvre of exceptional difficulty. But it was enough to get us down.

114

"What's it like?" Dave still couldn't wait. George's answer was enigmatic.

"No streamway – waterfall." There were sounds of him scrambling about, then quiet. We abseiled down to meet him. From the bottom of the rope, a sloping corridor filled with noise brought us to a wild, spray-lashed scene. A spout of water spurted from a tiny chink in the wall 20 metres up, landing amid waves and spume in a circular pool. John would have had to do an awful lot of hammering to have come out of there.

From the pool, Lago Victoria, the stream sank through the foot of a giant boulder pile, higher than the last pitch. George had already found a way through, crawling into a hole a few feet up. Dave followed him. "Jesus Christ!" he said, then, more calmly, "Richard, when you come through here, don't look at the roof." I failed to resist the temptation. It consisted of rows of razor-sharp boulders, rocky teeth all pointing down, some supported by tiny pebbles wedged at their sides. They were of a size and weight that could chop a man in half. It was impossible to say whether the act of crawling under them might cause a major collapse.

Beyond the hanging death was an easy climb into a stream-way. For the first time in FU56, the passage was an easy walk. It meandered with the stream, very large now, flowing in and out of clear pools. We charged along, scarcely able to take it in. This was something like the fulfilment of dreams. Horizontal de-velopment at depth: the start of the master cave of the region. Shortly we reached another pitch. We had no means of descent. The three of us sat there, jubilant, eating chocolate and throwing stones over the edge into the large cavern below. We scrawled 'OUCC 1982' in a mudbank by the lip of Tantalus, the un-descended shaft.

DAVID Our return to the surface was long and hard. We detackled the cave as far as the start of One Step Beyond, filling six bags, and helped George take more photographs. Two days later, after a great team effort of communal sweat, I was the last man out of the cave, with everything, except the ladder on the entrance pitch on which I was standing, removed. Lest a hard winter and poor spring completely fill the first part of the cave with snow, I carried a can of blue spray-paint, making a thick guideline along the roof up as far as I thought was the highest level such a blockage could reach. On the way down I had buried a bottle of pink Spanish champagne in the last snow before the entrance, and picking it up I slipped it into my prusik bag. The last ladder was pulled out and I opened the bottle as dramatically as I could, passing it round in the warmth of a perfect Picos evening. We all felt there was something to celebrate. The survey data had been computed and now we knew the depth to the top of Tantalus: 520 metres.

Next day I slipped off back to work, leaving the others to further celebrations and guilt-free trips to the beach.

RICHARD We had all agreed on putting up a memorial to Keith, but felt a little uneasy, knowing that he himself had been very rude about a similar plaque to a caver in Black Shiver Pot in Yorkshire. The caves are permanent, he had said, but we are transitory. In the end, we decided to put it at the bottom of Xitu's steep entrance climb, where it would be seen by future cavers and those making more than a casual inspection, but not by walkers on their way to the refugio. It was made of stainless steel and read:

> POZU DEL XITU −1139 METRES
> KEITH POTTER WHO DIED DIVING
> IN WOOKEY HOLE 14.11.81 THE
> FIRST MAN TO BOTTOM THIS CAVE

In successive years it has not tarnished at all.

7

Carbide Assist

DAVID By the time the British Cave Research Association conference came round again at the end of September, the survey of FU56 had been computed and drawn up. An enormous blueprint a metre high, it breathed excitement and allure, with its long series of plunging shafts and final question-marks where the Pyramids route led away from the Valley of the Kings and at the point where the stream sped over the last, undescended drop. It hung at the club stand in the fading sixties splendour of the Bristol University students' union, the team members clustering round. At a meeting convened during the lunch break it was confidently assumed that FU56 would be among the very deepest caves in the world. Was it not 300 metres further up the hill than Xitu?

Graham agreed to continue as leader for the following year. He even had a special jacket made by a well-known outdoor clothing manufacturer with an embroidered logo reading 'Pozu Jorcada Blanca '83'. He also continued to demonstrate his ingenuity by developing a waterproof rubber-lined bashresistant copper box for his Sony Walkman personal stereo. He showed it to Richard and me one freezing February day in Yorkshire, explaining that the tedium of waiting at the pitches in FU56 would be much relieved by his invention. And he could always boogie to keep warm. Later that day the car blew up, forcing us to spend a bitter night on the M6 inside it by the charmless town of Wednesbury. The stereo, if not the box, proved its worth.

RICHARD The real problem was Danny – Chris Danilewicz. He had done geology at Exeter College, where he had gloried in the reputation of a wild man. It is very hard to give him a personality profile – underground he was one of the safest of cavers, but, on the surface he was, well – suffice it to say that an evening with him was a pretty dodgy business. There are only three places that a guy like Danny can end up; in a debtor's prison, on an acute liver ward or as an officer in Her Majesty's Armed Forces. With Danny it had been the latter, but by how close a head I shouldn't care to speculate.

The Duke of Wellington's Regiment was now stationed in Gibraltar, and they stuck a rifle in Danny's hands and got him to march his men up and down the short border, knowing that whilst he was there Gibraltar was safe from the Spaniards. No Spaniard would want Danny on the same side of the border as his sister . . .

From the frontier post, Danny wrote to us. He was getting 'hundreds of pounds' from the army to bring a whole platoon of soldiers on our expedition. Only two of them had done any sort of caving before; the rest would make themselves 'useful'. They would carry heavy loads up and down the hill to our Top Camp day after day . . . Danny would order them to.

In Oxford there was panic. The squaddies were the last thing we needed. What was wrong with carrying our own gear up the mountain? The bored soldiers would surely only riot, burn down the bar or get Amador's daughters pregnant. We would be banned from Spain for ever . . . The worst possibility was that they would actually do as Danny commanded. Anyone who takes orders from a bloke like Danny must be a real psychopath. The whole idea sent shivers down our spines – it was unwieldy; it was divisive; it was too late. The post wouldn't reach him in time – our expedition had been taken over by a military coup.

There was other, better, news. Ian Houghton, the expedition letter writer, had saturated the business world with begging letters of the most brash kind. Crates of tins and jars and boxes began to arrive in Oxford, but better even than this was the rope. As we needed a great deal of new caving rope, Ian had written to all the manufacturers asking for some, free. In return we would let their managing director come for a while on our expedition. If they gave us enough rope, maybe we would even let him stay at home.

A fortnight later we got a reply, from Lafayette, Georgia, USA. Smokey Cauldwell, the owner and director of Pigeon Mountain Industries Inc., would be arriving mid-expedition at Bilbao airport with 1,000 metres of PMI flex, the finest caving rope in the world. He would bring it as hand luggage. This was talking – not only, at 80p per metre, much more than any of us could afford, it was also, at 1,000 metres, much more than any of us could lift. Smokey was obviously going to be a great help. The shame was that he could only stay a week. He explained in his letter; "my wife, MaryLou, gets kinda anxious if I'm outa state boundaries for too long."

We had the recurring problem of getting a van. Danny might at least have managed to borrow a tank or two, but he hadn't, and we had to get a vehicle to get our gear to Spain and back. By good fortune we had Steve Roberts in the club, a metallurgist from Cambridge who had sensibly moved to Oxford. He is a man who Knows About Engines. He had never been on an expedition before – the Cambridge Cave Club Expeditions are fairly select affairs, and Steve had never been selected. By contrast, we were desperate for manpower, especially people who Knew About Engines. We got Steve leglessly drunk (not difficult) and Graham and I held his arm as he signed the expedition deposit cheque. Knowing About Engines he was delegated to organise a van.

He got one on the cheap. Very cheap. He may well have known about engines, but not at all about bodywork, brakes, suspension or steering. The van had no windows for the passengers, but they weren't needed as you got a fine view of the passing scenery and of the road via the rust holes in the sides and floor. The starter motor was seized, and there was no reverse gear. The engine was, however, good. It always started when you pushed the van forwards. Graham fixed the electrics: "It's easy – to put the lights on, just push the *yellow* plug, on the end of the *red* wire, into the *blue* socket. Don't worry about the sparks."

Graham had also rigged his ghetto-blasting cassette recorder onto the dashboard, so we could listen to foreign language tapes, and reply in unison – *"Mais non, il ne reverse pas."*

The doors locked, but couldn't be unlocked. The only way in was to crawl in over the top of all the gear in the back, and it was a grade IV crawl. To keep costs down, five people were to go with the van to Spain. Three in the front, and two on top of the tons of rope, free breakfast cereal, free biscuits, free peanuts and free packet soup – notwithstanding all the tents, sleeping-bags, caving gear, cookers and water containers.

"Steve," I said when I saw the loaded van, "I don't like it. It's so difficult to get in and out – don't you think it'd be worth cutting some emergency doors in the sides in case of a crash?"

"Are you kidding?" He beamed back. "You don't need to worry about getting out in case of a crash. Any crash and all this gear will instantly crush us to death!"

DAVID We crossed the Channel and drove red-eyed through

France into the following day, pausing for pleasant interludes in roadside restaurants. Towards evening we sped along the geometrically straight highway that cuts through the forest which spreads out flatly between the Pyrenees and the Dordogne. Dusk was coming on and with it a tenuous dewy fog. In the back, unable to see anything past the mounds of luggage in our constricted cell, Iestyn and I dozed, and listened to the pop music from Graham's stereo. My brother Phil, driving, reached down for the awkward light switch.

Suddenly the van began to shake from side to side. The tyres thudded as they hit the kerb and bounced off again, making the uncontrollable oscillation worse. Steve managed to yell: "Phil, what the hell do you think you're doing?" and tried to grab the wheel, but then, with a large bump, the van mounted the verge and ploughed into the ditch. With a crack the stereo smashed through the windscreen and flew, still playing, into the field beyond. After a tremendous lurch the van was still.

I had been hurled forwards and lay upside-down on the front seat with blood pouring from my nose. Iestyn moaned behind me, his knee cut open down to the bone. Graham rushed round and opened the back to free him, but was met instead by an avalanche of free breakfast food, free biscuits and free packet soup, which tumbled out into the ditch. Midges began to cluster, scenting free blood. The stereo was still playing.

The van was wrecked, lying on its side in a ditch and surrounded by debris. We didn't even know where we were, except that it was a long way from any village, garage, hospital.

But things work in France. A Citroën ambulance whisked Iestyn and me to the hospital while the others were towed out by a rescue truck. Iestyn had his knee stitched up by a medical student who was going to pass his stitching exams with ease, but hadn't as yet done any anaesthetics local or otherwise. My nose was examined, and I was told to avoid violence for at least a month.

We re-met the next day, in the fly-blown yard of a deserted garage to inspect the remains of the van. "Lunch!" said Steve, producing half a baguette between five. The mechanics had all disappeared to sleep in the sweltering afternoon. It felt like thunder.

It was Steve Roberts who broke the torpor. Who needs a windscreen? There would be a Ford dealer in Santander surely? With indescribable nonchalance he looked at the wheel arches, and pulled. The old, soft metal gave easily – the wheels could move again. The head lamps were suspended with some wire.

The sides of the van had parted from the former, but . . . why bother? The old van, now christened 'El Sod', pulled creakily away onto the open road. Ten minutes later we were doing sixty on a dual carriageway. By now the storm had broken and hail blew from a Biscay tempest unimpeded into the cab, where Graham was driving clad in full caving gear.

That night we were in Santander. It seemed pointless to ask the sleepy Spaniard at the Ford dealer if he had a new wind-screen for an ancient Transit van, but unbelievably he did – from nowhere four mechanics appeared and beat it into place with their fists. By two the following afternoon we rounded the last bend to a damp, foggy Los Lagos, with 'Riot in Cell Block Number Nine' blasting out across the deserted moorland to signal our presence and give expression to what, improbably, had turned into euphoric, unrestrained joy.

There was no one about. At last we caught sight through the mist of a low line of orange tents, arranged neatly in line like an army camp. It was an army camp. Around the tents lay our new friends, all wildly, paralytically drunk, Danny most of all. Their officer was quite unable to give a sensible answer to the vital question – where was the rest of the expedition? He repeated again and again the slurred argument that he and his men had been waiting for us for three days in the mist, and had had nothing to do but visit the Los Lagos bars.

After tipping the van's contents into a huge heap on the grass we went down the hill to Cangas again to look for the foot passengers, who had arrived from England by train. It turned out that they had been sleeping under the seats of the Arriondas stadium for the last two nights, and they too were worse for too much wine. We drove back to the army camp. That first day it was immediately clear that there would be trouble. From either direction it looked like us and them: a bunch of over-educated toffee-nosed intellectual snobs or a gang of thugs who spent their evenings discussing 'contacts' experienced in Northern Ireland and what a shame they had missed the Falklands. The amount of common experience was minimal. Danny had, moreover, made a trip up the hill and sounded pessimistic: "It's been the worst winter here for years. They had snow as late as June and it's still lying everywhere. FU56 will be full of ice."

Next morning, Steve and I set off for FU56 with Andrew 'Nazi' Goring, one of the squaddies, so-called on account of his surname's resemblance to 'Goering', rather than his politics. Danny's gloomy report was immediately confirmed. Through intermittent rain we crossed huge snow-fields which we had never seen before. Even the Vega Aliseda, the little dale before the last steep climb up to FU56, was full of snow for its entire length, and big open shafts noticed the year before were concealed completely. It took some time to locate top camp in this changed landscape, confusing enough at the best of times with its web of ridges and depressions: at last, we found the tiny patch of grass, miraculously free of snow, and pitched a tent. The temperature was about minus two. Nazi crawled into the tent and got into a sleeping-bag, declaring that as far as he was concerned, the cave could wait. Hoping against hope, Steve and I took a small quantity of gear and made for the entrance. Even the south-facing slope leading up to the doline was snow-covered.

Yet nothing had quite prepared us for the sight which greeted us as we breasted the final rise and walked across the flat limestone pavement. Where last year the entrance scoop had been a great open gash on the hillside visible for miles, at least 20 metres deep and 30 metres across, there was only a vast iceberg. The snow level came up almost to the doline's rim. It had always been thought possible that there might be a blockage inside the shaft leading off from the bottom of the scoop, but the idea that the scoop itself would be snowed over had seemed unthinkable. For the second time in forty-eight hours it looked as if all bets were off. The only hope was a narrow gap between rock and snow at the back end of the scoop, just wide enough to insert a human body. It looked as if this led directly onto what should have been the entrance shaft. I kitted up, belaying a rope over the doline rim into this icy fissure, not bothering to put on a proper caving suit but just pulling a harness over my shorts. It started to sleet.

Shivering at the contact with the great white mass now surrounding me on three sides, I abseiled down, the rope pressing against the snow and rapidly becoming iced-up. Ten metres down I reached what had been the bottom of the scoop: now, a horizontal squeeze beneath the overhanging ice to gain access to the top of the entrance shaft proper. There, the belay, a great flake, was hidden under the snow. Where once the pitch had been a spacious, rocky tube, with just a little snow along one wall, the iceberg had almost filled it, leaving a tiny, body-sized chimney. Yet still I was able to slide down, though only too aware that the acoustic deadness meant an almost certain total blockage very soon. Fifteen metres from the lip of the shaft, it came. A solid, white floor, with densely impacted stones holding it together. It felt quite unshiftable, and there wasn't even any room to dig. My 1982 spray painted blue line was nowhere to be seen. I yelled to Steve that I was coming up. Disconsolately, we made our way to Ario. Alvaro, whose command of English had come on strides, was ready with some helpful thoughts: "It seems perhaps that FU56 is a system which man can only enter once in every 1,000 years. Your efforts, therefore, may well be futile." Never one to accept defeat without at least a token effort, Steve spotted a large shovel. "But of course you may borrow it," said Alvaro. He looked out of the window, at the dark spires across the gorge and a strange, purple twilight, a gale driving the clouds across the sky at furious speed. It felt bitter for the time of year. "I think tomorrow will perhaps be the commencement of a storm of many days' duration," said Alvaro. "I think it's a terrible misfortune."

Alvaro's weather forecasting tends to be as accurate as the predictions made by some geologists about unexplored caves. Next day dawned fine and clear, the beginning of a long spell of hot dry days which would eventually melt nearly all the snow which now bedevilled us. But first we had to get into our cave.

By lunchtime on the following day top camp was well-established. Phil, Andy Riley, and two new visitors to Spain, Steve Gale (an academic geologist in Oxford as a junior research fellow) and Steve Mayers (a member of the Sheffield University club invited by Ian Houghton) had joined Steve Roberts and me. Andy and I were seized with impenetrable depression. While the others took turns to descend the shaft and dig laboriously, risking being suffocated by a sudden underground avalanche as they undermined the impending iceberg, we looked for non-existent 'alternative entrances' on the surface. We believed that even a quite lengthy dig through scree and boulders in a blocked shakehole would be more quickly profitable than the grim struggle going on beneath us. Steve Roberts soon came up with a suitable name for the blocked shaft, which had been known only as 'the entrance pitch' in 1982. He called it 'Snow Joke'. It wasn't.

Steve recalls: "Objectively, it was a beautiful sight. The sun shone down the little hole at the top, reflecting off the snow plug above, and bounced down the glistening shaft like Walt Disney's version of the light that shone on the righteous. I couldn't take it. 50 feet down where snow met rock I looked up and suddenly wished very much I was somewhere else. I was meant to dig away at the base of *this*? I prusiked desperately up, dislodging loose snow which pittered down into the depths, waiting for the big rumble which must come any second. It didn't. I forced myself to shove away more snow at the top of the shaft, on the grounds that if it had to be widened all the way down it was better to start at the top."

Yet by teatime the digging parties were sounding unwarrantedly optimistic. They had cleared a space wide enough to dig properly at the blockage and evolved a system whereby one loosened the snow and the other stacked it. A short way down, the fissure widened, and throwing the snow to one side was quite easy.

Around the petrol stoves and encouraged by the ponche liqueur, spirits revived. Tomorrow we would go for it. After all, there was no choice.

Muzzling his fears Steve joined me for an early start and we descended rapidly to the blockage. Already, the scene had changed markedly from my first visit, the fissure considerably widened by the joint efforts of the sunshine and the diggers. We set to work in a frenzy, hardly pausing. After half an hour I noticed that bits of snow at the bottom of my excavated hollow were falling away below to one side. "Er Steve, I think we had better clip onto the rope," I said. If the blockage suddenly 'went' it might be 25 metres down to the bottom of the shaft. A few minutes later there seemed to be a small window opening up by my left welly. I kicked some more then crouched down, sticking an arm through a tiny hole which I speedily widened. At last I could stick my head through and whooped in exultation. We had cut under the blockage and the way on down was clear, my blue line a short way below. I took the spade and frantically widened the space, turning an undercut overhang into a wide hole going all the way down vertically. It was much easier work now, since all I had to do was hack wildly and let the snow fall down the shaft – it would take more than this to block the way on at the bottom of Is Necessary, where this dislodged snow was going to end up. Still whooping and yelling like a madman I set off down the rope: "Aha! FU56! FU56!" Below the former blockage, there was a large but harmless bank of ice on one side but there was no doubt now: we were in. I climbed back to Steve: "Shall we go caving then?"

We decided to behave as coolly as we could, knowing that Graham and other team members would have arrived at Top Camp expecting a long dig. Walking into camp still wearing our caving gear we answered the others' inquiries with sad looks, saying nothing. Trying to look inconspicuous we started sorting out tackle for the first ten pitches or so. At last we could contain ourselves no longer. To disbelief, then celebration, we relayed the news. In the afternoon we rigged the cave as far as the second of the Mistral Shafts.

Three days later, Sunday July 10, Steve Mayers and I were ready for what looked like being the first pushing trip of the expedition. Top Camp was now consolidated, with carries by most of the team and most of the squaddies having amassed a vast pile of stores and equipment. In the unbroken heat wave that was now shrinking the snow-fields at almost visible speed, this was a considerable achievement. To leave Los Lagos for the strenuous uphill climb of three and a half hours – a fairly fast time – much after dawn or much before dusk was to risk severe heat exhaustion. From the top of the gully between the Vega Aliseda and the slope down towards the Ario path, the mountains shimmered across the harsh white lapiaz, the rock radiating and reflecting additional heat. There was no wind. It was fortunate that for the time being at least, the melting snowplugs all around Top Camp gave a much closer and more copious supply of water than that used the previous year.

Changing into caving gear designed for the chill conditions of deep alpine potholes in this weather was unbearable. To have walked up the steep rocky slope from camp to the cave in close-hugging furry suit and PVC outer would have been unthinkable, but pulling on one's gear in the solar oven by the entrance was almost as bad. Between trips, one's sit harness would dry and stiffen, making putting it on exhausting, strenuous and sweaty. Once inside a furry, even pulling on a recalcitrant pair of wellies was enough to produce rivulets of sweat on forehead, back and chest.

Six metres below the lip of Snow Joke we had fixed a rebelay where the rope rubbed against a projection in the wall, and it was usually about here, during the few moments it took to negotiate this obstacle, that one would cool down. The sweat, previously felt only as an annoying dampness, turned icy. Lower down, FU56's average temperature was about three degrees centigrade. The brief period of heat before descent made the rest of the trip considerably colder.

On our last foray, two days earlier, the series of short wet pitches, the Bathroom Steps, had seemed far in. Today, we reached their end – we had now rigged them all as SRT climbs, much safer than the horrendous unlifelined ladders of 1982 – in only two hours, moving rapidly to keep warm and keen to reach new territory as fast as possible. Beyond the Steps, the chore began: ten pitches to rig again, improving where possible on the often inadequate or dangerous methods of the previous year.

This year, we hoped the pitches would be used many times en route to greater depths: there was no room for short cuts.

It was not until well after midnight that we reached the top of Wallop, the last drop negotiated in 1982 and the last pitch in the dry section bypassing the stream, One Step Beyond.

We rigged Wallop a little more conventionally than George had done on our brief visit the previous year and descended. Swollen by the great volume of melted snow water, the waterfall now thundering into Lago Victoria hurled an unavoidable spume way beyond its plunge pool, filling the entire area of the cave with spray. Gingerly, I led the way through Don't Look at the Roof, the flakes above as delicately threatening as ever. On the other side Steve pointed out the obvious: "Er Dave, you know there's a much safer way over the top of that . . ."

And then, at last, we crossed those question-marks left at the end of the survey. Where the stream flowed swiftly over the lip of Tantalus pitch, we climbed above it, as so often in Asturian caves: following the line of the water now 20 metres below, traversing on small ledges in the winding canyon. We expected to come eventually to a convenient spot to make the descent comfortably away from the rumbling water.

Instead, we reached an area of breakdown, where the cave walls had undergone collapse. A chaos of boulders and other geological litter now formed a floor, so that it was no longer possible to see or hear the streamway below. We stooped beneath projecting rocks, and irritating gritty particles detached themselves as we brushed against the wall, sometimes falling inside our furry suits to itch maddeningly, out of reach. A low slope led to a letterbox, through which issued a peculiar hissing. I squeezed through and exclaimed in amazement.

We had entered a cavern that dwarfed anything else in Pozu Jorcada Blanca, a chamber at least as big as Eton Palais in Xitu. We stood at the top of a scree slope, its bottom invisible in the blackness swallowing our lamps, which flickered and complained, the flames buffeted by a mighty wind blowing down vertically from the far distant roof. The hissing sound came from the crackle of water falling with the wind, tumbling from the invisibility above of some unknown pothole to lose itself in a jumble of boulders at the base of the scree. The chamber became known as the Hot Tub.

Gasping, we advanced. The scree slope slipped and slid a little as we descended, making a path among the rocks which had lain there undisturbed since first falling from the roof. At the bottom, we hurriedly skirted the pit choked with boulders beneath the inlet cascade, unable to avoid the water entirely, and reached the shelter of a narrow rift passage opposite the letterbox through which we had entered. Twenty metres further on the floor dropped away. The walls were covered in a brown, brittle popcorn formation, long-dried out calcite crystal, and here Steve unhesitatingly picked out the sole possible line of descent which did not require a rope, weaving backwards and forwards in the fissure to keep to the narrowest part where the friction of pressed-out knees and elbows might compensate for any deficiency in the provision of footholds. I baulked a little: "Come on, it's easy. Don't be a wimp!" It was 3 a.m. Bleary-eyed and yawning I cast aside wimpdom and followed Steve, above the stream again, in a slightly wider canyon passage with a rapidly increasing absence of floor. Soon we could go no further. We had reached the most unpleasant, most difficult to rig and probably most dangerous pitch ever encountered on OUCC expeditions. For two and a half hours we – mostly Steve – struggled to place a bolt, in each spot the rock shattering and splintering. There were no natural belays either. It was awful, monstrous. It fully deserved its political name, which stuck: Pol Pot.

At five in the morning, as I dozed, Steve was satisfied at the combination of bolts in loose boulders and wires placed round dubious chockstones and abseiled down. Soon he was out of earshot and lulled by the music of the stream below I slept properly, slowly becoming deeply chilled as the glow of activity faded. Some time later I was jolted awake. "Are you coming down?" I remembered I was on a pushing trip I had looked forward to for eleven months or so. "Yes. I'll be right with you. What is there?" His reply surprised me: "Hundreds of metres of streamway. I haven't reached the end."

After so much verticality, FU56 had flattened out. Below Pol Pot – its landing on a loose boulder slope 15 metres down as nasty as its top – a brief climb, exposed to ammunition from above, led back to the streamway. Upstream was the fine cascade of Tantalus pitch, the passage having passed beneath the floor of the Hot Tub. Downstream was a long, tedious, winding crabwalk, often kneedeep or more in water. After 200 featureless metres, marked only by the propensity of solid-looking ledges to fall at a touch into the stream, there was a climb over boulders: then more of the same. In all we covered nearly 500 metres, the bottom of the passage almost completely flat throughout. At last, on a right-hand bend, the floor lowered again and brought us to another pitch. Beyond it looked as if the passage was altogether different: a sluggish, wide meander. We looked at the drop and christened it Delta pitch. The stream before had to be the Mekong. Pleased by this ingenuity, benefiting from the second wind that often comes during long trips underground, at the time one might consider getting up at home, we began to make an efficient and speedy exit. Six hours later, most of that time spent climbing the ropes of what we were, audaciously, beginning to think of as the 'entrance series' – all the way down to Wallop at 520 metres – we emerged, blinking, into the Picos midday sun. We had been down twenty-three hours. Soon, we thought, this would seem like a brief excursion, once the cave *really* started to go . . .

An hour after collapsing in sleeping-bags and dozing, overheated, back at Top Camp, Graham arrived with several helpers, many of them from the army group. No one, it seemed, was ready to go caving, however, either that day or the next. Danny appeared to be doing very little for the squaddies and Graham felt responsible for keeping them occupied. Organising potholing trips had, for a time, taken second place.

Petty arguments kept breaking out, often centred on food – the squaddies despised the garlic and green peppers tossed in most Oxford stews, the cavers despised their total lack of drive. The soldiers spent nearly all their time at Los Lagos, sitting on the grass looking at the can of beer held between their legs. Their idea of a good time was having no orders to follow.

Eventually Delta got rigged, but that trip advanced only 20 metres or so, stopping at some deep pools. The team missed an obvious line of ledges a few feet above the water.

On my next attempt, with Steve Mayers and Richard, we negotiated the pools and reached a small round chamber, the Pleasure Dome, where several passages led off. One quickly choked with silt, and was later the object of a desperate digging expedition. The streamway ploughed on straight ahead, but in place of the lofty canyon of the Mekong and the wide gallery below Delta pitch, the Brahmaputra, it flowed in a constricted, strenuous rift, well-supplied with sharp, suit-ripping flakes. This, we thought, was surely an immature passage opened up only recently in geological time. We had lost the draught as well: somewhere there must be another way . . . This suspicion was heightened by what came next: a spray-lashed, 10-metre pitch gained by a slot of terrifying narrowness directly above the drop. We called it the Vortex and left it well alone. In the remaining four hours before we made for the surface we investigated the many possibilities for larger, high level passages radiating from the Pleasure Dome, where the draught seemed to disappear. Steve performed several daring free climbs to gain access to a large sandy tunnel that had our spirits soaring again. But to no avail: after a miserably short distance, the way was blocked impenetrably by massive fallen boulders. Our growing depression was intensified by leaving the tin opener behind. Again, a party had gone to push but exited without having added more than a very few metres of depth.

At least the cave was still 'going'. This time, a team was ready to take over without a day's gap. Graham and Phil felt fit and mentally prepared for some serious exploration and proved their point by getting up remarkably early. Then, as the log book records,

> this trip started at the incredibly early hour of ten o'clock, and around midday we had descended the entrance series to Don't Look at the Roof. An hour or so later we had reached the Vortex, the previous limit of exploration. Graham added another ladder to the top of this and descended the extremely wet pitch finding a small tight rift on through the waterfall. I then had the rather terrifying task of carrying three heavy tackle bags down this soaking wet pitch without a lifeline, getting thoroughly wet in the process. At the other end of the rift was a pitch, after which the passage opened out. Our hearts were really going now as we thought the cave was going strong again. However only 50 yards or so down the stream, involving some tightish traversing, the passage reached what we had all feared for so long: A SUMP.

And that, it appeared, was that. On their way out Graham and Phil looked, as the earlier party had done, for high level bypasses, but without success. A sump. The end. FU56 was not going to be the deepest cave in the world. It was quite deep – of course, without a survey, we as yet had no idea how deep it was – but it didn't really get near Xitu. So much effort and anticipation for this. I looked across at the sweep of white mountains as I heard the news and wanted to tear them apart. There were few that night who had the detachment to laugh at this predicament. All the water, the whole of Jorcada Blanca's very considerable stream, just slid into this dank, low sewer, airspace zero. And now what were we to do?

Most reacted in time honoured fashion, by drinking considerable quantities of alcohol and being inactive. Through the

129

ginebras y tonica, the tintos and the coñac Fundador, the depression was like a miasma.

Two less obviously affected individuals were George, who had recently arrived, and Smokey Cauldwell who now had just two days to go of his lightning seven-day visit. In his short time with us he had already proved his worth, not only with the gift of his excellent rope but also by his great experience and dry, Southern wit. "I guess you'd call it a carbide assist," he would say, describing an epic rescue he had directed in the States: "There was nothin' really wrong with the guy and all you had to do was light a lamp right under his ass and out that cave he'd go." Smokey and George decided to look yet again for a high level passage on the day after Graham's sad report. At two in the afternoon on the 17th, they set off, expecting to reach the surface again by the following morning.

RICHARD The possibility of an underground accident had always been a nagging worry on our expeditions. There were no rescue services within call, and the warm sunny weather, the wine and magnificent views belied the seriousness of our caving trips. Not only were they longer and harder and more frequent than in Britain, but the caves themselves contained sections of prolonged difficulty through which rescues would have been almost impossible. And the caves were new and deadly: no worn down mud to guide the way on, no guidebook descriptions. Every handhold or belay had to be tested – none had been used before and sometimes the friable Picos rock crumbled at the slightest touch.

John had once warned everyone of the dangers of loose rock. "Always have at least three points of attachment," were his unnecessary words. William, like all of us the victim of at least one heart-stopping slip, was more emphatic: "Always have at least FOUR points of attachment in new stuff."

Quite how one would then move, William did not say.

Despite the dangers, the only accident which had taken place during this expedition was when Al Cousins had fallen and cut his arm descending one night from Amador's bar. There had been near misses. Bits had pulled out of rock with people attached to them, holds had crumbled, cavers fallen on their heads. In Jorcada Blanca, Dave and I had abseiled down a pitch in One Step Beyond and later picked the belay up, rope still attached, with one hand on our return. Everyone feared that sooner or later, there would be the real thing.

As George and Smokey set off, we were surprised to learn that this would be Smokey's deepest trip in all his years of potholing in the 'beeg peeyits' of Georgia. They were unencumbered by tackle or the chore of having to derig. George had even left his camera behind. They bade Andy farewell and left him at Top Camp on his own, keeping a lonely vigil under the tarpaulin that served as cooking shelter, sunshade, rain guard and drawing room. Someone had to stay and wait to make sure they were all right. Soon Andy made for his sleeping-bag and stayed there.

In the morning, no one appeared to relieve him. And now, right on cue, as the caving was turning sour, so did the weather. As Andy huddled under the tarpaulin the mist blew in, the drizzle running off the edges into the washing-up. Huge sparkling droplets formed on his beard and hair. Nothing in the camp was quite dry. In the late afternoon, Graham, Paul, Sara and I arrived. We were not exactly raring to go. But Andy was now increasingly concerned about the two underground. They had been down for twenty-eight hours. The trip to the bottom and back would take about twelve hours, and everything that might need a rope was rigged. Surely they couldn't have been looking for a bypass all that time? Might they have found one and discovered a huge new extension? New pitches? A squeeze they had been trying to widen? A double light failure? All possibilities were discussed, and the final one only with the greatest reluctance – an accident.

"Surely," said Paul, "if one of them had an accident – broken leg say – the other would be out by now to raise the alarm?"

"Could be helping him out," I replied.

"One thing's for certain, you can't get lost in that cave." Something in his voice suggested that this was by no means the certainty he maintained. Andy, ever the master of logistics, came up with a foolproof plan:

"Right. If they're not out by eleven – that'll be thirty-one hours – Graham whizzes off down the cave, followed by Richard and Paul, who bring all the rescue gear. I'll go to Ario – should get there before midnight if I hurry. I'll mobilise the troops there, a group was supposed to be going there tonight. Sara stays here and cooks a MEGA amount of trough."

What should we do until eleven? Eat, of course. What was there, apart from the rice, asked Graham. Andy said: "Our best bet . . . is pilchard vindaloo and Mornflake porridge bhajee."

By ten o'clock things were fairly sombre. The daylight had gone, and the cold mist persisted relentlessly. It was impossible to see even across the tiny campsite, and the carbide lights spluttered as the mist seeped into the generators. Graham, Paul and I got into our damp, cold furry suits, belching up the taste of the meal as we did so. Graham stuffed his pockets with spare bulbs and batteries, and then grabbed as much chocolate as he could find. Between us, Paul and I had a lot to carry. There were two ex-army ammo boxes each, with the medical gear, food, a stove, more chocolate, carbide and more batteries. The medical set was quite well-stocked, with four bags of plasma expander, intravenous antibiotics, dressings and bandages. There was even a nurse's uniform (to clean things underground, although just about the entire expedition had had their photos taken in it). The pièce de résistance was a large supply of injectable morphine, carefully smuggled into Spain each year. It was enough to stop several horses.

Paul and I agreed that the best use for it if someone was really seriously injured would be to administer enough morphine to finish them off, so remote would the chances be of a successful rescue. Graham departed. We would see him at the bottom.

As Graham said goodbye, Paul attached the two ammo cans to his donkey's dick. They were heavy, and needed to be tied to him so that they didn't fall down and slip inside the cave. Normally, a donkey's dick, the standard way of carrying equipment by a short length of rope, is clipped into the main sit harness. Paul was short of a karabiner, however, and tied the donkey's dick cord directly to his harness attachment with a figure of eight knot. This act was nearly to cost him his life.

Meanwhile Andy stiffened his jaw and moved away into the foggy dusk to negotiate three miles of interleaving karst ridges, depressions and blind valleys, in order to tell a knot of rosy-faced, intoxicated cavers at the Ario refugio, "Right, I want you all out on that hill by 7 a.m."

Paul and I descended the cave with already tired eyes, Graham's cries of 'rope free' echoing from far beneath us. Our progress, weighed down with gear, was painfully slow, and by the time we reached the Meander of the Argonauts Graham was already out of earshot. At every opportunity the ammo cans jammed in the rift, and I also carried a large bag of food. I tended to rush ahead a little, knowing the cave much better than Paul, and mindful too of the plight of George and Smokey somewhere in the depths beneath. It was about half past three in the morning when we reached One Step Beyond, 400 metres down. Here the passage between the pitches doesn't really have a floor, but the slit in the bottom is so narrow that the only way on is to traverse to a wider section breaking into the next shaft series down to Valley of the Kings – 20 metres below.

I was about to abseil down this shaft when there was a cry from behind: "I'm a long way from a place of safety!"

The tremulous cry re-echoed in the big cavern below. There was more than a little panic in it. "What do you mean?" I asked, little realising that this was Paul's way of saying he was about to die.

Not knowing the cave well, Paul had forgotten about the traverse above the slit in the floor to the next pitch. Thinking he was still in the constricted vertical section which begins the One Step Beyond series, he had squeezed into the improbably narrow slit at what should have been boot level. This was not at all easy, and he had had to force his body through, breathing out to make his chest smaller. He had kicked his ammo cans beneath him through the slot and they hung below from his central maillon harness attachment, tied in place. He had raised his arms above his head and pushed to get his bum through the tightest part of the slot, and then his chest. Too late he realised his mistake. Below the slot the cave opened out onto the 20-metre pitch. When I arrived back to see what the fuss was about, Paul was dangling by his tensed shoulders, his body and legs waggling helplessly over the drop. The pull at his waist from the heavy ammo cans was dragging him inexorably downwards.

"Help me out of this, Richard." Paul's voice emerged with great strain, as he held his chest expanded to try to avoid slipping any further.

"Drop the ammo boxes, Paul," I urged, gripping his collar.

"I can't – they're tied to my waist." His voice became higher in pitch and more anguished. "Every time I move an arm I slip further down."

This was true. Paul's position depended on him bracing his shoulders; even the slightest relaxation allowed him to fall further into the mouth of the abyss. It dawned on me that he was really about to fall sixty feet. I gave a command designed to instil hope: "Stay there."

I reached over the fissure. Perhaps I could just reach down to his centre maillon. I couldn't, so went back to the pitch head to fetch the rope. I tied a figure of eight knot into a loop and clipped in a krab; reaching down with this, my arm pressed tightly between his face and the cold rock, I was able to secure it to the centre of Paul's sit harness. We both breathed a sigh of relief. "How the hell did you get here?" I asked after a long pause.

"I can tell you it was a hell of a job – probably the hardest squeeze I've done." As Paul said this, he relaxed, and fell at last through the slit into the gaping drop below. The rope took his weight and slapped against the rock as it became taut. I passed the rest of the rope through the tiny crack and it was clear that there was enough to reach the bottom, where his badly chosen descent route connected with the conventional pitch. After some fumbling, Paul sorted out his gear and abseiled down to the roomy chamber, where I joined him after re-rigging the rope.

"I've never been so scared in all my life."

"What about that time that huge nurse trapped you in a corner of the medics' disco?"

"Never, I tell you, never."

Resuming the descent, we abseiled on, past the dusty silence of the Valley of the Kings and the awesome free abyss of the Sphinx. At Lago Victoria, by the wind and spray of the re-entering stream, we met Graham, George and Smokey. Paul unpacked the stove, tea and biscuits and offered Yorkie bars, provoking a loud retching in Smokey and George. It transpired that Graham had found them below the awkward climb-down from the rift beyond the Hot Tub. Returning from another fruitless push, they had missed this climb and found only the impenetrable boulders beneath the floor of the great cavern. Eventually they had given up hope, and lain down to rest on one of the sandy ledges above the stream near the top of Pol Pot.

They had marked the walls with soot arrows burnt on by their carbide flames around their makeshift bivouac. Then they waited, snatching what sleep they could, miserable, cold, wet and hungry. "We talked for hours about whether to eat our last half Yorkie bar on Tuesday or Wednesday," George said later.

At last Graham showed up and disclosed the elusive way out. He had ten Yorkie bars in his prusik bag, which they wolfed down immediately. By the time Paul and I arrived, they were both quite ill from this, with chocolate bursting from their ears. The tea settled their stomachs a little, but even then they looked unwell.

On the way out, however, it soon became clear that George and Smokey, once warmed up by the exercise, were easily the freshest. Their rescuers were exhausted, and we made heavy weather of the 600 metres of strenuous rope work and endless difficult squeezes in the rifts between Lago Victoria and the entrance. I remembered the elation of twelve months before, when Dave, George and I had seemed to float out of the cave after our rediscovery of the stream. This time, as we broke surface towards 9 a.m., the 'victims' skipped down the hillside into camp, whereas we slunk out behind them, slouching and withered, feeling like hostages released after some prolonged terrorist siege. George and Smokey had been down forty-three hours. We met up again at the little circle of tents, the sun streaming down without much warmth in a way which old Picos hands knew meant that this was only a temporary break in the weather, not a proper improvement. The Ario team, goaded so dramatically by Andy the night before, were there in force, and Sara was ready with steaming plates of stew. Smokey came to thank us once again, with a genially unabashed grin. "Well," he said, "I guess you could call that another carbide assist."

George, oblivious of our desire to do nothing but collapse, was leaping about with his photographic gear, trying to organise a team portrait. Suddenly Smokey, who had been quiet for a few minutes, let out a loud exclamation, realising that he had missed a day and that there was no time to waste. He had ten hours to catch his flight from Bilbao, a steep mountainside and hundreds of kilometres of dreadful winding road away. George offered to drive him there. Within minutes they were packed and off down the hill like a couple of spring lambs. And they made it. Fifteen hours or so after being lost hundreds of metres below a remote Spanish mountain, Smokey was enjoying a bourbon on the rocks aboard a transatlantic aircraft. His three man rescue team, by contrast, didn't move much at all that day. We chewed our lentils in silence, then crawled into our tents like woodlice hiding from the daylight. We lay still.

DAVID The burst of adrenalin provided by the Great Jorcada Blanca Rescue soon faded. The torpor creeping up on the expedition was soon back, and with it, renewed appalling weather. Further attempts were made to find a bypass to the baffling, shouldn't-be-there-at-all sump, most determinedly by Steve Mayers, but to no avail. The survey, too, proceeded at a snail's pace. Meanwhile, the almost constant mist made any sustained search for new caves impossible. Parties were getting lost within a hundred metres of Top Camp and forced to orientate themselves by yelling at those wiser people who had not left their tents.

Relations with the soldiers might be said to have sumped too. If there was ever a nadir in the history of our explorations in the mountains of Asturias, it was now. At the end of July a large group of us drove down the hill towards the station at Arriondas, braving the vagaries of El Sod on the crazy bends and precipices of the Lagos road for the last time. And surely, I thought, this really must be the last time. What those left would get up to in their last two weeks was up to them, but the chances of another expedition after this seemed slim. Goodbye Picos, I thought, a complex of emotions – nostalgia, anger, disappointment and wistfulness for good times past – making a large lump in my throat. I thought of Keith: what would he have made of this? Goodbye, Picos. And maybe good riddance.

RICHARD That Dave's pessimism was eventually proven wrong was due to the efforts of those left behind. Those on their first trip to Spain – Ian, Steve Roberts, Phil – got on with it, in spite of everything. Two of the soldiers, Ray and Wingnut (so called because of his large ears), started caving, and relationships with the army started to improve.

In 3/5, the very small cave near Ario which was left over from 1981, Wingnut pushed through into new territory through a narrow rift, despite his ears. 'Wingnut's Rift' showed how things might have been . . . we could have had a great time. In Jorcada Blanca the various tasks were carried out: surveying, photographing. William's account of surveying the Vortex gives a chilling feeling: "One of the wettest pitches I've done, and the rope failed to run through my self-lining ropewalker! I just climbed up to the ledge where I pushed the rope through and tried to put off being frightened, the water pouring onto my back. At the top I remembered to be terrified and swore blue murder at the pitch – this one is DANGEROUS!"

The cave was detackled. "After John had chucked the traditional stone down the entrance," wrote Iestyn, "all that was left was to carry the tackle bags back down to camp in the dying rays of a gently setting sun."

Well, not quite all. The sun wasn't setting on OUCC caving expeditions just yet. There was one day of nice weather, one day that could be used to go shaft-bashing – an entrance was discovered, and marked as F7. Several small holes led into a chamber filled largely with ice. Phil, Iestyn and Ian went to check it out.

After traversing the entrance rifts we climbed down an interesting 8-metre drop to the top of the first pitch. At this point we decided to abandon the survey, and in our euphoria kicked about two tonnes of rock down the pitch, revelling in the crashes and booms from below.

At the bottom we swore for joy; to the right was a large onion shaped passage with a deep trench, while to the left the pitch continued. Following the latter way, we landed on a boulder slope . . . walking downsiope, back underneath

136

ourselves, we soon came across a draughting vertical squeeze. Casually we threw a rock down this, and then got the shock of our lives – after the initial extensive rattle there was a silence. "Great, it's going," someone said. "Boom!" the hole replied. "It's really going," we all agreed, but the hole still had the last word with a deep "BOOM!" Expletives were exchanged . . . the small hole turned out to be a shaft of impressive proportions; 20 metres down to a ledge at an inlet, and we rigged another 38 metres free hang down to a further ledge. Only 20 metres of rope was left and it was getting late. We threw some rocks down the next pitch. It sounded very big . . .

8

Donde Estan los Niños Muertes?

RICHARD It was a sombre return for me from Bilbao; I flew into Gatwick on a wet July afternoon and drove down to Torquay. My diary read '1.8.83; start work for the next 38 years.' Not only was I starting work, it was one of the busiest jobs conceivable, as a medical houseman. It was quite likely that I should never go caving ever again, beyond maybe the odd trip to Yorkshire. I felt that my youth was over. I imagined my framed survey of Xitu hanging above the fire for a few years, then being moved to the spare room, then into the bathroom, then finally being confined to the attic. Years later it would be discovered there, and used as a roof for a tree-house, or as a sledge.

I could picture Dave and me as old men, demolishing a bottle of port after a large meal, like veterans reminiscing about campaigns on the North-West Frontier.

"Now, *we* were here . . ." moves pepper-pot, "and Xitu . . . was *there* . . ." moves mustard. "If this is the resurgence . . ." moves decanter, "what were we to do?"

In November I went to the 1983 expedition reunion dinner, expecting to be really depressed. It was full of optimistic conversations and plans for 1984. The new expedition leader was Steve Gale, a junior don in a branch of geology, and his status in the university, as well as his rather formal manner, were helping things along. As we talked, we were drowned out by Phil Rose and Ian Houghton entering a spiral of hyperbole about the new entrance that they had found together. It would join Jorcada Blanca *after* the sump; it would be an independent, deeper, system containing huge pitches; it would reach a big master cave; it would . . . Steve Gale interrupted them.

"It will sump."

They were choked into silence, while he treated us to an exposition of cave geomorphology and genesis. The level at which the limestone is saturated, he said, is higher in the centre of the massif than at the edge of the massif, so the caves in the centre of the massif, he maintained, would reach the phreas at a greater altitude than the caves nearer the edge of the massif, now, as the area around Top Camp is in the centre of the massif . . . Everyone listened intently for a while, but soon lost interest, geomorphology never having been one of our strong points. Wild imaginings were much more fun.

Later Dave cornered me.

"Do you think there's any chance of you going next year?"

"Not really. I've a job which finishes on the first of August, and I'm not allowed to take any holiday at the end – continuity of the care of the patients and all that. Any other job I get will start on August the first, and by the time I get to be able to take some of my measly holiday allowance they'll be back from Spain. Anyway you can't guarantee that they'll let me take *any* holiday at all. Consultants are an odd bunch . . ."

"Give your job up."

"You give yours up!" Dave was still trying to make his way in the cut-throat world of journalism, where, as in the cut-throat world of medicine, holidays were frowned upon. We both liked caving, sure, but when it was a choice between caving and eating . . .

Steve Mayers had already made his decision. He had given up his well-paid job (with car) working for a drug firm, and was now climbing and caving on the dole. I just couldn't bring myself to do that, so the prospects for caving seemed hopeless.

As it happened, I got a job in Sheffield, starting on August 1, 1984. On the way back from the interviews with the stern surgeon I was to work for, the rain lashed the windscreen as hard as any Picos storm.

Later, as I lay in bed, waiting for the phone to go again, I heard the rain lashing against the windows of the NHS flat I had been given to sleep in. I thought how much nicer it would be to wake up at Top Camp, with the bright morning sun and the chilly mountain air, the perfect silence of the wilderness disturbed only by the rebeccos and the soaring of large black birds.

Mr D. G. Ferguson,
Consultant Surgeon,
Accident and Emergency Dept.,
Royal Hallamshire Hospital,
Sheffield.

Drs Residences,
John Radcliffe Hosp.,
Oxford.

Dear Mr Ferguson,

Thank you for offering me the job of Casualty Officer, starting on 1.8.84, which I should be glad to accept.

In this job I am allowed 3½ weeks holidays, which includes Bank Holidays, and I wonder if it would be possible to take *all* this holiday *starting* on August 1st 1984.

Normally I shouldn't ask a favour such as this, but I have had the great fortune to be invited on a major International Caving Expedition, which is going to discover the deepest cave in the world, in Spain, and is supported by the Royal Geographical Society, the British Cave Research Association, the University of Oxford, the Spanish Government, the Ghar Parau Exploration Foundation, the Sports Council of Great Britain, the West Lancashire Evening Gazette, Dunlop Ltd (Wellington Boot Dept.), Mornflake Porridge Oats Ltd, Rington's Tea Bags and John West's Tinned Foods.

Yours,

R. M. C. Gregson

I waited for the reply with bated breath.

Dear Dr Gregson,

I have arranged for you to start work on Monday, 25th of August 1984, at 9.00 a.m.

Yours faithfully,

Mr D. G. Ferguson, FRCS (Lond).

Steve Gale organised everything except the van. So once more this was left to Steve Roberts, the Man Who Knew About Engines. With what little money we had he bought a yellow second-hand Luton van, the sort of thing that the bailiffs arrive in to take away your furniture.

It had no windows and a top speed of forty, but one great redeeming feature. It was huge. You could stand in it, lie in it, change in it when it was raining, cook meals in it – you could hold roller-discos in it. If you were so inclined you could play the Eton wall game in it . . . it was the vehicle we had been searching for for all these years, a travelling caving hut. Unlike 'El Sod' it had lights, a windscreen, gears and started.

The van easily accommodated the huge amount of sponsored supplies that were hurled into it, and off the expedition went, with a whole new bunch of cavers. Most of the old lags from the previous expeditions who had actually managed to go on this trip were, like me, leaving a couple of weeks later. The team who arrived in the big yellow van were not a very experienced bunch. A few had been on the 1983 expedition; several had never been out of the UK before.

Quite unlike the jaded lot who were depressed by the great let-down of the year before, this new team were determined to find a going cave as soon as possible. No sooner had the van arrived than there was a titanic effort to carry the gear up to Top Camp. Phil Rose made the first entry in the 1984 Top Camp log book and brought up his tent, caving gear and enough rope to start the exploration of the new entrance the following morning. His partner was to be Fred Wickham: one of the very keenest.

Phil and Fred went back a long way. They had been at school together, and had hitched through South America at the height of the war between Britain and Argentina, getting into Argentina just before the border was closed to British nationals. Fred had collapsed soon afterwards with appendicitis on a remote hillside and had had to crawl down from the snowline to a rubble track where Phil had managed to hire a donkey from a bewildered villager to take him to hospital. He still bears the scar – a wide vertical one, which is known as the battle incision.

It was Dave who had persuaded his brother to take up caving, and Phil had persuaded Fred, though that hadn't been difficult. Fred had taken to it with ease, and now, only a few months after his first trip below ground in Yorkshire, he found himself rigging a new pitch under a hanging choke of ice some 2,000 metres up in the Picos de Europa. What would happen? There was only one sure fact, and that was that Fred wasn't going to get appendicitis again.

The entrance to Pozu de las Perdices, as F7 was now known, was a huge gash in the mountain which was nearly completely filled with snow. Below the snow plug the cave had a howling gale blowing through it, and a freezing spray as the snow melted onto the heads of the cavers below. The first new pitch was marked by a man-sized block at the top, standing upright like a sentry. This was the 'Obelisk', and it had given the pitch its name the year before. Fred, though, intent on making his mark on the cave right at the start, managed to topple the whole thing off with one touch – it fell 36 metres onto the head of the next pitch. Phil told Fred that he had to get used to this sort of thing.

In the few days that followed the assault team laid siege to the cave. Only three – Phil, Ian Houghton and Ursula (Ukie) Collie – had done any caving in Spain before. All the others were novices, not only to Spain, but also to caving itself. Nicola Dollimore, who had left school only a year before, and had done hardly any outdoor activity previously, now found herself writing accounts in the logbook of the discoveries that she had made:

Obelisk Pitch was *brilliant* – superb shaft 36 metres down free hanging, then into unknown territory . . .

Another novice, Sean Hodges:

> Then the descent. Phil rushed down shouting inaudible exclamations. I followed with a couple of tackle bags. The pitch goes on for ever! Beautiful smooth fluted walls, opening out on the way down to a large flat chamber. The 80 metre rope was almost exactly the right length. Immediately Phil found another huge drop – 3 to 4 seconds.

The cave was clearly dropping down like one of the wild imaginings from the previous year. It was not very hard to follow, but with every pushing trip the place became more and more of a proposition and less of a simple caving sortie. It also required a lot of new names, and after dinner, at Top Camp, they decided to call the 80-metre pitch which had so excited Sean after its tube-like appearance at the top – The Nostril. Presumably the 3–4 second drop which followed should be called 'the Bogey'! The trouble was, the word 'Bogey' can have more than one meaning, and the joke was very nearly on them.

Andy Riley was about to arrive. He had told me many times that there were three distinct phases you have to pass through when learning any dangerous sport. In the third phase you are safe, because you have so much experience that you understand and appreciate all the dangers. In the first stage you are also safe, because, knowing nothing, you are so absolutely scared rigid that you can't make any dangerous move without checking and re-checking all the things you are supposed to have done beforehand. The dangerous stage, and he would wag his finger at this point, the dangerous phase is when you have lost any initial fear that you may have had (pause for sip of beer), but you haven't yet gained mastery of the activity. At the start of the 1984 Expedition, Pozu de las Perdices was being pushed by just this sort of people.

Fred and Ukie descended to the Bogey and rigged it. It was Ukie's first pushing trip, and she felt a little tentative. Not long after beginning to abseil, she realised that the rope was too short. It also hung for most of the way in the full force of the water. She came up again, and as she did so, a rock fell spontaneously from the roof and hit her hard on her helmet. She sat down on the ledge to recover, while Fred changed the rope to a longer length. He too went part of the way down and fixed a rebelay, hoping thus to avoid the water in the lower part of the shaft.

Ukie's electric back-up light was broken, but she had asked particularly to be the first one to the bottom of the pitch, so Fred climbed up once more. With any luck, the rebelay meant that the water wouldn't extinguish her carbide flame. Below the rebelay, Fred had not taken the rope out of the tackle bag but left it stuffed inside, clipped to the anchor. Ukie went down, passed the rebelay, and attached the heavy sack to her harness. She was now 'spidermanning', feeding the rope out of the bag as she continued the descent. A second bag at her waist held the heavy rigging equipment.

Fred finished spirited renditions of 'House of the Rising Sun' and 'Whiskey in the Jar' and sat alone at the pitch head. Time passed. Then he became aware of shouting from a long way below, with the distant but unmistakable sound of a large volume of water falling on a PVC suit. His rebelay had failed to avoid the water, and now Ukie's light was out. In the blackness she decided to carry on abseiling in the hope of reaching the foot of the shaft where she could get her flame going in more congenial circumstances. Unfortunately, a large tangle pulled out of the bag all at once and jammed itself in her descender, bringing her to an abrupt halt. Her only option was to perform a changeover in the dark: climb up a little way to unload the tangle so she could sort it out.

This too, she now found, was impossible. The loops of her ascending system must somehow have become incorporated in the mess. Isolated in space in a sit harness which was slowly cutting off the blood supply to her legs, Ukie was trapped in pitch blackness with icy water falling on her head. There was no way to escape without a light: even if the water were somehow to stop, her hands were becoming numb with cold.

Caving is not a good solo sport. Fred didn't know exactly what was wrong, nor how he could help Ukie, but as time passed and her cries echoed up the pitch he knew he had to do something. It is impossible to abseil on a rope loaded with another caver's weight from below, but Fred still had the shorter rope he had rigged on the drop the first time. With luck it would get him down to Ukie. If it didn't . . . he would have to think again.

Out of the 45-metre length, he had about fifteen centimetres to spare. With Fred's fading electric illuminating the scene, Ukie was just able to reach the cow's tail he passed her, and use it to clip in above the tangle, stand up and undo the knots with frozen fingers. Exhausted, she prusiked back to the top and lay panting on the ledge, listening to the thud of the stream as it hit the two tackle bags now tied to the end of the rope 45 metres below.

When they made it back to the tents, Phil had a large dinner ready. He was emphatic. Ukie must go down again the next day and conquer the pitch, otherwise she would never get her confidence back. It's an old argument – pilots should take off immediately after a crash in order to stop them being for ever incapable of doing so. Ukie, still rattling the spoon against the side of her bowl through fear, realised that Phil was right. Tomorrow she would go down and 'crack the Bogey'.

Phil went with her. He knew the way to the Bogey pretty well by now, and the two of them made 'swift progress', as he later wrote in his no-nonsense log-book account. "First I went down the pitch and managed successfully to take the two tackle bags from the previous day's epic, and get them to the bottom. Then it was Ukie's turn. All went well until the rebelay, when the dreaded light struck again – a splash put it out, leaving Ukie in total darkness."

Once again Ukie was swinging in icy spray above a huge drop in total darkness. It was rather like waking up from a nightmare only to find that the dream doesn't stop. She had learnt from the day before and brought a spare battery, yes, but could she fit it into her lamp by touch alone without dropping any of the vital parts down the pitch? Much more sensible to move back through the rebelay and prusik up to a dryer, less awful spot. She began to do this, transferring her weight and undoing the vital karabiners by touch, but just as the day before she had become tangled because she had the two great tackle bags, so now she became tangled because of her reluctance to let go of another rope she carried. After quite a lot of kicking and struggling she discovered to her horror that once again she was trussed up, unable to move either up *or* down, and couldn't see what was holding her in the darkness.

This time Phil began to climb to the rescue. In the course of getting tangled, however, Ukie had dislodged the rope from the small rebelay spike. This meant that he transferred his full weight to Ukie's sit harness, climbing over a series of appalling rub points which the rebelay had avoided. Slowly Ukie felt him strangling her leg, but she had no alternative. She didn't complain.

With the arrival of Phil's light the mess was quickly seen to, and Ukie was released. They headed out. Once again the two bags stayed under the waterfall.

Back at camp, a meal inside her, Ukie made an entry in her diary: "Two mega cock-ups in two days. This is not good going. At the moment I'm being neither hard nor useful; perhaps I'm on some other list. Try looking under liabilities. I'm not very happy with myself."

She took the next two days off, but the exploration of the cave carried on. Phil and Nicola vanquished the Bogey at last, descending a small pitch beyond. The following day Fred and Graham pushed on further to a great discovery – a very big pitch indeed. They hadn't got the rope to rig it, and reluctantly came out. As chance would have it, the fresh team available were Phil and Ukie again.

In her description of the trip Ukie made no mention of the Bogey at all. She passed it without difficulty – so much for the have-to-get-your-confidence-back-by-going-straight-down-again nonsense. They had an uneventful trip down, and the account began at the head of the large pitch:

It wasn't difficult to find Graham and Fred's six-second drop, and we spent some time staring out into the blackness and dropping rocks down. "OK Ukie, I'm dropping a rock down now," says Phil. Pause. "Well, go on then, drop it!" thinks Ukie. Pause. "Boom!" goes the rock. "Shit!" go Phil and Ukie. Eventually we decided to get on with it and rig the bugger. At last Phil was ready to go down. "Here I go into the unknown!" he cried, and vanished over the edge.

He seemed to take a very long time to go down. Then the call came – "Rope Free", and I followed; an incredible pitch. It was a straight free hang in the middle of a vast chamber. On my way down, enveloped in a cloud of steam, I had to look at the rope running through my rack to convince myself that I was moving at all: walls, roof and floor were all out of sight. 110 metres below the belay I landed in a bouldery, shafty, sloping chamber and headed off down a little rift, with popcorn stuff all over the walls. A few minutes later Phil stopped in his tracks and said – "Hey! I've been here before . . . This is FU56!" A piece of peanut wrapping was evidence that we were NOT THE FIRST – the big pitch had landed us in the Hot Tub of Pozu Jorcada Blanca.

We got out at 12.20, after a twelve-hour trip with a strangely historic feel about it . . . what will happen to the expedition, now?

It was an interesting question. The inexperienced bunch of cavers who had arrived to push the new entrance had just re-explored, photographed and surveyed a cave nearly 500 metres deep in only a few days. They were now experienced cavers with the rest of the summer to play around with.

Whilst the frontiers of caving were being pushed back further up the mountain, a great deal had been happening at Los Lagos. The Spanish families who drove there for picnics were greeted by the sight of a khaki-shorted Englishman darting about with a butterfly net.

This was John Hutchinson, the expedition biologist. He was collecting not only butterflies, but also beetles, which he religiously pinned in neat rows on cards and stored in his tent. At night he would lie curled up in his sleeping-bag surrounded by the corpses of dozens of innocent creatures. They didn't call him 'Hutch' for nothing.

Apart from seeing off insects, John (the Impaler) Hutchinson had another function; he was Steve Gale's driver. The only other drivers (Steve couldn't drive) were swinging about on ropes in the big pots up the hill, so John was co-opted into driving about on the terrible Picos roads with Steve navigating and giving commands, like a tank commander, except that instead of a Sherman they were driving a yellow bread van.

Together they bounced up the road that followed the valley of the Dobra into the mountains. It was Steve's plan to set some dye-detectors in this rarely visited place, just in case it was from these springs or resurgences that the water from the Jorcada Blanca system re-emerged. The road deteriorated the further they went until after a few miles Steve looked up from the map on his knee and pointed up a disgraceful shambles of a track to one side.

"Up there, John." It was a steep rubble path, fit only for donkeys, which led to a small clump of houses and, beyond them, to a large spring. His not to reason why, John took a run-up and careered up the hill with the engine screaming, then lurched into the tiny village.

Rare as it was for the sleepy hamlet to receive visitors, it was unprecedented for one of the village's own sons to be flying off to America. At that moment, though, one of the young men was packing his bags into his cousin's Land-Rover. The Land-Rover was to take him to Santander, then the train to Bilbao for the late afternoon flight. By morning he would be in the United States!

The lucky chap kissed his mother goodbye, then jumped in – his cousin already had the engine running – and as the Land-Rover rolled off he looked back at the house of his birth and waved. Next stop New York.

Wrong. Just as they turned into the village centre they saw that the way was blocked by a huge yellow van that had tried to get around the corner by the Ramirezes' house. It was wedged across the street with the nose up against the wall on one side, and the square back leaning against the wall on the other. What kind of cretins would bring a van like this here and what could they be delivering? The street was totally blocked!

The two cousins pushed through the crowd that had gathered around the wedged vehicle, and it was only then, when they were quite close, that they saw the sticker 'GB'.

"What's he say, Hutch? – Look, I reckon we need to go back about six inches, then try turning left a little."

"It's something about an aeroplane, I can't catch the rest."

"Well tell him a helicopter would be better, it could lift it out for us. Hey – do you think we've enough *people* to lift it out?"

"No, not nearly enough, and anyway they're all old folk. *Qué, Señor?* . . . He says we've got to move the van straightaway."

"Can't he *see* that we're stuck?"

"He's got to get to Santander, hang on . . . he's got to get to Santander . . . to catch a train . . . then a plane . . . from Bilbao . . . this afternoon."

"Well, look, tell him we can't bloody well take him to Santander, because we're bloody well stuck here! Jesus Christ! He'll just have to make his *own* way to Santander. Do you think they'll let us demolish the wall of this house?"

"We can't demolish a house!"

"Try it."

"Er . . . Señor . . . Eso es possible . . . er . . . el muro . . ."

It is a remarkable thing how, if he is sufficiently motivated, one Spaniard can destroy the entire wall of a house single-handedly. It can be difficult to imagine, when you see the Picos villagers sleeping in the sun, just what dynamite they can be. No wonder the Moors never conquered them.

The wall was soon down, and there were cheers as the yellow van lumbered away with a massed helping push, hotly pursued by a Land-Rover.

This use of John Hutch as chauffeur was in keeping with Steve Gale's view that the expedition was his private research group. We had, of course, always tried to foist the idea on grant-giving bodies that our Spanish trips were scientific expeditions, pushing back the limits of knowledge, and not just superb adventures at the limits of human endurance. The grant-giving bodies knew the truth of it, naturally, and we knew they knew, and they knew we knew they knew – it was quite a knowledgeable charade.

This year it was to be different. Steve Gale was in charge. His position as a proto-don had added weight to our begging letters, but the corollary was that we had a whole list of 'projects' to complete while in the Picos. One was to measure the daily rainfall at our three camps, another to make a systematic study of the insect life in the hills. Each camp had a weather station, and detailed meteorological records were expected to be kept. At Los Lagos this soon proved impossible, because the rain-gauge was stolen by someone who no doubt wanted to turn it into a still. At the other two camps there was no one to steal the rain-gauge, but one glance at the log-book reveals that the cavers' hearts weren't in it:

DATE	MM OF PRECIPITATION & COMMENTS
20th July	None. Found one fly (dead).
21st July	None. One beetle (dead).
22nd July	None. Two beetles (one dead, one v. ill).
23rd July	
24th July	Rained so hard yesterday no-one left the tents to read the gauge. Overflowing today, with one ant (dead) as well.

Steve Gale spent much of the expedition walking at high speed from one camp to another, exhorting the cavers there to carry on with whatever they were doing and why hadn't they read the weather stations yet? He was discovering, he confided, that it rained more at the foot of the mountain than at the top of the mountain, and this would be the basis of a paper he intended to write. As the reader may by now be well aware, it was generally good, hot weather at our Top Camp, whereas it was reliably foul at Los Lagos. This was the fact that Steve was now purporting to have discovered, namely that the Rain in Spain Fell Mainly on the Plain.

DAVID While the newer members of the team had spent the winter speaking of Perdices, I had never been inspired by the idea. I too had been listening to Steve Gale's theories and firmly believed the cave would either end up in FU56 or sump. One February evening Richard and I nursed pints in the New Inn at Clapham, refreshed by a pleasant excursion in the Gaping Gill system. I had a new job, as a reporter for the *Guardian*: I had to work harder, with daily, not weekly deadlines, and weekends away were more valuable than ever.

"There's one cave at Ario with great potential we haven't really looked at," Richard said. "Cueva del Near Miss. Remember? It was never looked at after 1981."

I remembered all right. "But how would we break through that four inch slot? Colin Nicholls tried jumping up and down on it and it seemed impenetrable."

"Dave, I know we once scoffed at people who hammered their way through Picos caves. But we've got to move on."

Slowly the concept grew. Steve Roberts was also taken with the plan, and during a pleasant journey by train through France we psyched ourselves up into a lather of anticipation. As soon as we arrived at Lagos at 7 p.m. we would be off up the hill with a lumphammer. Next day we would set to work, and break through to the booming space into which Colin had thrown rocks in 1981.

We were pre-empted. By the time we arrived, days of work by Ukie, Graham, Dave Horsley, Ian Houghton and Sean had already done the job, and 12/5 – Pozu la Cistra – was 200 metres deep and going.

It had been back-breaking work. Colin's description of jumping up and down had not given a clear idea of what the slot was like. I had imagined a thin flake would be all that blocked the way, and smashing through would be as easy as it had been at the top of The Chair in FU56. But the four-inch slot was in solid rock, and the cave was very constricted, making it very difficult to swing a hammer. I would have taken one look and given up. Sean and Ian were more determined.

At the end of a particularly hard session, Sean tried once more to insert himself into the fissure. This time, he said, he thought he could do it. Rigging a rope through the squeeze, he forced himself down. Squeezes are one thing. Vertical squeezes are another: it is always more difficult to climb up through them than to slither down, aided by gravity. This was a vertical squeeze above a 30-metre drop.

Had there not been a ledge 3 metres below the narrowest part the obstacle would have been more serious still. As it was, it was possible to rest there, sort out normal SRT gear and carry on down; and on the way back up, to remove equipment and free climb up to the daunting hole with an ascender clipped onto the rope for protection. The squeeze was so narrow that even the thinnest members of the team could not pass it wearing harnesses. To descend, Sean wore only a waist belt. He could not have got through with the bulk of a descender in the normal position at his waist: it would have jammed between his chest and the wall. He clipped it on high above his head, joined to his belt with a length of tape.

But the Newt – so called because it had been 'really hammered', – had been passed. Below, the cave was human sized again, with a series of six dry, pleasant pitches. The last landed in a horizontal passage with a stream.

Sean slipped back up through the Newt as easily as he came down. Ian, a bulkier fellow, had more trouble. "He looked like a cork trying to force his way out of a bottle," Sean said later. It was all very well for anorexics, but for others, the Newt was extraordinarily strenuous. Once committed, there was no turning back: the jammer prevented one from going back down for a rest, and if anyone was silly enough to try it without a jammer, they risked falling down the 30-metre shaft. In the early days of its exploration, Cistra was pushed by little people.

Steve and I are big people. Our first trip ended in abject failure. I forced myself in. Thick wedges of rock jammed against my thighs, bottom and groin. There was no way I was going to get through. Put off by the sight of my bursting veins and purple face, Steve didn't bother trying. There was only one thing for it: a whole lot more hammering.

Eventually we got bored. It was still early afternoon: if we made good time, we could get back to Lagos and set off for the shops in Cangas – the expedition was in dire need of restocking with food. Freed from the narrow confines of the cave, we skipped down the hill in glorious sunshine, piloting the big yellow van towards the shops with reckless abandon to the sound of James Brown.

Many big boxes of groceries, tortillas and beers later we turned back onto the road. With only two people on board, the van coped with the bends and inclines of the Lagos road effortlessly. "Steve," I said, "don't go *too* fast. . . ." It had been a booming day for the bars and restaurants at Lagos, and the downside of the road was crowded with holiday traffic. We had a near miss with a coach not far from Covadonga: the road was not built for two vehicles this size. Then, on a short descent at the point where forest and pasture gives way to mountain limestone and scrubby grass, we saw a large, very new, white Peugeot saloon. There was a bang. We were on the outside: "No worries," said Steve, "no danger of going over the edge, plenty of room."

"Er Steve, don't you think we should stop?"

"Nah. I think it was only their wing mirror. By the time they get to Covadonga they'll have forgotten all about it."

We drove on, at a more leisurely pace. As we pulled onto the Lagos meadow we were in high spirits again. "Yoo hoo! Lots of lovely Rioja, anis, ponche, cuarenta y tres, eggs, bread, jamon, chorizo, pimentas, tomates, ajos, cebollas, naranjas," I yelled, demonstrating the command of Spanish five years in the Cangas supermercados had given me. I leapt out of the cab: "Come on, you buggers, give us a . . ."

I had meant to say "hand". Instead I said "Señor?"

The Peugeot had not forgotten about its brush with speleologists. It had turned round very fast indeed, chased us up the hill and had just screeched to a halt. Its driver, a smart and paunchy man, was standing in front of me and he was angry. His wife and two children sat in the car, visibly seething too. Along one side from end to end we had left our calling card: a yellow groove, with three deeper dents at front, rear and doorpost.

Steve stayed calm: a big mistake. After a pursuit of 3000 feet and seven miles up a mountain, the packs of AA Five Star insurance forms which he coolly attempted to persuade his victim to sign were of no avail.

"*No fiamos!*" the man kept saying, as Steve pointed hopelessly to the dotted lines. "We don't trust you!" Steve tried again, filling in a graph with a map of the accident, underlining the impressive list of Lloyds underwriters which, his Spanish was in no wise equal to explaining, offered cast iron security. The lady, as angry as her husband and only slightly thinner, got out and joined in the fun. It was she who produced the solution which suddenly seemed to her husband to be the only possible way out:

"*Ingleses, no fiamos ustedes. A Covadonga hay una oficina de la Guardia Civil.*"

Either, she went on, we could follow her family down the hill and explain the situation to the officers voluntarily. Or she would go and fetch them. The Guardia Civil, she added, did not like having to disturb their evenings with unnecessary trips into the mountains.

We had no choice, and wearily got back in the van. On the way down I began to feel angry. This was absurd. All the Guardia could do was tell the woman to sign the insurance forms. We had been supposed to go to Ario that night: now it would be too late.

The Guardia post at Covadonga is very small. It normally deals with nothing more serious than elderly people fainting

151

with emotion in the sacred basilica. "What we've got to do is get to them first," Steve said on the way down. Tonight, there was one thin adolescent on duty, chain smoking Winstons. We were beaten: as we pulled into the car park the youth was surrounded by our antagonists.

Steve tried again with his forms. The Señora remained implacable. "No fiamos." Finally I lost my temper, summoning up all reserves of indignation and linguistic skill.

"Hombre! Es una pequeña problema!" ("Man, it's a small problem.") I pointed at the two sleek kids. "Donde estan los niños muertes?" ("Where are the dead children?")

As an attempt to soothe matters it was not well-judged. "Assassin!" the woman screamed, clearly interpreting my words as a death-threat to her little ones. This time we really were in a pickle: I could see the callow cadet getting on the blower to Interpol to check me out any minute . . .

His response was less sensational, though tedious. "We will have to get los trafficos," he said. "They are the specialists for this affair. They must come from Ribadesella." Ribadesella, I remembered glumly, was 40 kilometres away.

In the end – two hours later – the trafficos sorted it out. Six strong, armed to the teeth, they pulled up in a fortified Land-Rover. They inspected the damage. "For *this*," they said, "for this we have come all this way?" Smiling now, Steve produced his forms once more. "Lady, sign here. And good night."

There was just one catch. "Señor Roberts. We will require your passport. You may retrieve it after one week from the Palace of Justice in Cangas de Onis."

Seven days later Steve tried to get it back. In Cangas they explained that it was in Covadonga, because the accident had occurred in that jurisdiction. In Covadonga, he was directed to Arriondas. No, they told him, you are mistaken, it is in Cangas. In desperation he tried the ordinary police station, where the men are armed only with joke guns clipped well out of harm's way. The passport was in a drawer.

"Ah, Señor Roberts. Señora Lopez is not going to bring an action, so you are free to go."

"Great," said Steve, reaching for his documents.

"That will be 25,000 pesetas." Steve stopped short.

"Ask him what will happen if I don't pay the bloody fine – it's over a hundred quid!"

"He says that in that case you must go to jail until your insurance company coughs up."

"Do they take travellers cheques?" Steve asked.

The entrance to Pozu la Cistra lay on the very rim of the Cares Gorge, at the furthest extremity of the Ario plateau. On one side, the great bulk of Jultayu rose above sweeping lines of strata; below, the sun played many-coloured tricks of lighting in the clouds welling in the canyon. Somehow or other I was going to have to find a way to pass the Newt. The Skinny Team was advancing rapidly: a boulder choke had given way to a fine 60-metre shaft, the Armadillo, and the streamway continued beyond.

After some hours of hammering Steve, who is smaller than I, at last felt ready to go for it. The squeeze was still too narrow for me, but after forcing his body through, he was able to get a better hammer swing from below and widened the slot more rapidly. Not really knowing how I planned to return, I breathed in and followed. We advanced swiftly to the limit of exploration and rigged two short pitches.

Back on the ledge below the Newt, reality sank in. I prided myself on having tackled some of the narrowest Yorkshire caves with impunity, despite my size. But this was different. Steve took ten minutes to get through, ten minutes during which his legs waggled helplessly above 100 feet of space before brute strength won the day. He had taken off his helmet and I passed it through on the rope. Breathless and panting he urged me on: "Come up, Dave. It's not that bad."

Foolishly, I tried without removing any clothing. I handed him my hat and light and struggled in the dark, barely able to insert a shoulder, let alone my chest. The surface was five minutes away beyond this squeeze: an eternity. Desperate and exhausted, I lost the little ground I had made and slid back to the widening, dangling from my single ascender clipped to the rope and my waist belt. Steve passed me my light again: somehow I found footholds and unclipped, climbing unprotected back to the ledge.

I took off my heavy oversuit, and despite the risk, my belt. My only chance was to remove every protuberance. I hung the ascender on the rope with a footloop, hoping that it might give me some purchase for my feet. It had been a long time since I had been really frightened underground, and I was not enjoying the reminder.

Delicately up the chimney; helmet off and up to Steve. Push jammer up as high as possible; lift leg into footloop and push . . . I gained two feet further than before. The rock compressing my belly thudded with the constriction of my aorta. The jammer was too low to be of use now and I flung an elbow up and across the top of the slot, grinding it into the walls to pull me those last few inches. At last it was over: my chest was free. My buttocks were still stuck fast but now I could push down with both hands: easy.

"Christ, Steve. I've got to do that every bloody trip."

Cistra carried on. There were fine tubular pitches: Camshaft, Geselschaft, Thompson's Gazelleshaft, Eddie Shah, all rigged on a glorious push by Steve, Phil Sargent and me next day. Ukie – her epic in Perdices a distant memory now – carried on in a series of trips with my brother, Fred and Phil Duncan down drop after drop, split by winding, marbled streamway and wet, sporting freeclimbs. It was Orwell's year: the last pitch descended was Room 101, and the four-second drop beyond had to be Big Brother. Richard and I went surveying with his fiancée Sara – her sixth caving trip since taking up the sport was a long mapping session down to 400 metres. Each shaft landed in a high, round chamber, with clear pools on the floor. The passage between was nowhere very large: often we had to crabwalk sideways, squeezing past sharp mineral projections and the same blood red stalactites we had seen in Xitu. The weather was hot and settled, and we emerged from long trips into quiet, windless nights lit by more stars than I had ever seen, even in the Picos. Expedition perfection was back; a shared excitement as each push returned and related its discoveries and the promise of more to come.

The only discordant note came from Andy, sparking off an intense debate. When Steve and I widened the Newt to enable ourselves to pass, he said, thinner cavers could already get through. What we had done was therefore unethical.

Caving has never had the developed system of ethics and principles evolved by climbers. Its approach has always been: get down the hole without leaving a mess by whatever means appropriate. Andy argued that as techniques and equipment had made the sport safer and easier, it was high time that ethics were introduced. If the fatties like Steve, Richard and me wanted to go underground, Andy said, he had the perfect hole for us – Andy's Rattler, F20, a deep and barely investigated shaft with a huge snow tower, on the hill behind Top Camp. By widening the squeeze, we had lessened Cistra's challenge. Yes, we retorted, but we've also made it safer, and quicker to widen still further in the event of an accident and rescue. At the time, I contested Andy's point hotly. Now, I am not so sure. Several of us would never have seen Cistra without our action: probably, the thin team was too small to have bottomed it without our help. But undeniably we had changed the cave for all time. Still, the Newt got no easier with practice. It was, and remained, a problem of sheer dimensions.

As Cistra grew – well over 500 metres deep at the top of Big Brother – I began to wonder if it was going to snake on slowly down to the very bottom of the gorge. Its entrance was not far from the line of Xitu, but there was no sign of any connection. It didn't appear to be collecting its own inlet tributaries either: perhaps it was a smaller, but equally deep parallel system.

One morning Ukie and Phil appeared at Ario soon after dawn, the grassy plateau white with frost. Their excitement bubbled over: "We've found a huge master stream passage. Boy oh boy it's really going now. We followed it upstream a little way to what looked like a tricky freeclimb; the other way there was a 20-metre pitch, seemed very wet . . ."

Recognition stirred. Stream passage . . . free climb . . . wet pitch. It sounded like Xitu: Cistra must be the wet aven above Dampturation where I had shivered in a showerbath while Skunk took pictures on our derigging venture in 1980.

"Don't get carried away, Phil. I think you and Ukie have done it again."

Steve and I confirmed it later that day, entering the main cave via a last, spectacular 60-metre abseil. Round the corner Graham's dreadful bolts still stuck out half an inch where he put them in in 1980. The Xitu stream ran clear and cold, the carbide tipped into it four years earlier having long been washed away. The first person down that pitch was Keith, I thought. Only 500 metres to go to the bottom. To the point of union, Cistra was 610 metres deep.

Up at the refugio, the donkeys bearing ham, casks of wine, wheels of cheese and enough tinned food to keep a supermarket stocked for a week had announced the arrival of the Barcelona caving talent. The SIE were back to push Cabeza Muxa. They had suffered more than their fair share of mishaps over the years we had shared base campsites. In 1979, they had run out of rope halfway down the Gran Abisu, negotiating a final 30 metres on a dynamic climbing rope which bounced them up and down like yo-yos every time they took a step. In 1980, they reached the bottom of the abyss and found another immediately beyond, a mere 120 metres deep. After that, already 600 metres down – and less than 100 metres from the entrance horizontally – they hit a major river. Not a stream, but a river which made the Xitu torrent look puny. It clearly accounted for about nine tenths of the water emerging at Culiembro. Before long they were forced

155

to wade above their waists, and then to take to a rubber dinghy at a 'marmita' – a swirling pothole in the floor. Halfway across the dinghy sank. There remained the possibility of bolting a tyrolean traverse round the obstacle, a kind of aerial ropeway. The work went well at first; then someone dropped the only boltkit into the water. It was swept away.

In 1981, they abandoned the Picos for the Pyrenees. They were back the following year, armed once again with a gastronomic prowess which made us drool and feel glad that we were spending more time at Top Camp, away from the smell and sight of their meals. This time, Muxa ended at a boulder choke not far from the marmita.

In 1983, they arrived as we were on the point of leaving. The weather, which had been vile in the early part of August, turned obscene. The Gran Abisu, normally watered by a few drips, became a raging waterfall 247 metres high. Somehow they passed it, but at the bottom of the succeeding shaft the river level was 10 metres higher than normal. A way was found through the boulders into more river passage which in those conditions was nearly lethal. A member of their party was climbing one of the many short drops when the rope swung him into the full force of the water. This was not like getting caught under a wet pitch in Yorkshire: it was like being hit by a tidal wave. He could not breathe. His companions, endowed with the strength that comes with sheer desperation, pulled him clear. Muxa was left alone again.

We had grown fond of the Catalans; sometimes, when we looked particularly hungry, they would give us a few leftovers. There had been some good sessions shared between the two clubs, which had sometimes benefited from the Barcelona group's familiarity with the increasingly liberal Spanish laws concerning the use of marijuana. A day after Cistra was connected to Xitu, they found the bottom of Cabeza Muxa at last: a beautiful, deep green sump 918 metres down. Tentatively I asked their leader, Giuseppe Victoria, if some of us might have a trip down on their ropes. "Mais bien sûr," he said. And afterwards, we agreed, there would be a fiesta. Leonardo, a graphic designer and another of their regulars, pointed surreptitiously at Sara. "Et la blonde?" he said. "Elle va venir à la fiesta también?"

We were a large party: Sara, Ian Houghton, Phil Sargent, Fred, Ukie and myself. Giuseppe directed us across the hillside with his umbrella towards the entrance – a conical depression 50 metres deep and 75 across. The first pitch followed. There were two bolts, sticking out a little too far. I waved goodbye to our guide. "Adios." To retreat now without reaching the bottom would be a national humiliation.

The next pitch followed immediately. There was only one bolt, badly drilled. I took a deep breath: Giuseppe was still seeing off the others, so it would be impossible to jack the trip, lie low for a few hours and return. Oh well. If it's supported all those gourmets it'll support me.

The rigging all the way down did not conform to BSI standards. At the top of the Gran Abisu, the psychological strain was too much for Phil, and he left for the surface, mumbling about responsibilities to his colleagues at work which meant he couldn't afford to die. The SIE's approach to rub points, most noticeably at the top of the last 120-metre pitch, was eccentric. Instead of rebelaying, they rigged a rope too long for the shaft. Each time the abrasion cut it to the core, they simply pulled up a few more yards of line and tied it to the belay. When we got there, there were about twenty loops already in place.

But the Muxa river was the master cave we had always dreamed of. Its scale was continuously and terrifyingly vast. For most of its three kilometre length, the water was like the Colorado, and progress possible only by teetering on tiny ledges. The passage was about ten times as big as Xitu's. The pitches were rigged on old 8 mm rope, often badly frayed. No wonder Giuseppe had said that they wouldn't bother detackling below the entrance series.

Nearly 800 metres down, Ian began to suffer the psycho-somatic effects as well: in his case, diarrhoea. At the same spot, I broke my carbide generator trying to fill it too enthusiastically. It was Sara's ninth caving trip, and she felt quite deep. The three of us turned round. Fred and Ukie made it to the bottom, and caught us up at the 247-metre abyss. Giuseppe was waiting for us at the entrance, a little concerned. It was 7 a.m.: he thought we should have been able to finish the trip in ten hours, not sixteen. This, I thought, is what unlimited smoked ham does for you.

Back at Ario, the water supply was worse than ever. There was none at all. Fred said he was dehydrated, and dressed still in his caving suit, consumed half a bottle of brandy by eight o'clock. As the sun rose and replaced the frost with bleaching heat he collapsed insensible. We began to think the heat might not do him any good and undressed him. His limbs stuck fast in the attitude of rigor mortis as we manipulated them to remove his stiff PVC overalls; later he said he'd been dreaming of nurses in an orthopaedic hospital.

The Muxa excursion had cemented international friendship between speleologists but delayed the detackling of Cistra by several days. Ian was particularly keen to get it over with. After further setbacks with the completion of the survey, he finally managed to get the team in a state of readiness. Then he announced a modification to the original plan.

RICHARD It wasn't because of any personality disorder that Ian wanted to go alone into a desperately severe cave at six in the morning. It was the challenge of the idea, the physical and mental stamina it required, the total self-sufficiency. Ian had been reading too many climbing books in fact.

Solo caving was not a new concept, or even new to Ario. There had been Steve Worthington's solo 'push' down Xitu in the utumn of 1980. Steve Worthington had been Ian's guru at the Sheffield University club and his exploits had thrilled the fledgling Houghton when he had been just learning how to screw up his karabiners. Ian remained captivated by the idea of a solo assault on a deep cave. Now, he announced on the eve of the great detackle, he would accomplish his ambition.

The plan was to detackle the entire cave in one push. There were only nine active potholers left: all hands would be needed. Everyone would go down in a series of waves, bringing out all the rope, ladders, belays, tapes and litter in a gradually enlarging group. Ian said he would be wave one: he and no one else. As always on expeditions, the longer the trip, the later it was likely to start. Ian said his departure at 6 a.m. would give us an incentive not to dally. He would begin the detackling of the bottom, meeting up with the next wave some time in the morning. "Then," he said, "by the time we're back at the entrance series it will be only ten at night, and I'll feel completely fresh because it won't be the middle of the night." Yes, we agreed, but you would still have been up since four and underground for sixteen hours. Ian was unshaken.

He rose before dawn, and by six was climbing down the entrance ladders. Well before eight, he had passed the 60-metre Armadillo: this had been a badly rigged pitch, but a few days earlier Ian had rearranged things with a remarkable three-point belay which both avoided loose boulders and gave him considerable aesthetic pleasure. All alone, he moved quickly; there was no one to wait for at the pitches, no one to talk to, no other light to disturb the cave's darkness. There was no need to shout 'rope free' after a descent, no other footsteps to echo from the walls. He adjusted to the noise of falling water, which seemed strangely quiet as it tumbled down the shafts. Did the drips make any noise at all when there was no one there to hear them?

He paused for the first time at the top of Camshaft. It had been one of the trickier rigs in the cave, for there was a rub point a short way down which had proved curiously difficult to avoid with rebelays. A few days before, a party found the rope cut to the core, and sensibly they cut it, leaving only just enough for the descent. They arranged a more gymnastic way of getting on the rope which required a shorter length.

Despite the fact that Ian was on a de-rigging trip, he found himself unable to avoid re-rigging this pitch again. He knew that the take-off in this case would be so much simpler and less strenuous if there was an extra back-up from the boulder by the stream, and if the main hang were achieved via a triple belay . . . he pulled up the rope required and made his adjustments. What he didn't do was to check if there was a knot on the end of the rope. *All* the ropes on the expedition had knots in the end, even, as was usually the case, if the rope was much longer than required. There was still a knot in the end of the spare rope coiled on the floor. It is tempting to speculate whether a companion would have pointed out to Ian that he should check the rope's end, but Ian didn't have a companion.

What Ian did was to use about fifteen feet of extra rope in his re-rig, so that when he slid down the rope he sailed off the free end and flew bum-first into a serendipitous deep pool of water. It was about nine o'clock in the morning. Back at the camp, above all the pitches, squeezes and across the fell, the other cavers lay dozing in their bags. Not one had started to stir.

Neck-deep in his pool, Ian was far from asleep. His plight was straight out of a caving pub-yarn; at once desperately serious and totally absurd. The rope dangled enticingly above him way out of reach. There were no walls anywhere near to it, nor any movable rocks he could use to build a cairn and get to it. When he recovered from the shock he had a go at climbing up in the downstream passage, where he could bridge with one foot on either wall until he was way, way above the floor, perhaps half the height of the pitch. It wasn't possible to get any higher, and he could see the rope dangling only metres away out of reach. Did it occur to him to leap into space and grab for the rope, or did he accept his fate at once? Whichever, he was marooned.

Underground the only way to keep warm is to move. Ian raced off down the cave to get at least some of the de-rigging done. Soon he was puffing and panting again, and feeling had returned even to his wet behind. Not far from the final shaft he stopped. It was now well past eleven. The first wave of the main party was due down at ten, and they would be well into the cave now. One thing he couldn't allow was for another sucker to come whizzing off the rope end . . . he had to turn round and race back *up* the cave.

At Ario, some people were up, cooking breakfast. There was no sign of anyone going caving before lunch. Time passed. Soon the pre-prandial bottle of Ricard anisette was being passed around.

"Hello!"

"Hello!" After all these hours of sitting in the dark and the deafening quiet, the sound of another voice came as a shock.

"Don't . . . come . . . down . . . until . . . you . . . rig . . . the . . . rope . . . again. It . . . is . . . too . . . short."

"What?" The echoes and falling water made communication of this subtlety very difficult.

"ROPE . . . TOO . . . SHOrrrrT!!!!"

"What? Look, we're not coming down till you tell us what's wrong."

"What?"

DAVID Cistra was finally derigged on two trips, not one, although by eight next morning sixteen heavy bags lay poised beneath the entrance pitches. Each pitch got a little harder as the weight of gear increased. Between them, we made a human chain and passed the bags from one end to another, before moving the chain on a few yards and beginning the process again.

Taking a leaf from the SIE's book, I brought copious supplies of ham, tinned fruit, cheese, chocolate, olives and smoked mackerel. The cave seemed almost a merry place, lit by the lamps of the whole expedition remaining, warmed by the exertion of group activity. When we reached the surface, the sun was rising slowly above the mountains' rim, running through the spectrum on the rocks and cloud from red to blinding white.

We sat for a long time, half dozing, half marvelling at the intoxicating beauty of the Picos. Only one person was missing. Ian had gone out early: wet, frozen and traumatised. He huddled alone at Ario, making tea.

160

9

Dancing in the Dark

RICHARD Cave diving is the epitome of what most people consider perfect torment. Swimming down a constricted tunnel filled with bone-chilling water is bad enough; just try getting lost, or damaging your gear, or staying down too long, or going too deep, or any other mistake. They all mean certain death. Usually initiates dive alone, but going with a partner only introduces the added risk that he will run out of air and kill you for yours.

There has been very little diving in the Picos. In the 1970s, a Swiss team lost a diver in Cueva Culiembro, the Xitu resurgence, and since then the bureaucrats in Oviedo have been reluctant to give permission to the few who have applied. Meanwhile the business of supplying divers with air, compressors and other specialised items, all of which weigh a great deal, means that any non-diving team with a diving contingent would find itself with little time for anything other than 'sherpa-ing' for the divers.

All these points were made to Danny at a meeting called to plan the 1985 trip. He agreed with them all: they were the very reasons he wanted to go diving with four of his friends in the Picos – almost no one else had. The great systems of the western massif were all undived: Osu, Hoyo la Madre, Xitu and Culiembro, where the Swiss found a bypass to the sump where their diver was drowned, leading to more passage and a virgin sump which Danny was sure would lead straight to Xitu and the deepest 'through trip' in the world. But Danny was still unpopular in the club. He had not been forgiven for bringing the soldiers in 1983, and no one wanted to waste 1985 looking for his body. He left the meeting in a huff.

The planning of expeditions had, by now, been honed to a fine art. The timetable of things to do was well-established, and Steve Roberts, who had been volunteered as the new leader, whisked things along with his word processor. Dave and I never went to the meetings in Brasenose bar any more, but the young blood went there still, fantasising.

161

The Bay of Biscay looked as if it had never known a storm since the day it was formed as the ferry ploughed steadily toward Santander. We sat on deck on a circle of mats around a big box, from which we helped ourselves to cheese, pickle, bread and Ricard.

"It's just incredible, a seventeen-year-old winning Wimbledon." I took another swig.

"Soon enough, seventeen-year-olds will win everything," replied Steve Mayers, "there are plenty of seventeen-year-old climbers who can climb the pants off anyone."

"God how depressing! Only twenty-nine and already over the hill. Look at us . . . the average age of these expeditions is getting higher and higher. They'll end up like a P & O cruise."

The combination of sun and Ricard was making me depressed, and it was all the more depressing to be sitting, as we were, next to York University Caving Club Expedition, who had just started caving in the Picos not far from our Top Camp. Their area was large and new; unexplored by cavers.

"We've got these three brilliant leads, and there are dozens of entrances all around just waiting to be looked at. We're going to have our work cut out this summer I can tell you." It was a very brash and muscular youth talking. He looked a bit like Boris Becker.

"Well," I replied, grabbing the bottle as it passed by again, "we've got three poxy leads: 3/5, which is a tight horrible pot that'll drop into Xitu; F20, which is a 200-metre shaft entirely full of ice; and Sima Tras la Jayada. The trouble with Sima Tras la Jayada is that it's already been bottomed by two Spaniards who couldn't find a way on. They were probably right, but they've been wrong before, and we're clutching at straws now."

If the Ricard was making me depressed, it had had the opposite effect on Dave.

"But there's Ridge Cave! You haven't mentioned Ridge Cave!" He started bouncing up and down. "We'll find Ridge Cave! We'll find Ridge Cave! Ridge Cave, Ridge Cave! Yeah! Yeah! Yeah!"

The yellow Luton van coughed along the north coast road with its 2½ kilometres of rope and eight cavers. It was one of the hottest days of the year. Here we were driving through Cangas de Onis once again, the bartenders leaning against the same walls as when we had said goodbye in August 1984. Even the road works were unchanged, and the half-completed house stood just as it had done for five years, with its upper storey still only a pile of bricks and a tangle of scaffolding. It was as if the entire townsfolk had deserted the place as soon as we had left, and had returned a few days before as part of some monstrous conspiracy of permanence.

We unloaded the van then ambled over for the celebratory drink.

Shock number one was soon coming. A note from Alvaro, explaining that he had left a crate of cider for 'my bestest friends, the most wonderfuls peoples ever to came at Ario'. Beside this was an addition, in scrawled but better English, from . . . Danny! This said that he had helped himself to one of these bottles in a moment of severe cash crisis, and so sorry and all that. Only a week and a half before he had rolled up with his bestest cave diving friends to do the diving he'd wanted to do for so long. When challenged by the Park Warden Danny had showed his true resource. "We are the Oxford University Cave Club Expedition. The permits for us to cave here are coming out in a couple of weeks. We're just . . . er . . . an advance guard."

Their trip had been unimaginably successful, a snook cocked at us good and proper. The bunch of them had dived all the easily accessible sumps around . . . Cueva Trumbio hadn't 'gone', but Cueva de Osu had. This cave, which had been visited by so many French, Spanish and English cavers over the years, ended in a sump only 2 metres long! There was a lot of cave on the other side . . .

Hoyo la Madre, the massive resurgence lying at the foot of a deep ravine not 3 kilometres from Los Lagos, had had a 100-metre long sump beyond which was another long section of passage, where the entire stream could be followed up a small waterfall before another sump barred progress again. Only a few days before we had set off – probably as Danny and Co. were diving in Hoyo la Madre – we had finally analysed the dye-detectors from 1984 (it had taken us ten months to get them out of Steve Gale's loft). It looked very much as if Hoyo la Madre was the resurgence for the Top Camp area – the dye put into Jorcada Blanca had come out in the big resurgence. The depth potential was enormous. All we needed now was to get a cave going up there, one as good as Xitu. The breakthrough was just waiting to be found – 'el exito' – the Spanish for 'success'.

The first breakthrough, such as it was, came in 3/5. This cave had been first pushed by the SIE, the Barcelona caving group, in 1978, and rejected – it was tight, horribly loose, and as unattractive as a Picos cave can be. In 1981, we had decided to have a look at it, and so William had been despatched to see what it was like. As a 'thin man', he had loved it . . . but he totally failed to get anyone else interested. After Xitu was bottomed, 3/5 was ignored, for it lay directly above the line of the Xitu survey. Obviously, the best we could hope for was merely another entrance to the main system. Why bother?

In 1982 we had been too busy looking for the deepest cave in the world elsewhere, and 3/5 was forgotten. But the following year, the depressing end to FU56 forced us to set our sights lower. Wingnut, the army character with the big ears, managed to force a way through the final rift into new territory. The passage continued to get still tighter, and as Wingnut didn't want to risk getting his ears stuck, he turned round and headed out. There were no plans to go back – 3/5 was a sordid place.

But we hadn't reckoned with the SIE. At the end of the 1983 expedition, as we were about to leave, we showed them our survey of 3/5. They recognised it as the hole they had abandoned in 1978, and no sooner had we left to catch the ferry, than they went down it. They got about five metres further than Wingnut, and claimed that the passage now really was too tight.

William was undeterred. "Look," he said, "I mean I know the Spanish have got through the rift and say it doesn't go, but dammit, that's what they said about Xitu. I've simply *got* to have another look before I write it off. Simply *got* to."

So here we were, at Ario once more, ready for that other look. William had been pressed into taking some of the novices, Steve Roberts believing mistakenly that 3/5 was an 'easy introduction' to expedition speleology. After the second unsuccessful trip, William was not pleased. He wrote in the log book: "Total abortion. I feel sorry for Dave Horsley who's now had to go down twice with . . ." He never finished the sentence, being far too polite to name the culprit who had brought matters to a halt.

DAVID The culprit's name was Gerhard: one of the strangest and most colourful characters ever to grace an OUCC expedition. He hailed from Bavaria, and was in Oxford conducting some extremely cerebral mathematics research. Not only in the Picos, where it was far too hot but only marginally ridiculous, but also among the spires of the university city, his normal dress was lederhosen. On his second caving trip, a beginners' outing in Wales, he fell 20 metres down a narrow fissure, unfamiliar with the principle of traversing above such drops. He had since endured a series of similar mishaps, yet owned an array of SRT equipment larger, newer and more impressive than the rest of the team put together. Each new setback only redoubled his enthusiasm.

In 3/5, the team had been poised at last to make the great breakthrough when Gerhard attempted to pass Wingnut's Rift. There were grunts, groans and strangled cries. He tried it on his back, on his front and on both sides. There is a common conceit among cavers to deny that a narrow bit is too tight for them: "It's not tight, only awkward," they say, lying through their teeth and regretting the greed of preceding weeks. Gerhard's approach was more individual. As Dave fretted and froze on the far side he kept insisting: "It's much too wide. The passage is too wide for me." What he meant was that he couldn't get a purchase on the broadest part of the fissure, and slipped down into the impassable trench at floor level. But after the trip was abandoned, and Gerhard repeated his explanation back at camp, he passed into folklore as the only man to be defeated by a rift that was too big.

Steve tried hard to persuade William to go down 3/5 again next day, this time to show the capable Phil and Fred the way on. Beyond the 'wide' section, Dave Horsley had found another way on, obscure enough to have been missed by the SIE – a tight slot with an echo, suggesting a pitch. Only William could be relied upon to find it again.

"Look, Steve," he complained, "I've been down that cave too bloody often and I don't see why I should go again. My gear's all wet and I'm fed up with it." But Steve worked on him, and true to form, William gave in. He set off, still grumbling, with Phil and Fred skipping along in front.

RICHARD Phil and Fred were soon pushing ahead, down the slot at the far side of Wingnut's rift and down the 45-metre pitch which followed – a big change from the awkward short pitches that 3/5 had offered previously. The passage which followed was even worse than Wingnut's . . . '(No) Picnic Rift'.

"I say, wait a moment, it's just like the Teresa series," William said as he led off down another narrow passage. "Grunt, grunt, I'm sure that I've been here before! Grunt, but no! God! Hell! I haven't. You know it's NOT Xitu, grunt, grunt, definitely not! Oh Hell! this rift is truly awful!"

When they made it out onto the surface again William was effusive . . .

"Look, I mean, I'm going on a pushing trip tomorrow, and, I mean, no one's going to stop me."

The next trip found the link with Xitu. 3/5 entered as a pitch coming straight out of the roof above Graham's Balls-Up pitch – "we came down into a big chamber with a huge pile of boulders and we soon spotted a tell-tale pile of used carbide. We were in Xitu. We found some truly appalling bolts sticking out of calcite veins. Back on the surface only 2½ hours later."

3/5 was finished at last. It was the 'last adios' – not only to 3/5, but also to Pozu del Xitu, now a magnificent cave system with three entrances, all 1,000-metre potholes in their own right; the original, and highest, was much the easiest. The whole of the plateau had now been explored; it was adios, too, to Ario.

DAVID In our propaganda for sponsors, we had made much of the potential for the 'third system' – the putative cave which ought to exist in the huge expanse of broken limestone between Ario and Top Camp. Previous investigations in this area had always been sporadic, and unsystematic, as Richard and Sara had shown towards the end of 1984. Idly leafing through the journal published by the club after the 1981 trip, they came upon descriptions of cave 3/7: "Cave 3/7 lies further along the ridge away from Ario at the head of an obvious gully. The entrance is an open shaft 9 metres by 3 metres. Stones thrown down took between five and twelve seconds to hit the bottom." In other words, no one had ever been down to have a look. They discovered a fine 80-metre shaft. It was blocked at the bottom, but the rain falling on this huge sector had to go somewhere.

There was only one major cave known – Pozu Jou Tras la Jayada, the 315 metre pothole explored by the SIE. But they had only sent two people to the bottom of the shaft, and unlike Keith who made an abortive 'discovery' of the cave in 1981, they had descended in the freezing showerbath emanating from a huge snow pile on a ledge halfway down. The extensions to 3/5, and the fact that it had taken the SIE so long to bottom Cabeza Muxa, hardened my belief that there might be a way on that they had failed to investigate.

On first inspection, the shaft was a very different and more serious proposition than it had been in 1981. I realised just how serious as I screwed a hanger into one of the old bolts at a rebelay 50 metres down. I heard a deep, forbidding rumble, roar-rattle-crash-BLING-BLANG-BOOM!!! . . . spontaneously. I looked down and saw the cause: car-sized boulders made of ice hanging on the wall. On top of the icebergs, stuck precariously above the route of 1981, were snow banks, which in turn were full of lethal little rocks. Swinging from the rope I spent a long time trying to dislodge the icebergs in reach: each one fell with the same terrifying, and lengthy sound. There were far too many.

I was back next day with Phil and Fred: good men to have in a crisis. There was, we found, a way to avoid the worst of the ice . . . at least until we reached the bottom. To one side, the shaft bifurcated, and we followed a route of unremitting verticality guarded by an overhanging roof. Phil went off first from a small ledge 100 metres down, abseiling past bulges where we needed bolts to avoid abrasion. Like the Xitu big pitch, the shaft sloped outwards, requiring an interminable series of rebelays. But our techniques had advanced a long way since those days. Dangling over nothing in a harness, trying to find a purchase on the smooth, glistening wall, was merely uncomfortable.

Phil banged in two or three anchors, then prusiked up for Fred to take a turn. We waited on the ledge, the only place to sit or stand for 100 metres in either direction, the only sounds the hissing of the showerbath on the far side of the shaft and the pinging of Fred's hammer far below. Three hours passed, then at last a cry to break the monotony: "OK . . . come . . . on . . . down . . ." The echo prevented any further communication. There was little we could do but comply.

Fred had got himself a little niche, from which a rift led behind him into the side of the shaft. It seemed to be another parallel pitch, covered with calcited popcorn. Rocks fell down it for a long time. The original bifurcation had rejoined the main pothole now, and I prayed we were out of the line of fire. The day was a little chillier: there had been fewer avalanches of late. It was my turn to carry on. Fred's fissure was difficult to rig, so I returned to the main abyss. The rock was wet and fractured, bolting impossible. I chipped and scraped at the poor, crystalline wall; the rope twanged ominously on a rub-point lost in the blackness above. What I need is a nice, natural arch to make a thread belay, I thought. Some fat chance . . . but no, there was one two feet above me. I slid a wire round the solid handle and abseiled on. Looming out of the darkness was terra firma. A proper ledge at last, big enough to unclip from the rope after so many hours of collective dangling. Ten metres further was the real bottom. So it had one after all.

At the back of the ledge was another drop . . . a window into another parallel shaft, presumably Fred's fissure further down. I dropped a rock – it was deeper, much deeper, than the main pot opposite! El Exito! Success!

I yelled up: "Rope free. I've found the third system!" As the others heard my call, their excitement matched mine. We regrouped on the ledge, whooping and dancing. La Jayada had been cracked: the SIE *really* blew it this time.

For form's sake, we kicked the spare rope to the bottom of the main shaft and abseiled down. A flat-floored, matt-black cathedral, chilled by the snow, wind and water which ended its hissing in a deep, clear pool. The floor was an impenetrable choke, on top of which were clumps of moss and wild thyme. We had knocked them off at the entrance – the only sign that the shaft, whose twists and turns blocked the daylight, was open to the surface.

We had three bolts left: we had better make them good ones. The first went in at the top of El Exito, the second a few metres down. Really very excited indeed, I descended. Below, a steep, loose slope in a high rift. I advanced gingerly: another pitch was probably very close.

Around the corner the floor changed to hard mud. Then there was a wall: a dead end, with only an aven bearing a tiny splash of water. It was the cruellest moment of my life. We were about 5 metres deeper than the bottom of the main shaft reached by the SIE.

By the time we reached the surface at 11.45 p.m. we were drenched by the sweat of more than 300 metres of vertical ascent. The final changeover, just two metres from the top, was the most strenuous: as I fought and steamed in a warm summer wind I couldn't get the stiff dry rope out of my chest ascender. The Picos had won again. The third system was a flop.

Richard and Sara had come up to Ario with Steve Mayers. They consoled me with appropriate doses of cumbres de gredos, the clarete wine which the new refugio warden Vlas sold in cartons – a sign of progress, since more cartons could be packed onto a donkey than the old plastic bottles. "Don't worry, Dave," Richard said. "There's always Top Camp. You might even find Ridge Cave."

"Richard," I replied, "fuck off will you?"

RICHARD Things at Top Camp were only going in a sort of so-so fashion. Despite the hard winter, the snow was very low, which was good for finding caves, but it also meant that we were going to have a bit of a job finding enough water to drink.

At the best of times the water supply at Top Camp was precarious, for there was no surface water at all on the colander-like hillsides. In previous years we had been able to fill our water containers from the streams which ran off the bottom of the ice-sheets. The run off would fill the containers quickly if you chose a big enough snowfield, although the water had a liberal dash of glacial filth in it. This year our old favourites had shrivelled and we were forced to fill washing-up bowls with shovelfuls of snow from the small piles that remained in the shadows. Inside a black plastic bag the contents would melt within a day or so, and there was a queue of them waiting to be used. Every morning there was the ritual 'spooning of the crud', as handfuls of the filth were decanted off the murky water that remained. A cup of tea made with this stuff had a head of scum on top which made it look like a draught of Birmingham canal water.

Some Spanish walkers appeared, and were grateful for the drink which we offered them in the sweltering heat. They sat in their shorts as Steve Mayers and I laid out the plaited ropes on the grass, assessing what lengths had made it up to Top Camp.

"Why are you here?" one of them asked, in good English. She was a blonde, heavily made-up lady, dressed improbably in a bikini, and sweating profusely.

"Well," I began, quite slowly, "we want to discover where the water goes which falls on these hills . . . in the caves, underground."

"Ah, yes, the water." She examined the icy cupful she was sipping, and the tide marks of scum which ran around the sides of the tin mug. "But there is very much water at Los Lagos?"

"Yes, well, we know – it's just something that we do on our holidays." I felt foolish.

"Where are the caves?" she asked, but soon wished she hadn't, for Phil Duncan let out a barrage of enthusiasm.

"F20 is just over there on that ridge – up by that snow field and left a bit. It's a vertical hole right into the ground that leads down 100 metres to the top of an ice tower over 150 metres high!"

The opening at the surface was small enough, but as you abseiled down the colossal nature of the shaft became obvious. The light at the entrance grew less and less noticeable as the sides of the shaft sloped away on all sides, and the last 70 metres of the rope were free-hanging well away from the walls, landing on the top of what was, in effect, an up-ended glacier. There was a bergschrund on all sides between the snow and the walls of the shaft, and tossed stones indicated that the depth of the cleft between ice and rock was over 100 metres in places. Phil Duncan and Steve Roberts had been unable to rig much further down, however, as the ice slowly squeezed them towards the limestone wall. The rope cut into the ice tower, making the ascent into a

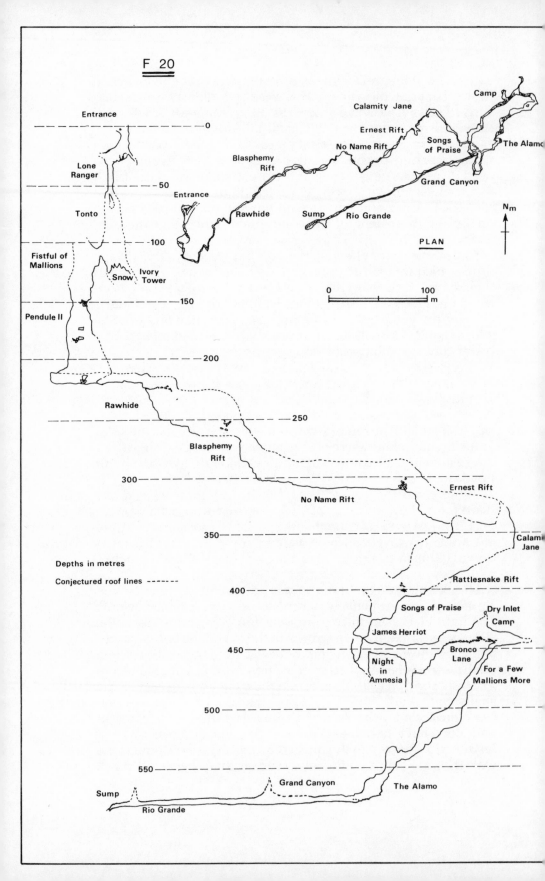

F 20

PLAN

Camp

Calamity Jane

Ernest Rift

No Name Rift

Blasphemy Rift

Songs of Praise

The Alamo

Rawhide

Sump

Rio Grande

Grand Canyon

N m

Entrance

Lone Ranger

Entrance

Tonto

Fistful of Mallions

Snow

Ivory Tower

Pendule II

Rawhide

Blasphemy Rift

No Name Rift

Ernest Rift

Calam Jane

Rattlesnake Rift

Songs of Praise

Dry Inlet Camp

James Herriot

Bronco Lane

Depths in metres

Conjectured roof lines - - - - - -

Night in Amnesia

For a Few Mallions More

Grand Canyon

The Alamo

Sump

Rio Grande

0

50

100

150

200

250

300

350

400

450

500

550

0   100
m

nightmare. Worse still, the top of the glacier was slowly receding, so that on successive trips the anatomy of the place changed considerably. It wasn't anything that we were expecting, and the cold dripping of the meltwater had frozen them both in the process of their getting to know it. Steve Roberts, in particular, was a jibbering wreck. He described the cave as 'obscenely vertical':

"The 70m puts you by the wall where there are two bolts – though you can't get at them now of course, the traverse needs re-rigging. Take some of the rope from Tonto and re-tie to a bould . . . by the way take two hangers. God the ice! It collapses and skids off down the gaps around . . . brrrr." Phil Duncan interrupted him.

"There's this faint blue glow, you know . . ."

"Not in F20 there isn't, it's so dark! I know all caves are dark but . . ."

"I didn't mean in F20," Phil replied, "I meant in the gins. There's this faint blue glow to the gin at Los Lagos . . . I think we need some."

It's important, I thought to myself as the two of them made their way off, not to suffer any vitamin deficiencies on an expedition. That included Vitamin G.

They had left the four of us, myself, Sara, Steve Mayers and Dave, to crack on down the wet, drippy shaft to what we hoped would be the ice-cold streamway below. At least the water there would be clean.

Dave offered to carry some rope to F20 for Sara and me, while Steve went off for more from La Jayada. The way to F20 from Top Camp was so long and difficult it was impossible to do any more in one day than get there with your caving gear. Perhaps a kilometre of landscape to cross, but in all that way there was not one patch of grass to put up a tent, only the unforgiving Picos boulders which was why we couldn't camp any nearer the entrance. Our problem was how to find the cave in all this chaotic wilderness – the descriptions left in the log were awful: "From the camp go down the hill to the big pile of boulders and follow up the green valley. From there take the brown gully and leave it at mid-height, then branch off right and climb. From here the route is too complicated to describe. PS the map I've drawn is useless actually."

By late morning we were still struggling up the green valley with our heavy packs, and the sun was debilitating now. We identified the brown gully, only when to leave it? We puffed our way up . . . and on and on, scrambling on the knife edges of rock that lined its sides. One slip here and you would slice your leg off. No sign of any cairns, only a large snowfield that was softening in the heat. Munching some of this we eventually found ourselves struggling over the top. I threw my pack off in frustration – it was soaked through with sweat, and started attracting a swarm of flies. I cursed at our bad luck, and turned to Dave – perhaps if he went left, and I went right we should manage to find the entrance without having to reverse the awful gully. He didn't reply, but furrowed his forehead in a strange way.

"Do you know, I think that I recognise this view?" I looked out across the new expanse of featureless wrinkled rock. I looked back towards our camp. The view was almost exactly the same. Dave had shot off and was poking about in the rocks right on the top of the ridge, whereas we knew that F20 was half way down.

"For God's sake, Dave, let's find this cave and get on with it – look, it's half past one already." The heat of the sun was unbearable; all around there was a shimmering of haze from the baking rocks. Sara had taken refuge under a small overhang and was sullenly chewing some snow, knowing full well that nothing could hurry Dave up. I looked at her and shrugged my shoulders when we heard a distant shout. It was Dave; he'd gone for miles down the ridge in obviously the wrong direction. We ignored him, and then he appeared on the skyline a couple of hundred yards away.

"I've found 2/6!" He seemed very excited about it. "2/6 is the cave that I found straight after I found Ridge Cave . . . look, I've just got to find Ridge Cave now, it must be really close."

After all the hyperbole and embellishment since 1980 I couldn't conceive of Ridge Cave being anything other than a legend, and I certainly wasn't impressed now. As I negotiated the ragged top to the ridge, with its loose scree and blind shafts, my head beat with throbbing pain . . . perhaps I was getting sunstroke?

"Look," said Dave, "there it is."

And there, indeed, it was. Above a long sausage of snow was a short, flat wall. Some two feet above the top of the snow was some paint; faded black writing. It said 'OUCC 1980 1/6'. This was the legend, Ridge Cave itself, re-discovered after five years. It was probably the least impressive cave entrance that I had seen for a long while, for the massive pellet of snow all but filled the oblique cleft in the rock from which it issued. There was just enough room to squeeze between the snow and the rock and walk into what might be a cave. After Tras la Jayada it was quite pathetic. No wonder we had been unable to find the place. Dave's writing was only just visible today, with the snow at a low level – in other years the inscription and the cave entrance itself would be completely covered.

"Go inside," Dave said, smugly.

I slid past the snow and slipped into what suddenly belled into a very large cave – a 3-metre diameter tunnel headed straight into the hillside. The snow soon stopped, leaving a sandy floor and easy walking to the head of a short pitch. No one had ever been down this pitch, but for five years Dave had been boring us stupid with its potential.

"What I think we should do is this – Richard, you and Sara have your caving gear here, so go in now for a 'cheap and nasty' trip, just to see if the place goes, while I get more gear from Jayada. Tomorrow all four of us will push it as far as we can, with all the rope we can get, and we'll forget all about F20 and then go and have a massive meal in Cangas. Maybe even a wash."

"Don't you want to be the first down that pitch, Dave?" It was, after all, his cave.

"No, I've waited five years, so I can wait another twenty-four hours." He also knew that he wouldn't be able to stop Sara and me going down. "See you later."

We came out of Ridge Cave quite late, with the sun just starting to redden the top of La Verdellengua with its dying rays. Way, way across the expanse of nothing there was a tiny orange blob – one of the tents at Top Camp. I gave a loud, meaningless call, and it echoed back and forwards across the slopes. A minuscule figure appeared and stood on the top of a boulder – we could just make out its arms waving.

"Does . . . it . . . go?" Dave's voice came perfectly clearly across the amphitheatre. Sara and I called back together.

"YES!"

Straight away the figure began jumping up and down, and waving its tiny arms, but only after a long delay did we hear the sound of Dave's simultaneous cheers.

"What . . . happens?"

"Two . . . short . . . pitches . . . in . . . vadose . . . canyon . . . then . . . three . . . second . . . drop."

By the time that we got back Steve Mayers and Dave had prepared a large meal for us. Dave was still excited.

"For *five years* I've waited for this cave. Five years. I was a completely different person then – a second year undergraduate just turned twenty."

I thought about what I had been five years before . . . researching in an obscure branch of speech analysis. Living on a student grant in East Oxford with my cat. Now I was in Sheffield training to be an eye surgeon; mortgaged, engaged, responsible.

So four of us went on a pushing trip all together – an unusual event, but it meant that we could carry all our caving gear over to the cave as well as a huge amount of rope. The only limitation that we set ourselves was that we shouldn't cut any of the lengths of rope – otherwise we would carry on caving until all 250 metres of it was used up. As we changed in the cool of the entrance chamber, sheltering from the furnace outside, Dave made a speech. He stood on a boulder and pointed one finger in the air.

"This trip," he pronounced, "this trip will change the course of speleology in the Picos. After five years the mountains are at last ready to give up their secrets. We will need luck, yes, and why not, a certain deontology?" He was pushed off the rock by Sara as she went out of the cave again, clutching a loo-roll. Never pass up the opportunity to pass water, especially before a long caving trip.

It was a truly magnificent trip. Pitch followed pitch as the cave led on downwards, with squeezes and false leads between them. There being four of us, it took very little time to find the way on, even when it was not obvious. At one point the cave seemed to fizzle out into a tiny slot, but five minutes later we were rigging another pitch, which had been obscured behind some jammed rocks . . . kick the rocks down the drop and off we go another 30 metres . . . towards whatever was at the bottom. The tiny stream vanished not far inside, leaving most of the route through old, fossil caverns. When we ran out of rope we had rigged eleven pitches and were rather more than 200 metres down, sitting at the top of a very large pitch. Hunched on a ledge we ate some olives.

"What really gets me," said Dave, "is how *nice* this cave is – no ice, no freezing wind, varied caving. I told you, didn't I?"

"Yes, Dave, you told us. I can't say I believed you."

DAVID Finding Ridge Cave was a moving moment. I thought of all the parties I had blithely sent off into the mountains with the vaguest of instructions on its whereabouts, certain that its proximity to 'the ridge' would make it easy to locate. I recalled a walk with George in 1982, when we had searched every crest for miles, ending the day with burning thighs . . . every ridge but

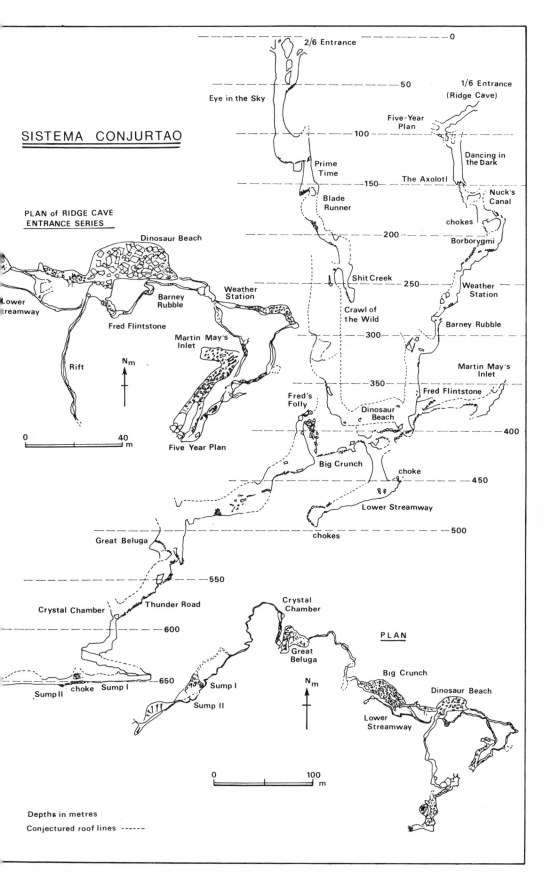

this one, which I had so often seen from Top Camp but ruled out because it seemed too far from Ario for Dave Thwaites and me to have explored on that distant July day. Each time we struggled up a scree-filled gully I was convinced that *this* was the ridge at last. How the old lags – absent friends on this expedition, Graham and John – would laugh when they heard the news. And we had been so close to it in 1983: finding it then would have changed that bitter year entirely.

The first pitch after Sara and Richard's two short drops was a beautiful, circular shaft with white, fluted walls. I called it 'Dancing in the Dark', and sang the Bruce Springsteen song all the way down. Next morning Steve Roberts appeared at camp bright and early.

"Well? What happened then?"

"Oh, we rigged eleven pitches, got into some really nice stuff; it's still going at the top of a biggie."

"So you got to the bottom of the glacier then? How deep's the shaft?"

"There is no glacier, Steve. I'm talking about Ridge Cave."

"Come on now, Dave. Don't piss about. What happened?"

Eventually, our leader was convinced. He sounded relieved: he wouldn't have to go back down F20.

RICHARD "Let's start with the calamares, and then, perhaps, the steaks. That way we could have several glasses of sherry – fino – with the first course, and that good Navarra wine later."

"It's just that I'd rather have the trout, you see, and that's a main course. We can't be going drinking red wine with trout, and there won't be any white worth drinking in Cangas. It's just going to have to be champagne before the meal *and* during the meal."

"Oh look. We're at Lagos." We had been so engrossed in our plans that neither of us had noticed the walk down was over. All the years of caving in the hills meant that we could tramp down the mountain on auto-pilot. We'd be walking up again to-morrow, of course, but in the meantime we should have to go shopping. And have lunch. We arrived at the tents at 10. The wind was beginning to pick up. Dave began to butter some bread: "Better have some breakfast too. It wouldn't do to be too hungry, or we won't enjoy it so much."

As he spoke, a strong gust rocked the old frame tent we had used for our kitchen since anyone could remember. An empty Coke bottle flew across the campsite at high speed, and as we watched a Spanish tent of poor design collapsed onto its two thrashing inhabitants.

"Serves them right," Phil said. "They shouldn't be doing that in a Catholic country." The wind became more continuous, and it suddenly became obvious that we were going to have to take drastic steps or have all our tents destroyed. The kitchen didn't appear capable of lasting much longer.

From the store tent we dragged out several lengths of caving rope, and unravelled them on the grass. The wind was getting even stronger now, and it was enough just to throw the rope up into the air for the wind to send it flying over the top of the kitchen tent. Some of the ropes were attached to pegs, or large rocks – some were simply tied to the wheels of parked cars. A crowd of Spanish campers had assembled, wondering what the 'locos ingleses' were doing, then all at once seemed to understand – they fled across the campsite in the direction of their tents, which, one by one, were being demolished. My own two-man was torn to shreds before I had a chance to get there – mangled poles jutted out of the blue nylon which flapped uselessly. Cavers began rushing about, giving each other orders, and ignoring all of them. Steve Gale, fearsome in his Assyrian beard, barked commands in all directions.

"Don't pull that, we've got to get a line across to there. Quick! Help me with that peg someone!"

"Take this thing and tie it around that thing!" came the reply. In the heat of the moment vocabularies seem to contract.

"Grab this pole! Somebody grab this pole!" A voice came from within the store tent. "Help me hold this tent up!"

"Help me pull this tent down!" shouted Steve Gale on the outside, and a struggle ensued, culminating in the inevitable collapse.

The Yellow Van now was beginning to lean alarmingly. I leapt in, started the engine and did a three-point turn to bring it unto the wind, scattering a generous top dressing of cow dung round the campsite as the wheels spun to get a grip. As I was doing this, our pavilion tent leant back under a particularly strong gust. Like the other base camp tents, it was borrowed and useless. Climbing expeditions always seem to have superb, high-technology tents that will put up with anything that's thrown at them, but we cavers, as usual, had a rag-bag of ancient cast-offs. The pavilion was a tent of the gypsy palm-reader's variety, and had in its time been half eaten by a grizzly bear in northern Wisconsin. Now the Los Lagos wind was about to send it home.

"The pavilion's about to go, Steve." Steve Gale turned around and stroked his beard.

"Don't worry, it's quite safe." His reply seemed very well-thought out. The tent collapsed only a moment later, and the single central pole shot through the roof. The blue canvas fluttered down to the ground as the pole stood to attention for a moment, then majestically toppled.

The Spanish holidaymakers were faring no better with their trendier gear. One tent, looking like a telephone kiosk, was ripped into the air, revealing a startled Spaniard sitting on his thunder-box. He skipped into the safety of his car hurriedly pulling up blue trousers over white legs.

Only one other tent remained, its owners absent. It was a large purple frame tent, and it was taking a terrible hammering. The rubber thongs which held it down were snapping, one by one.

"I say, let's go over and tie it down," suggested William.

As we advanced towards it with a hammer and a long length of SRT rope, the owners re-appeared. They asked us just what did we think we were doing, in complex Spanish subjunctives. I began to try and explain, but just then the whole tent was lifted bodily from the ground, revealing only for an instant its aluminium frame before another vortex of wind tore into it, twisting and snapping the tent into a conical spiral, rather like a miniature Matterhorn. It then fell onto the grass, a useless crumpled heap which flapped for only a moment longer. The wind had suddenly stopped.

"What a shame," said Phil Rose, and farted aggressively.

"You must be English," said one of the men.

The discovery of Ridge Cave charged all of the expedition with a new vigour. There was now a single objective – to push the caves at Top Camp. The mass keenness which afflicted the cavers gave me the same marvellous feeling of unison of effort experienced by a rowing eight pulling wonderfully well, or in an orchestra getting it just right. I was no longer tempted to feel a useless old fogey.

Whilst we repaired Base Camp and indulged ourselves in Cangas, the aficionados of the huge, cold, wet shaft made another assault on F20. Ian Houghton, in particular, was tormented by the place. He had seen it the year before when the glacier (now called 'the Ivory Tower') had been over 50 metres higher. Now, day by day, it was getting smaller, and consequently Tonto pitch, which landed onto it, was becoming longer and longer, coupled to which the landing was onto a treacherously slippery ice ledge. We couldn't really carry on any further down the shaft without ice-axes and crampons.

The solution was simple – a twenty-foot sideways pendule through a waterfall and into a parallel shaft which, although reasonably wet, was free of ice. The shaft dropped for a further 33 metres before it broke back into the main one again, and met the snow pillar once more. The solution was simple – a six-metre sideways pendule through another window and another parallel shaft with a 30-metre drop to a ledge, from where 33 metres further down there was the floor; solid rock at last. The Ivory Tower filled half the height of the whole shaft system; half of the 225-metre sheer drop from the surface – a pile of snow higher than St Paul's Cathedral.

Unlike La Jayada, this big pit didn't end in a large chamber with no way on. Instead of a dismal mud floor the shaft dwindled into a small trench which carried away a stream. This passage ran directly below the Ivory Tower where there was a drenching shower of meltwater tipping in from the roof – the explorers dashed through in an attempt to keep their carbide flames alight, to the dry passage beyond. It continued, carrying its stream, but the passage became loose and winding, both in the horizontal and in the vertical, and paradoxically smaller and smaller, so that in the few metres before it belled out into a pitch head it was a tortuous, squalid thrutch. After the icy grandeur of the entrance shaft this came as an unpleasant surprise.

DAVID In Ridge Cave, where the four of us had come to a halt, Steve Roberts and Phil Duncan had rigged the pitch from a jammed boulder. It descended 30 metres, passing through geological ages – from loose, dry re-eroded crumbly stuff to hard, clean limestone. The next drop was round the corner. It sounded big. Steve, Nicola and I pushed on. The shaft was complex, with several ledges and bulges, but by employing some complicated knitting techniques with tapes and wires I was able to get away with only one bolt on the way down: 67 metres. Below was a sloping ledge and a further drop. Steve was waiting at the top:

That Dave was bolting on the end of a 70-metre rope was fine by me and Nicola: we had lots of chocolate. Eventually the clinking down below was replaced by 'Rope free' to cheers from the chilly upper duo. Cavers must have reptile blood . . . waiting in the cold results in floating torpor after about half an hour. We called the pitch Fred Flintstone; Barney Rubble was the one above. It was thoughtfully split into 20-metre lengths between rebelays, facilitating conversations as we descended: 'Big pitch, this eh?' and other gems of Varsity wit. At the bottom, a small bouldery slope and another drop in the rift. My turn. A quick ferret through the bags produced only one 9mm length despite our cunning ferrying forward of ropes as we came down. Ho hum. Out with the bolt kit.

Rope backed up, to put it loosely, to a boulder which Dave sits on, just in case. I walk backwards to the edge of the pitch and lob stone off down . . . weee . . . eeee . . . bonk. It lands in the base of the rift, 25 metres or so below. If I smile enough I won't have to look at the rope or what it's tied to. Bolting off the walls fails miserably, so I put one in the rock I'm standing on. The rack slips alarmingly once or twice as I make pinging music with the hammer, but Dave and Nicola have reptilised and take no notice.

Electric on. Teeter, swing and twang. I'm hanging on the belay rock which looks comfortably large and solidly jammed. Wary of my worn rack (well, it's an excuse,) I descend slowly, watching the wall and the floor . . . kick and spin and the rift suddenly isn't a rift any more. In the far off blackness, colossal boulders fade up and back to no wall that I can see. There's no echo. At the bottom, I'm unable to move too far . . . the vast cavern has a silent, dark presence that is only accentuated by the faint and regular drips coming from somewhere behind me.

Dinosaur Beach. It felt like the end of the trip: we all sat boggle-eyed and silent, occasionally nodding our heads meaningfully (and chewing chocolate – so much for the rapture of the deep). A tour revealed the chamber's true size, and the chaos that lay underneath. Boulders heaped on rocks heaped on rocks heaped on pebbles. Many routes were looked at, climbing up and down. The most horrible was a squeeze past an egg-timer poised pair of rocks that on the other side proved to be nastily balanced on not much and also holding up the roof. Beyond this was a rift down which stones fell a long way, and which was declared not to be the way on. Somewhere in this horrible, loose maze a draught was found again, and it led us to the obligatory undescended pitch. We called it a day and went out to find that it very nearly was. I lay outside in my sleeping-bag facing east to try to see the dawn, but as the sky got redder the sandman finally found me.

Three days after my rediscovery of Ridge Cave, it was nearly 400 metres deep. We had come a long way since the days when pushing parties would set off into Xitu with one ladder, find a pitch, spend several hours rigging it and fail to descend. If Ridge Cave had continued on down in similar fashion we would have been 1,000 metres below ground within a week. It didn't.

RICHARD The next trip was also a threesome, and the three of us, Steve Mayers, Geoff Hogan and I, all knew we were unlikely to get another look at Ridge Cave. Dave and I had to take a turn in F20, and then departure loomed. He would be back to writing about racial attacks, I to removing cataracts. It seemed very far off.

Beyond the pitch, a long, descending rift took us down a steep slope without the need for rope. At the bottom we heard the sound for which we'd hardly dared to hope: a streamway.

"We've cracked this cave, Richard," Steve said, "all we gotta do now is follow the stream!" He nipped off down the passage but soon returned, crawling back at stream level, dripping with water.

"It's a boulder choke all right," he said, pulling himself up into the streamway passage again. "If you want to follow it at stream level it's going to take a long time . . . it's quite tight and there's a biggish rock blocking the way."

"Well, we've nothing for it but to look at some higher level, then. Let's leave the bags here." I refused to be put off by the setback.

On the continent, cavers refer to boulder chokes as 'chaos'. What they are is nothing more than a passage which has been completely filled by boulders falling from the roof in some ancient collapse. Although it is not likely that one of these boulders is going to fall out of the roof while you are there, the ones that have already fallen are more often than not poised one on top of each other in a most delicate way. Quite large boulders can be made to settle, or wobble, or sometimes the passage of cavers through the choke slowly undermines the supports of the whole pile, and it can suddenly collapse into a new pile through which there may not be a passage. No one who has ever seen it can forget the boulder-choke in Langcliffe Pot, where the way through is to crawl down an avenue of car-jacks which are supposed to hold the choke up – only as you thrutch along you can see between the rocks into inaccessible gaps where lie the mangled remains of the car-jacks which held up the choke not so long ago.

The stream which we had only just found, and which seemed

181

to be the key to the rest of Ridge Cave, had vanished through the tiny chinks between the boulders; what we had now to do was to try and find some devious way through the bigger chinks in the boulders at a higher level. I have a recurring dream, which I was now trying to suppress, of crawling through a Spanish boulder-choke only to find that it collapses behind me, trapping me on the far side . . . I concentrated instead on the bright, clean-washed rocks that had jammed themselves in the canyon. We climbed up them, showered by a series of drips.

We each decided to try at a different level, so as to explore as much as possible at once. Steve Mayers climbed up very high and wriggled between some boulders jammed many feet above where Geoff and I were looking. This was wise, for it meant that the two of us couldn't drop anything on his head. Geoff vanished like a rabbit down a lead to the left, and I pressed on through a small hole into a chamber where the drips drummed rat-a-tat-tat on my helmet.

This chamber was simply a space between the boulders, which were the size of sofas. There were many smaller ones jammed between them, and most of these smaller ones were loose. I managed to kick a few out of the way and opened up a hole into another chamber directly in front of me, and thankfully free of drips. One particular fist-sized rock didn't seem to want to move, and I tugged at it a couple of times to try and make the hole a little wider; only later did I realise that this little rock was supporting the entire roof of boulders above me . . . I crawled into the second chamber *very* gingerly indeed.

"I don't like this, I don't like this at all." I said it to myself but Geoff was quite close in some other hole and replied in a very jolly voice.

"Oh, I'm enjoying it actually." He began to hum, kicking loose rocks away in time with his tune, causing great crashings and bangings that put me even more on edge. One of the boulders in the roof above my head could rock to and fro, and because of this I decided that it would be better to try and move downwards instead.

I could hear the stream now, shooting down some small cascade probably about 3 metres below me, and the noise was coming from a hole by my feet. I took off my belt and hat, and, holding these in my right hand, I slid down through the hole into the blackness below, flailing both legs about in order to try and get a foothold. The place I had dropped into was the shape of a sentry box, with the only way out at roughly face level, into a similar sentry box on the other side. To get through I performed a sort of slow-motion dive through the hole, so that I was left standing on my hands upside down, with my helmet dangling from my chin-strap. It was absurd.

After a long struggle and many contortions I managed to turn upright, only to discover that there was no way out. I had to perform another handstand in order to reverse the move, accompanied all the time by the distant crashes of Geoff and Steve settling the boulder choke. Just let me out of here, I prayed. There are no atheists in loose boulder chokes.

On the other hand, once out of the choke, sitting down eating pineapple with the other two, it seemed most implausible that Ridge Cave had been designed by an all-knowing deity. Who would take the trouble to carve out a splendid passage and then fill it up with boulders just so we couldn't enjoy it? After all the promise, Ridge Cave was going to fizzle out, with no way through the choke. Bored by the hours of poking about, we glumly made our way back to the surface. We got lost.

"Is this Dinosaur Beach?" Geoff asked. We had stumbled into a massive chamber.

"I don't think so . . . there's water running down that wall."

"Oh well, we must have discovered another big chamber then."

"Yep, sure have."

This second chamber was as big and impressive as Dinosaur Beach, but was flat-floored and square. Lying like monstrous dice on the floor were two rocks as big as houses with a third glued to one wall. Why didn't it fall? Above us the walls stretched into nothingness, darkness blacker than any night. Drips fell out of the dark like shooting stars as they caught our light and then fell into the boulder floor – they were the same drips that had rattled on my helmet 50 metres below. The floor of this chamber was the top of the boulder choke, 50 metres high – a pile of rocks bigger than a hospital. It suddenly occurred to me that I would rather someone else found a way through them.

Two nights later, the night before Geoff, Dave and I had to leave for Britain, Fred and Phil came back from the cave, whispering in the dark so as not to wake anyone. In fact they woke everyone, because we were all wondering whether they would have managed to force a way through the boulders in the stream. Or was Ridge Cave just another Picos joke?

"What's the time, Phil?" Dave's voice. It was pitch black and very cold.

"It's half past four. Is there any food? Oh great!" He had found the congealed stew we'd left them.

"There's no way through the boulders at the bottom." Fred's voice joined in, a very quiet, depressed voice. I could hear him unstrapping all his gear, the swish of PVC against grass. "We managed to get past the boulder in the streamway, and down a little pitch beyond, but there's no way out of the final chamber – the stream just flows on through chinks in the rocks and that's it. I had a look at your climb though, Richard."

"Think you can do it?"

"I'll give it a chance. Will you leave your belay plate?" Through the nylon skin of my tent I heard the unmistakable sound of two men eating cold lentil curry, by carbide light.

The climb which was the only possible way on was a long shot. It was also a long climb. In the second huge chamber was a large boulder poised halfway up one wall. We called the chamber 'The Big Crunch' after the noise that this boulder would make should it eventually fall, a time which seemed overdue. This far wall, complete with suspended boulder, was on the down-stream side of the cave, and above the boulder was a passage which seemed to carry on in that direction. What we had to do was to climb up this wall and into that passage. If it 'went' it would carry us over the top of all the boulders and on into the rest of the cave. I had showed the climb to Steve Mayers, just before we left. He said it looked 'hard'. Steve can climb to the standard of E6. The hardest climb in the world is graded E7.

I wondered if Fred would manage it. If he didn't that would be the end of Ridge Cave. In Britain a choke like that would be blown to bits . . . they say that in Craig-ar-Ffynnon they blew up the boulder choke every day for six months before they got through – perhaps we could get hold of some dynamite and smuggle it into Spain . . . no one ever searched the van on the way *in*? No – I dismissed the idea. The climb was our only chance. As Dave and I cruised the Escort into yet another restaurant car park on our way back to England next day I thought to myself that Fred would just have to go over the top. Certainly there was no one else mad enough to try.

Fred had soloed up to the boulder on his first try – that is to say with no protection by a rope. However, six metres up, under-neath the huge block he found it possible to arrange a sling and clip the rope to it, so that if he fell the rope would save him by suspending him from the sling. For every foot that he climbed up above this sling he would fall two feet before it held – twenty feet above the sling and a fall would finish him off. Next morning, William put in a few bolts at the level of the sling and just a little to the right – the way was now clear for Fred to keep what he called his 'appointment with fear'.

Ian climbed up to William's bolts and examined the rest of the climb. It looked impossible. Fred was lifelining him from below, and shouted up encouraging words, but much of the way was overhanging, and the tiny holds snapped off in Ian's hands. Any parts that weren't overhanging were merely ledges of loose choss, and as he moved about looking for a possible way to climb up, Ian had to kick steps in all the rubbish, rather like ice-climbing. Below, Fred huddled under an overhang as bucket-loads of gravel tipped down.

All at once the rope went taut, and there was a squeal from above – a hold had snapped away and Ian had come off. William's bolts had held.

Ian came down, and it was Fred's turn. The appointment could be put off no longer. He prusiked up to the bolts and eyed up the overhanging boulder. All he could do was to put in another bolt to abseil on – not trusting the one that had already taken Ian's fall. As soon as he started abseiling, though, Fred found that he could pendule around the side of the boulder and into a small gully on the other side, which presented easier climbing. Fred began, gingerly, to make his way up.

"Suddenly a large handhold went," he wrote later, "and I was flying past the bolt, wondering how long it would be before the rope caught me. Then I hit a knob of rock, landing on my back and ripping my glasses off. I ended up dangling, with a sharp pain . . .

"I abbed down, had a bite to eat and then set off up again. I got to the top of the gully and ran out of rope. Ian would have to come up to one of the bolts before I could carry on. By the way, all this time I was scared absolutely shitless."

Whilst Ian came up, Fred had to hang from a dodgy-looking spike, which threatened to snap off at any moment, so that he was almost glad when the time came to start climbing again. This time there was no easy way around – nothing for it but to tackle the final overhang.

Like all limestone climbs, the holds were slightly smaller than one would like, and on these Fred had to haul out backwards on arm-power alone, in the manner that sloths hang from Amazonian branches. Sloths don't wear wellington boots, but there was no point changing into smaller, climbing boots, because if a welly boot didn't fit on a foothold, then the hold would snap off for sure.

To Fred's surprise, the holds didn't break, and he wasn't sent spinning off into space again; instead, he managed to pull over the lip of the overhang and onto a fairly good slab with some solid-looking boulders only a few feet away. All he had to do now was to mosey up the slope. But he couldn't move! His lifeline, which zig-zagged up from bolt to bolt was stretched over the lip, and the combined friction made it impossible for Fred to pull up any more of it. He was a victim of the dreaded 'rope drag'.

He tried to haul up some spare rope with more and more frenzied efforts, but he couldn't do it, having to use one hand to hang onto the rock. His options were limited now . . . He couldn't climb back down over the overhang; far safer to jump right off into space, and hope that Ian would save the day. He remembered, though, that he wasn't on some Derbyshire edge, but at the bottom of a Spanish pothole . . .

There was nothing where he was to attach the rope to, so one possibility was to simply untie the rope and walk up the slab unfettered, only, what would he do then? If Ian couldn't throw a rope up to him, he would be stuck at the top of this remote cliff, for a very long time indeed. He only had one serious chance, although it was a while before it dawned upon him. He was still wearing his SRT gear, so what he now did was to dismantle it with his spare hand and tie all the cow's tails and footloops together. He clipped these to the end of the lifeline, and length-ening it in this way he could move up the slab a few more steps until the rope became taut again, with the boulders still tantalis-ingly out of reach. All he had left now was his thin shock-cord, an elastic strap that he sometimes used to pull his ascenders into place when climbing a fixed rope. With this knicker-band on full stretch he made it up the slab at last. Standing now behind the big blocks he could heave up all the spare rope he needed, and belay it for his descent.

"What's happening, Fred?" Ian intoned from below.

"Oh, nothing, just scared shitless again."

DAVID Fred's Folly was a gamble, but it paid off. At the top of the climb, the passage continued: an ancient high level, who knew how far above the stream which we hoped to regain. There were pitches down again, including one of 70 metres, and yet another big cavern, the Big Beluga. Phil and Ukie pushed Ridge Cave to its 1985 limit there during a 30-hour surveying and de-tackling trip. A loose climb led on through the floor, bearing a howling draught. The depth was 460 metres; the prospects excellent.

The three and a half weeks Richard and I spent in Spain in 1985 were the longest period of fine weather we had known in the Picos, but after our departure, there was a sharp change. While Britain endured the worst August (after what had seemed to me the worst May, June and July) for many years, snow fell on the mountains again. The team was much reduced in size, and those who remained had their work cut out. F20 was going too: an endless series of vicious, bewildering rifts, all with many ways through and none of them pleasant. Occasionally, a pitch provided relief as the passage widened to at least a couple of feet. Frequently, parties became lost among the different traverse levels, mysteriously bypassing pitches or having to retrace their steps when they came upon shafts for which no ropes were in place. The cave ended with another pitch into the unknown: 360 metres deep and still going.

Everyone hoped that F20 would drop into Jorcada Blanca at the Hot Tub, but back in England Steve Roberts fed the survey data into his computer and produced an accurate line. There was a long way to go towards Jorcada Blanca, and it looked as if the cave was already too deep to reach the great chamber where Perdices and FU56 met. There were no further inlets big enough to account for the F20 stream in the Jorcada streamway: to gloom from those who knew the place, but excitement from those who didn't, it was realised that F20 really might join the main Jorcada stream beyond the sump. Or, of course, become flooded itself at the same level.

A brilliant icy day towards the end of January, 1986. Two figures, cocooned in duvet jackets, pick their way across the frozen, snowy moorland towards the gritstone summit of Outer Edge, the loneliest spot in Derbyshire.

"What about this summer?" asks Richard. "I don't suppose I'll be getting away. Got to be getting into the operating microscope."

"That was definitely my last expedition," says Dave. "Climbing in the Alps this year."

"How about a long walk in the Andes? Ecuador or Peru?"

"I've always fancied climbing Mount Kenya. And they have great beaches at Mombasa."

A short pause as they skirt a peaty grike, and turn to gaze at the white emptiness of Kinder Scout.

"I'm glad we found Ridge Cave. It's going to whizz under all that limestone near Top Camp, join a really big stream – I knew it was a winner the day I first saw it in 1980."

"There's a bloody big problem if it is."

"What do you mean? It'd be great."

"Exactly. That's the point."

It sinks in. "Oh no. Oh my God. You mean we'll have to go back there again."

"Yup. I just don't see how we can escape."

In silence now, they pass the summit stones and begin to descend, almost in sight of Sheffield but high and remote in the winter hills. Hands in pockets, wriggling toes inside their boots to maintain circulation, they trudge on into twilight, down, down to the valleys below.

Postscript

The 1986 expedition, in which we both took part, discovered a lot of cave: but alas, the Picos was up to its tricks once more. Ridge Cave, which 2/6 entered at Dinosaur Beach via a series of magnificent, roomy shafts, ended after a long section of re-discovered streamway at about 650 metres depth. Its objective dangers caused three accidents: a loose rock knocked out one of Fred's front teeth not far from the entrance, Steve Mayers was hit on the neck while climbing Fred Flintstone and, more seriously, Ukie fell from a loose climb at the very bottom, while looking for a sump bypass. Unconscious briefly, and unable to move for half an hour, she eventually got herself out with an immobilised left arm and a black eye with the aid of Richard's jokes and hot soup.

F20, far the hardest system explored by OUCC, continued as foul as ever. At last, just as it appeared to have hit the big time in a large chamber with waterfall inlets, it too sumped, 582 metres down.

With this, Top Camp area would appear to have been worked out. Yet still possibilities remain within OUCC's designated area: the back of Jultayu, and the hills between Ario and the gorge must contain something to take away the rain and have hardly been examined. A team returns in 1987 to find out.

Glossary of terms used

Abseil: Sliding down a rope with a metal thing to slow you down.

Arthritis: What old cavers get.

Ascender: See Jammer.

Authigenic: Geologist's word applied to crystals. Ask a geologist what it means for certainty, but something like 'all pointing the same way'.

Aven: Hole in the roof.

Belay: Secure point of attachment for rope or ladder.

Bobbin: Type of descender.

Bolt: Steel cylinder which expands when driven into rock to provide artificial belay.

Buggered: What young cavers feel like. What happens to gear used underground.

Carbide: Chemical compound used in lamps which produces inflammable acetylene gas on contact with water.

Cave: Latin for beware.

Changeover: Manoeuvre performed during SRT at intermediate rebelay or knot.

Choke: Device used to start cold vans; blockage of boulders or mud in a cave. Alternatively a passive verb, as in 'the cave is choked with yellow vans'.

Choss: Loose rock. Very common in the Picos. Occasionally applied to bowel movement: "Doctor, I am frightened by this cave and my stool has turned to choss."

Clinometer: Surveying instrument used to measure inclinations from the vertical.

Cordellette technique: Way of solo caving whereby complex system employing lengths of household string enables rope to be pulled down pitch after descent and hauled up again on pulley system to climb back up. Dangerous but economical on rope.

Cow's Tail: Safety cord used at top of pitches, to protect cavers from the vertical.

Descender: Friction device attached to harness to enable safe abseils.

Doline: Depression in limestone which may have cave at bottom. Or may not.

Donkey's Dick: Rope attached to harness used for carrying tackle.

Footloop: Integral part of SRT system whereby a caver can stand in a loop from a jammer.

Free Hang: Ideal position for the rope to fall down the pitch, free of all the walls; a penalty imposed by Spanish courts at no cost.

Furry Suit: Fibre-pile romper suit worn next to the skin (see oversuit).

Hanger: Device attached to a bolt enabling a caver to descend the cave.

Hangover: Device enabling caver to avoid descending the cave.

Harness: Nylon truss which attaches the caver to the rope.

Helectite: Curly stalactite. No one knows how they are formed: can be metres long with many bends.

Jammer: Device which will slide up the rope but not down.

Jumar: Obsolete form of jammer now used only by climbers.

Karabiner: Universal linkage for ropes etc.

Karren: Yugoslavian geologist's girlfriend's name, now applied to bleak expanses of cave-bearing limestone.

Maillon: Universal linkage for ropes etc. Cheaper than a karabiner but more awkward to use.

Natural: Any feature of the cave such as a knob of rock or a large boulder that can be used to provide a belay without having to drill a bolt-hole.

Olives: Something unique to Spanish caves.

Oversuit: Tough PVC one-piece suit worn outside of the furry suit.

Petzl: Famous French caver and now maker of SRT gear.

Phreatic: Cave passage formed when completely flooded. Usually round and undulating.

Pitch: Vertical drop, pitch black when peered over.

Pothole: Vertical type of cave (see cave).

Prusik: To move up a free-hanging rope using a system of jammers and harnesses.

Resurgence: Spring where underground water re-emerges into daylight, except at night.

Rift: Tall thin passage with or without a floor; a disagreement between members of the expedition.

Rope-protector: Sheath of thick PVC which prevents damage to the rope where it touches the rock. Far better to have a free-hang.

Rope-walker: Device like a jammer which is more awkward to use. Better to have a jammer.

Rub-point: Place where the rope rubs against the rock. Better to have no rub-point.

Sever: Result of rub-point which has been ignored.

SRT: Single Rope Techniques. See chapter 1.

Shaft: Vertical underground drop. The most feared obstacle underground.

Shakehole: See Doline.

Slot: Body-sized fissure, sometimes poised over very large pitch, when highly inconvenient.

Squeeze: Excessively tight point in the passage, usually requiring a great deal of effort to get through. The most feared underground obstacle.

Sump: Point in the cave where the water fills the cavern entirely. Probably more feared than either a shaft or a squeeze.

Thrutch: Way of passing a squeeze by unco-ordinated whole body effort.

Vadose: Cave passage formed by a stream with air space above. Opposite of phreatic.

Wetsuit: Rubber suit that keeps you warm by a thin layer of water next to the skin, and also keeps you cool by a large number of holes.

Wire: Thin metal used to construct a belay; also what you send to the editors of the *Guinness Book of Records* when you have found the deepest cave in the world.